RAILWAYS OF EAST SHROPSHIRE

THROUGH TIME

Neil Clarke

T0307347

AMBERLEY PUBLISHING

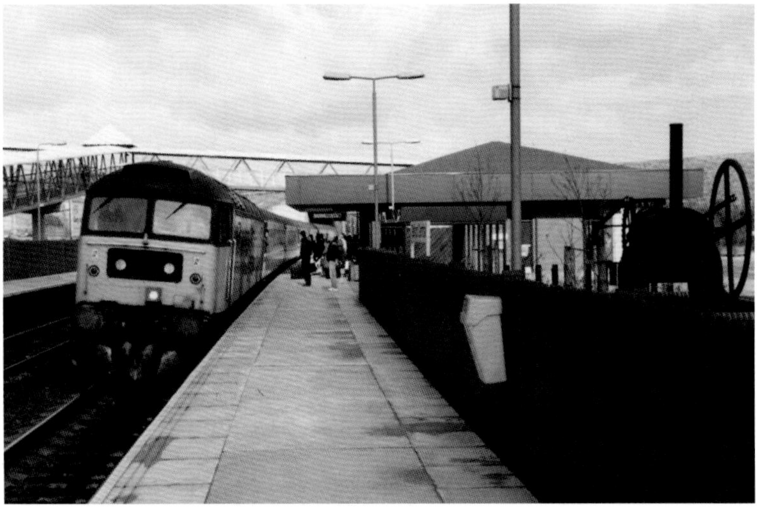

Above: Ancient and modern at Telford Central station, 1988.

Front Cover
Top: Madeley Salop station, 1897.
Bottom: The popular but short-lived Wrexham & Shropshire service to London Marylebone.

Back Cover
Top: LNWR bridge plate, Coalport.
Bottom: GWR boundary marker, Jackfield.

First published 2015

Amberley Publishing
The Hill, Stroud, Gloucestershire, GL5 4EP
www.amberley-books.com

ISBN 978 1 4456 4022 8 (print)
ISBN 978 1 4456 4031 0 (ebook)

British Library Cataloguing in Publication Data.
A catalogue record for this book is available from the British Library.

Typesetting by Amberley Publishing.
Printed in Great Britain.

Introduction

Vibrant and busy, East Shropshire is part of a county noted for its contrasting scenery, unique geological structure and wide range of ongoing human activity. As diverse as the county as a whole, the area at once incorporates the old market towns of Wellington, Newport, Shifnal, Much Wenlock and Bridgnorth, as well as the 'new town' of Telford. Distinctively, the centre of this area, bisected by the River Severn, was the Coalbrookdale Coalfield, and it was here that developments in the coal, iron and clay industries from the sixteenth century onwards earned area the epithet 'Cradle of the Industrial Revolution'. Today, the area centres on the Ironbridge Gorge as a World Heritage Site, and its rich industrial history is proudly displayed by the Ironbridge Gorge Museum Trust.

A significant factor in these developments was innovative transport systems. The Roman-built Watling Street was the forerunner of the Holyhead Road of the coaching era and the A5 trunk road of the motor age. For centuries the River Severn was a major transport artery, boosted during the Industrial Revolution by its link to the area's unique tub-boat canal system. Some of the country's earliest railways, known as wagonways, were developed on the Coalbrookdale Coalfield, and nineteenth-century railway development saw companies competing for a share of this area's mineral wealth and passenger traffic.

In national terms, public standard-gauge railways came relatively late to Shropshire. Many other railways had been built after the opening of the Liverpool & Manchester in 1830, so it is surprising that Shropshire, one of the major pioneering areas of the Industrial Revolution, was one of the last English counties to be connected to the growing national network of steam railways. In fact, the first public standard-gauge railway in the county, the Shrewsbury & Chester, opened as late as 1848; it was another year before the first railway to pass through the eastern part of the county was complete.

Why did an area at the forefront of industrial progress take so long to adopt this new means of transport? It's the old story of pioneers getting left behind with the march of progress. In East Shropshire, the remarkable industrial developments of the eighteenth and early nineteenth centuries had led to the growth of an equally innovative transport infrastructure. Wagonways and plateways, the River Severn and tub-boat canals and turnpike roads all served the area well, but continued to be relied upon when other, newer industrial areas were developing a more efficient means of transport – the public standard-gauge steam railway. This finally came to East Shropshire in 1849.

While it was mostly local coalmasters, ironmasters, landowners and entrepreneurs who had sponsored and funded earlier transport projects, the first public standard-gauge railway to be planned in this area attracted additional outside financial interests. There were several schemes to build a railway from the Black Country through the Coalbrookdale Coalfield to Shrewsbury, but the one that was finally authorised by Parliament in 1846 was the Shrewsbury & Birmingham Railway (SBR). This was to run from a joint station with the Shrewsbury & Chester Railway in the county town to Wellington, and this section was to be built jointly with the Shropshire Union Railways & Canal Company (SURCC), whose own line would then go on through Newport to Stafford. From Wellington, the Shrewsbury & Birmingham line was to pass through the northern edge of the Coalfield to Shifnal and then on to Wolverhampton, where it would join the proposed Stour Valley line to Birmingham.

Building commenced in early 1847, but the wet summer of the following year held up construction, particularly on the large embankment near Shifnal and the tunnel required at Oakengates. The tunnel was not ready by the time the joint line from Shrewsbury to Wellington was finished and so, on 1 June 1849, the Shropshire Union line was opened through to Stafford, though the Shrewsbury & Birmingham could only open theirs as far as a temporary station at Oakengates. It was another five months before Oakengates Tunnel was completed and the Shrewsbury & Birmingham line through Shifnal to Wolverhampton was opened.

For the next few years, Shrewsbury & Birmingham trains continued to terminate at a temporary station near the present High Level Station in Wolverhampton, at first because of a delay by the London & North

Western Railway (LNWR) in opening the Stour Valley line to Birmingham, and then because of their reluctance to give Shrewsbury & Birmingham trains running powers into Birmingham. As a result of this, in 1854 the Shrewsbury & Birmingham Railway was wooed into amalgamation with the Great Western Railway, and a connection was made into its newly opened Low Level Station at Wolverhampton. Two important consequences resulted from this amalgamation. Firstly, the GWR would now push its main line northwards from Wolverhampton through Shropshire to the Mersey; secondly, for the next hundred years most London-bound passengers from Shropshire would arrive at Paddington and not Euston.

Over the next decade or so. These included: a number of branch lines were built by the GWR (or by companies soon to be absorbed by the GWR). These included: the Madeley Branch to Lightmoor, which opened for goods in 1854 and for passengers five years later; the Wellington & Severn Junction line through Ketley, Horsehay, Lightmoor and Coalbrookdale to Buildwas, which opened in stages from 1857 to 1864; and, beyond the Severn, the Severn Valley Railway and the branch to Much Wenlock, both of which opened in 1862, and the extension from Much Wenlock to Craven Arms five years later.

While the Great Western was empire-building in East Shropshire, its arch-rival the LNWR, which had absorbed the SURCC, stole a march and built a branch line to replace the ailing Shropshire Canal it had recently purchased. This line ran from the Shropshire Union line at Hadley, through Oakengates, Stirchley and Madeley to Coalport, and was opened for goods in 1860 and for passengers the following year.

The local railway network was completed in 1867 with the opening of the line from Wellington to Market Drayton. This connected the hitherto isolated Nantwich & Drayton Railway to the Great Western system and provided a new route for East Shropshire traffic to Crewe and Manchester.

These railways were to have a dramatic effect on the social and economic development of East Shropshire. The initial impact was recorded by contemporary observers. William Smith, a toll-gate keeper on the Holyhead Road, said that 'the road that was once considered the best in England ... in a few months time was almost deserted'. W. G. Norris, manager of Horsehay Ironworks, wrote that with 'the opening of the Wellington & Severn Junction Branch ... the conveyance was such that iron could be rolled, loaded and into Birkenhead before it was cold'. Revd Thomas Priestley, vicar of Albrighton, commented that the village station 'began to serve a large district, especially in the way of coals, timber and agricultural produce'.

The impact the railways had on the area was greatest in Wellington. It had a pivotal position in the network, and railways helped the town to become the administrative and commercial centre for the adjacent Coalbrookdale Coalfield by the end of the nineteenth century. The industries that grew up in and around the town – malting and brewing, timber yards, engineering and the cattle market – had easy access to the railway via the two large goods yards to the west of the station. Wellington became the 'Clapham Junction of East Shropshire' – not only did it have the through expresses on the Paddington-Birkenhead main line, but also local services to Shrewsbury and Wolverhampton, Newport and Stafford, Much Wenlock and Craven Arms, Madeley and Coalport and to Market Drayton and Crewe. Late nineteenth century railway timetables show how busy Wellington Station was.

Four years after the end of the First World War, the country's railways were reorganised. The 'Grouping' of 1923 created four large companies – the London, Midland & Scottish, the London & North Eastern, the Great Western, and the Southern; East Shropshire was on the boundary between the LMS and the GWR. The 1920s and 1930s saw some erosion of passenger and goods traffic on the railways as a result of the growth in the use of the motor bus and lorry on the roads. Locally, the GWR tried to fight back with the opening of a number of local station halts, but the number of expresses actually increased and Wellington was still a thriving junction. This situation continued until well after the Second World War and the nationalisation of the railways in 1947. The lines of East Shropshire were placed in the Western Region of the newly created British Railways.

Away from the main line and its branches, mineral lines and sidings served a number of local industries. The most extensive of these was the railway system that grew up in the second half of the nineteenth century to serve the Lilleshall Company. This operated with its own fleet of locomotives over an extensive network, linking coal mines, ironworks and brickworks with the LMS at Donnington and Priorslee, and with the GWR at Hollinswood. The eventual decline of the Lilleshall Company led to the closure of most of the system by 1959, but the line from Donnington still served Granville Colliery for another twenty years.

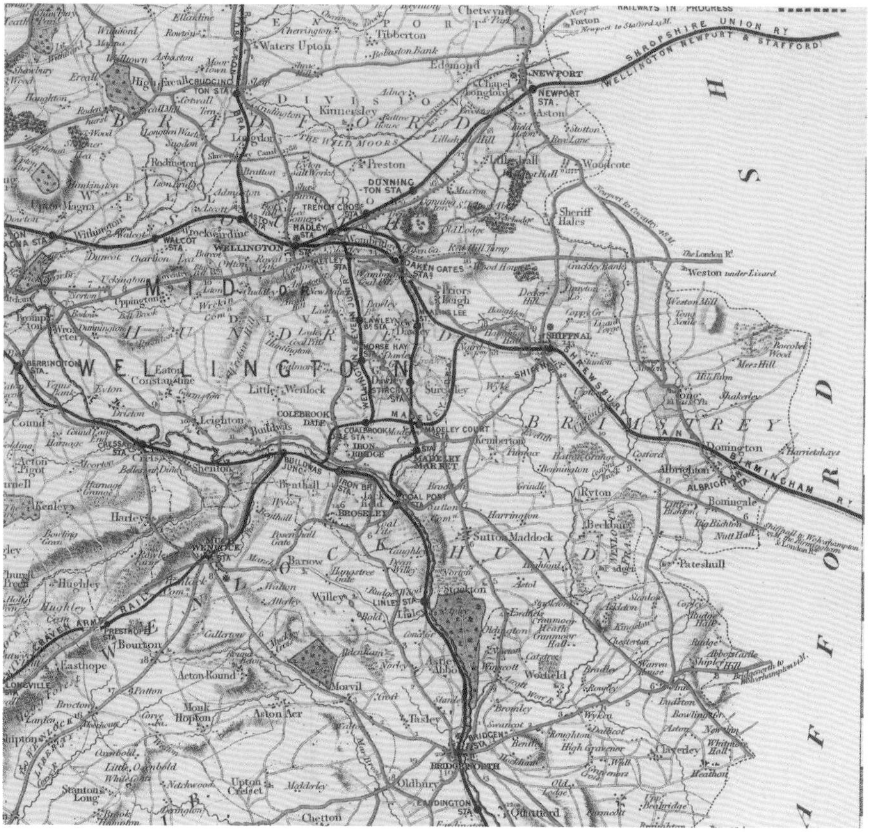

A section of Cruchley's map of the railways of Shropshire (from around 1870) showing the eastern part of the county.

In the late 1950s, government disquiet at the cost of running the nation's railways culminated in the controversial Beeching Report of 1963. In East Shropshire, four local passenger services were withdrawn even before the impact of the Beeching Report: those to Coalport in 1952, Much Wenlock in 1962, on the Severn Valley line and to Crewe in 1963. Some of these lines remained open or partially open for a few more years for dwindling goods traffic, but gradually all the local goods yards closed.

Included in the implementation of the Beeching Report, which began in earnest in 1964, was the closure of local passenger services and stations on the line that had been the first railway to be built in East Shropshire, that between Shrewsbury, Wellington and Stafford. Services were withdrawn on 7 September 1964, and the line beyond Donnington was closed completely two years later. Some freight traffic continued on the Wellington–Donnington section until 1991; but the track, initially removed, was reinstated in 2008 in preparation for the opening of a new freight terminal at Donnington. The remaining East Shropshire branch line that still handles regular freight traffic is that from Madeley Junction to Ironbridge power station, until recently carrying trains of coal but now carrying biomass.

Passenger services on the main line have undergone a number of changes in recent years. In 1967, through trains from Shrewsbury to London switched from Paddington to Euston, and from 1986 served the newly opened Telford Central station. Reduced to a single service each way in 1992, this was discontinued seven years later, leaving only feeder services from Chester (later Holyhead) and Aberystwyth/Pwllheli, through Shrewsbury and Telford, to Birmingham. A direct link to the capital was reintroduced by the enterprising Wrexham & Shropshire Company's service to London Marylebone in 2008, but this was withdrawn within three years. A new twice-daily return service between Shrewsbury and London Euston was begun by Virgin Trains in December 2014.

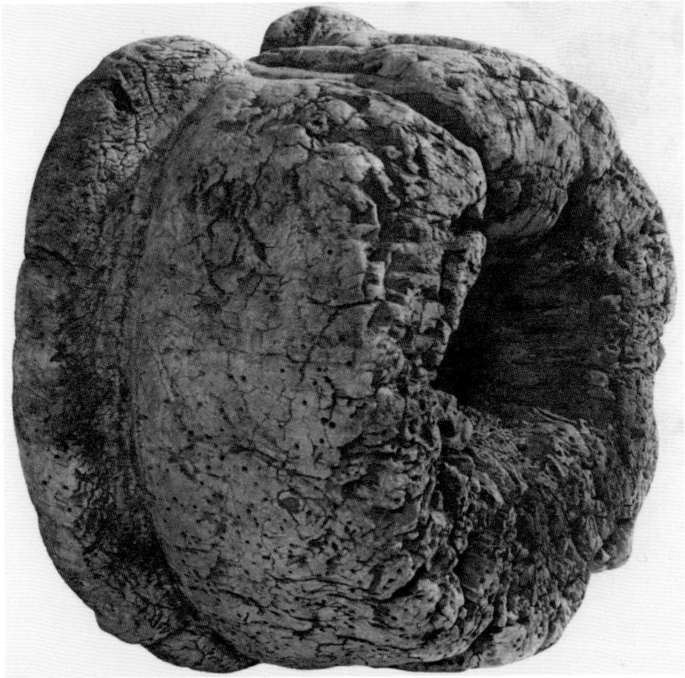

Early Railways

One of the earliest recorded railways in this country ran from a mine in Broseley to the River Severn at the Calcutts (Jackfield). The wagons on this wooden wagonway of 1605 would have used wooden wheels similar to that found in a pit at Caughley (above), which has a diameter of 9½ inches. The riverside wharf at the Calcutts is depicted on an early eighteenth-century estate map, redrawn below.

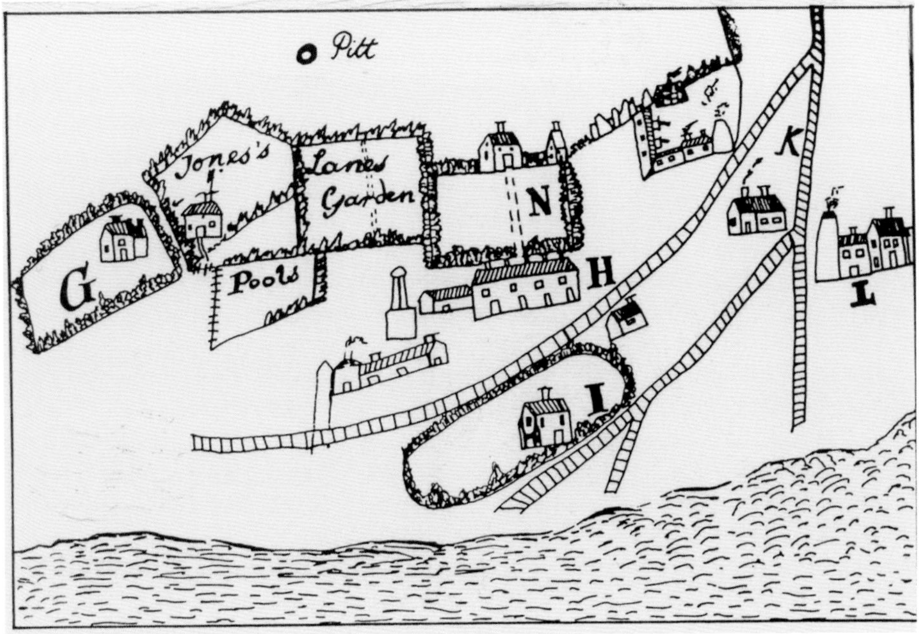

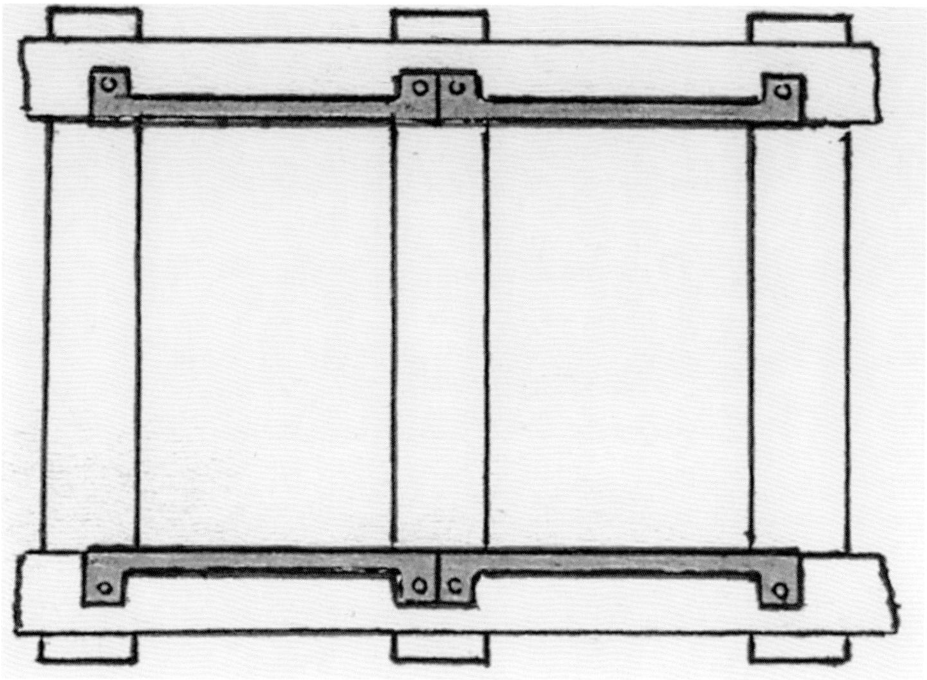

First Use of Iron
The Coalbrookdale Company made the first flanged (rimmed) iron wheels for use on wagonways in 1729 and went on to produce the first iron rails in 1767. These were attached to the top edge of the wooden rails to prevent wear, as shown in this plan view (above), and were used on the company's railway system linking their ironworks and mines. A railway bridge from around 1760 survives at New Dale, near Ketley (below).

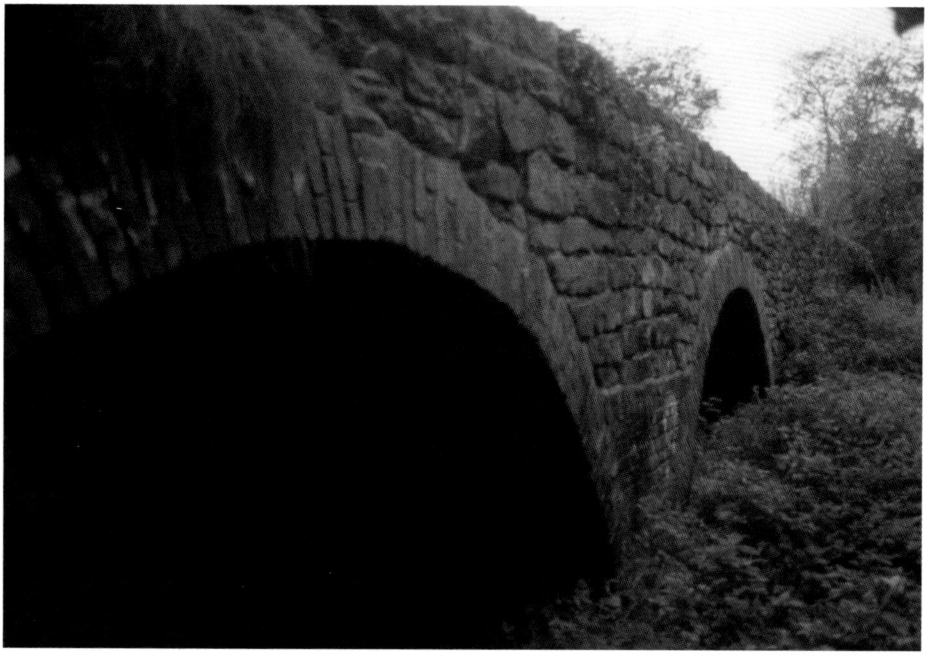

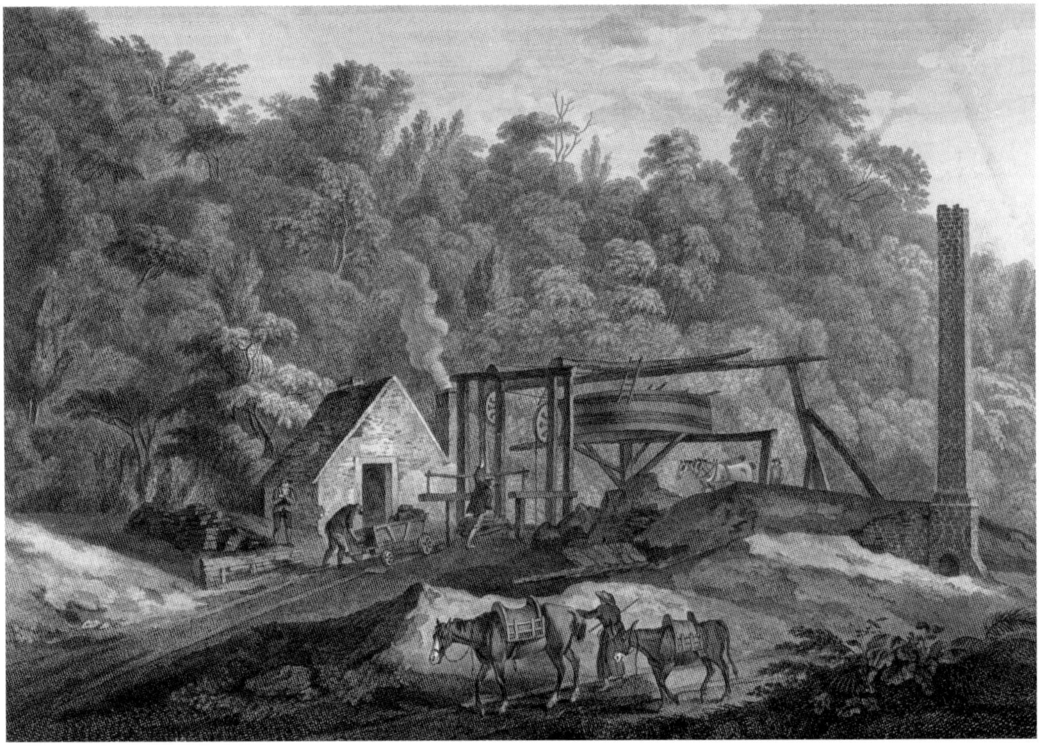

Other Wagonways

Some of the hybrid wood-and-iron wagonways continued in use during the late eighteenth century. They can be seen on the depiction of a coal pit near Broseley in 1788 (above), and the ironmaster John Wilkinson carried iron from his furnaces at Willey to a wharf on the Severn (below) along such rails, before introducing all-iron rails.

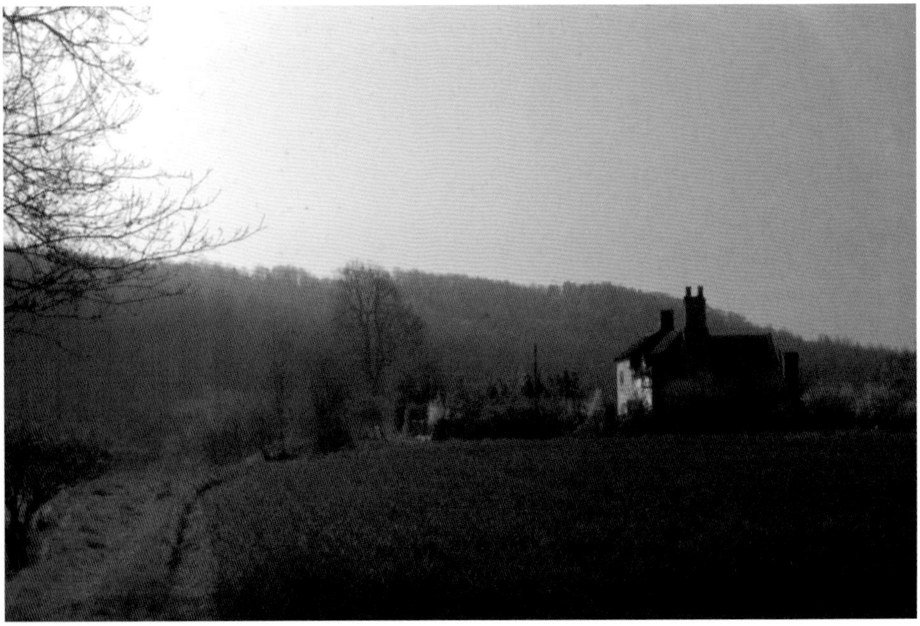

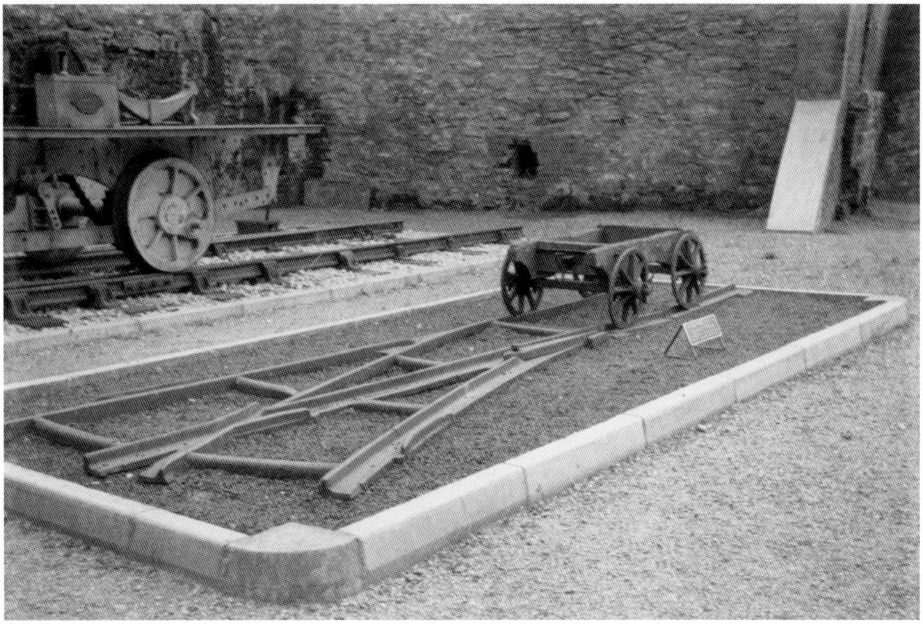

Plateways

At the very end of the eighteenth century, cast-iron L-shaped rails (plateways) were introduced; on these flanged rails ran wagons with flange-less wheels (above). These plateways, or tramways as they are sometimes known, were soon adopted throughout the coalfield, and remarkably survived on a small scale, in places such as Horsehay Works, into the twentieth century (below).

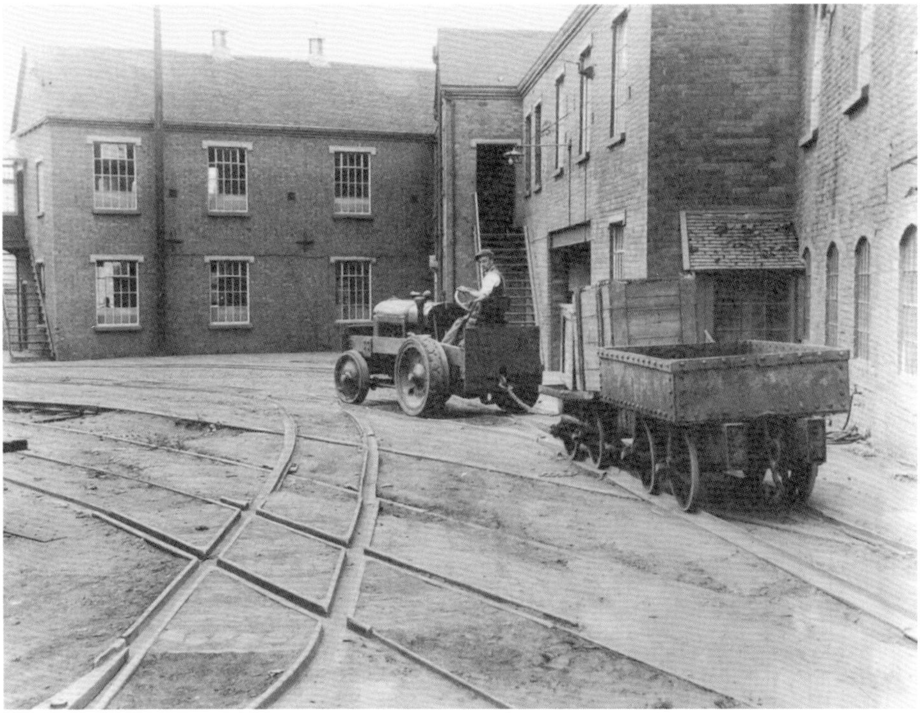

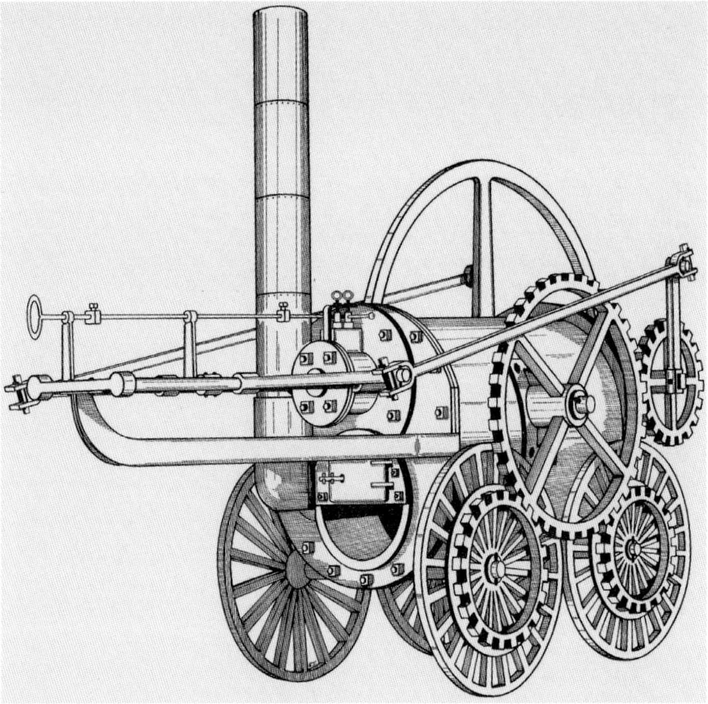

Early Locomotive

What is generally considered to be the world's first steam locomotive, designed by Richard Trevithick and sponsored by William Reynolds, the Ketley ironmaster, was built at Coalbrookdale in 1802-03. With teething troubles and the early death of Reynolds, the idea was not pursued further locally. Based on a 1803 drawing in the Science Museum (redrawn, above), the replica of the locomotive, built by GKN Sankey of Hadley, now operates on a plateway at IGMT's Blists Hill Victorian Town (below).

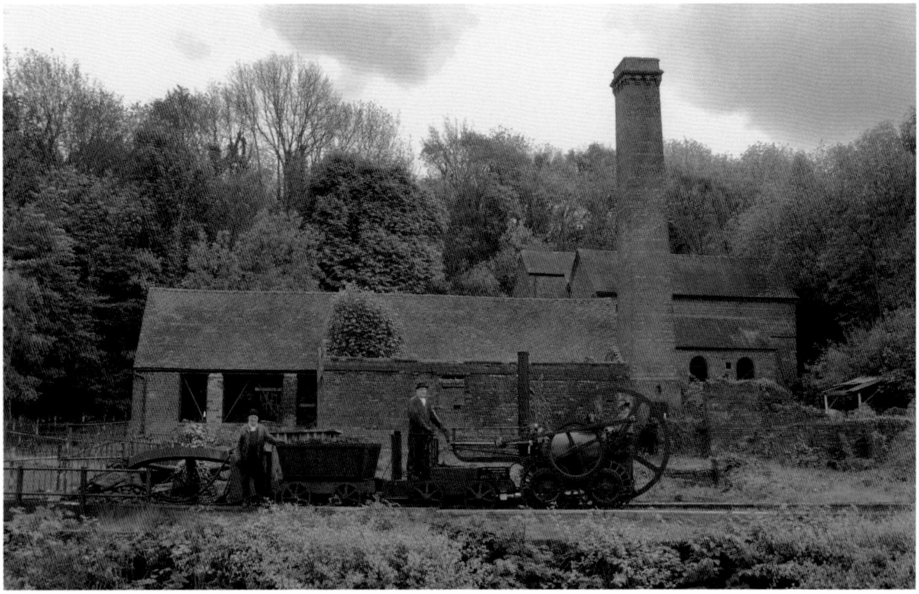

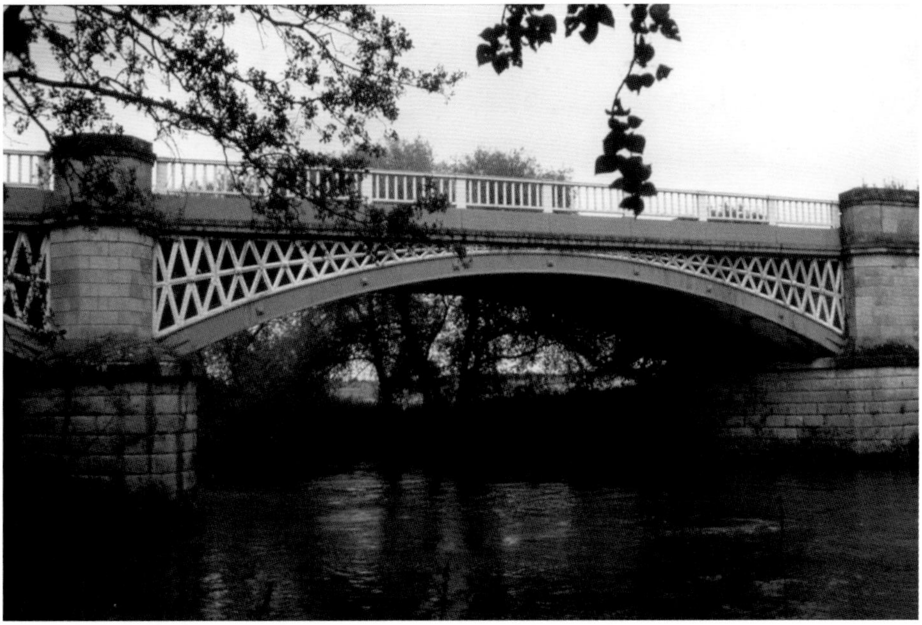

The Main Line

After crossing the Severn at Shrewsbury, within two miles the railway has to bridge the river again at Belvidere (above). The two cast-iron spans were built by the Coalbrookdale Company. On the joint Shrewsbury & Birmingham (SBR) and Shropshire Union Railways & Canal Company (SURCC) line to Wellington, the three intermediate stations all opened 1 June 1849 and closed 7 September 1964. All that remains at Upton Magna are the railway cottages (below). Notice the adjacent bridge on the SURCC-owned Shrewsbury Canal.

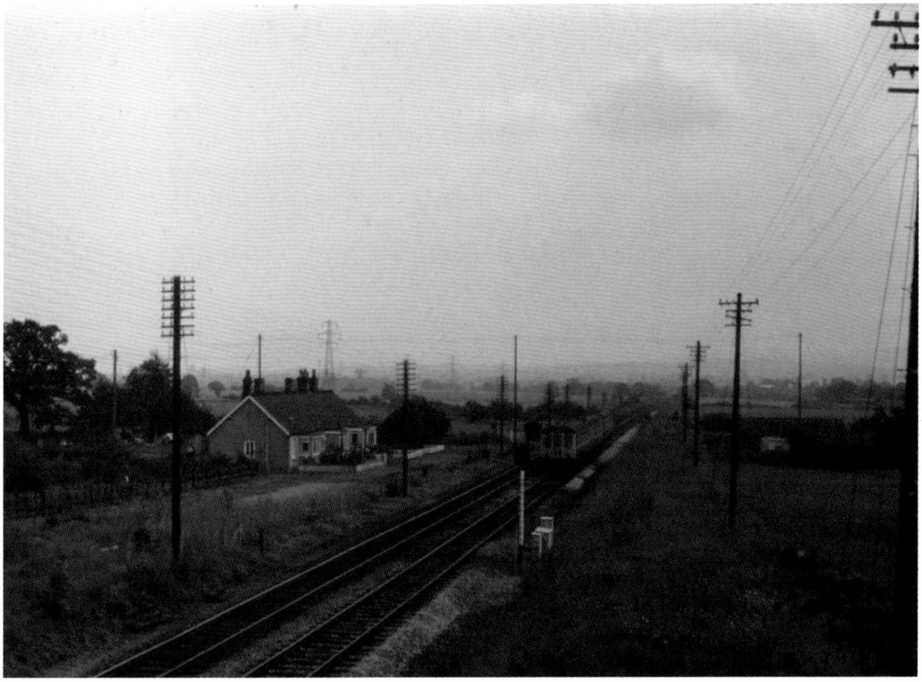

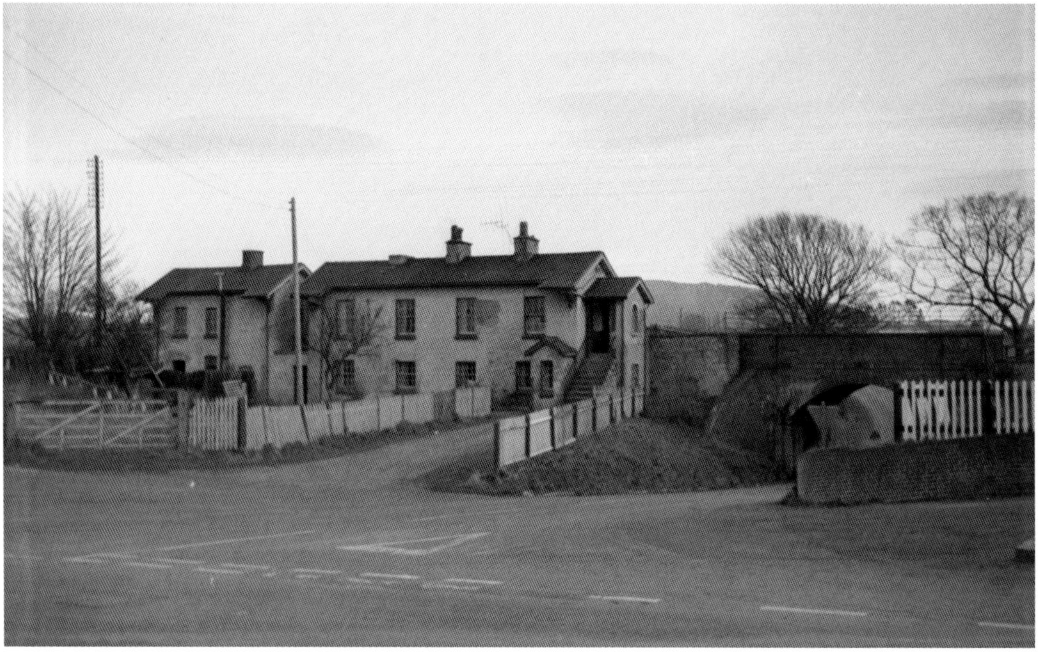

Walcot

Because of the slope of the land on the Up (London-bound) side, the station at Walcot, which served a scattered rural community, was a two-storey building at the front (above) and a single-storey at platform level (below). It was demolished soon after closure.

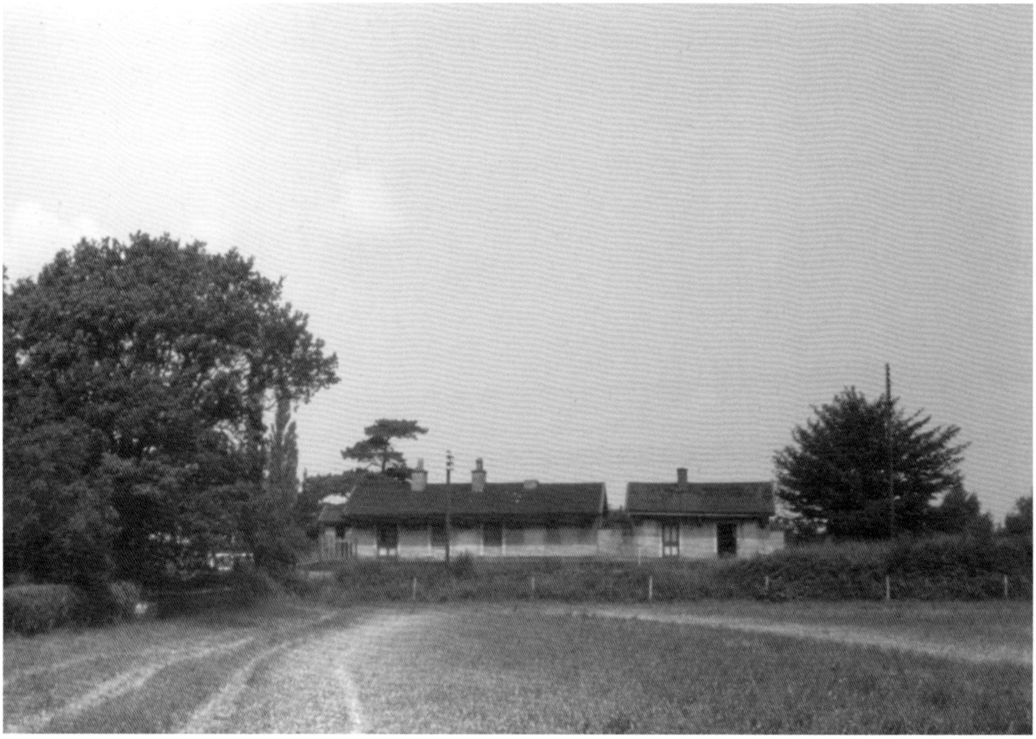

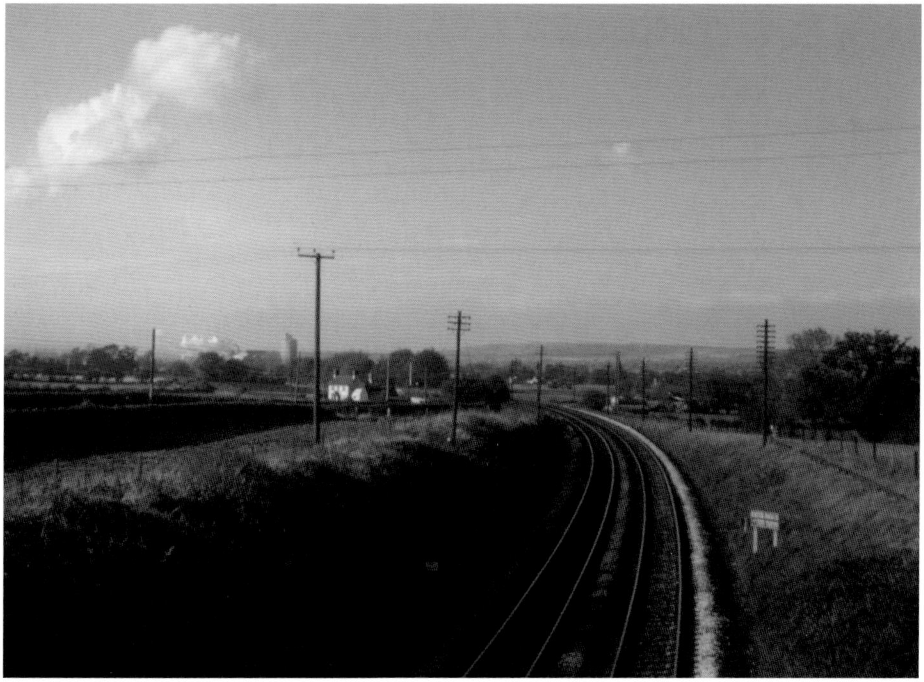

Admaston

Sidings served the Allscott Sugar Beet Factory (1927–2007) until 1983, and the main line was built in a cutting (above) on its approach to Admaston. The station here, also used by residents of nearby Wrockwardine, was below the level of the station master's house (below). Its name was changed to Admaston Halt in 1952.

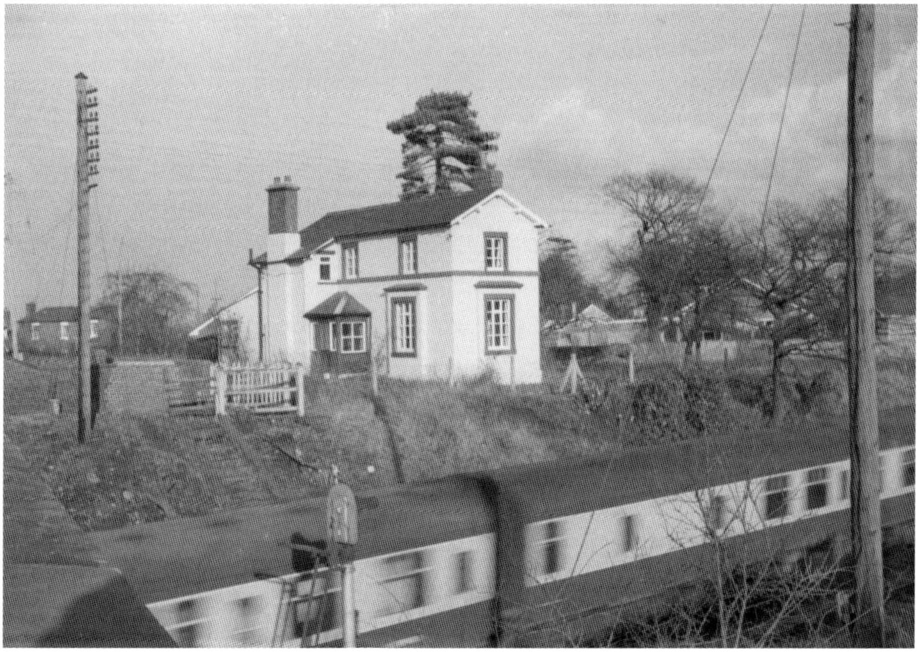

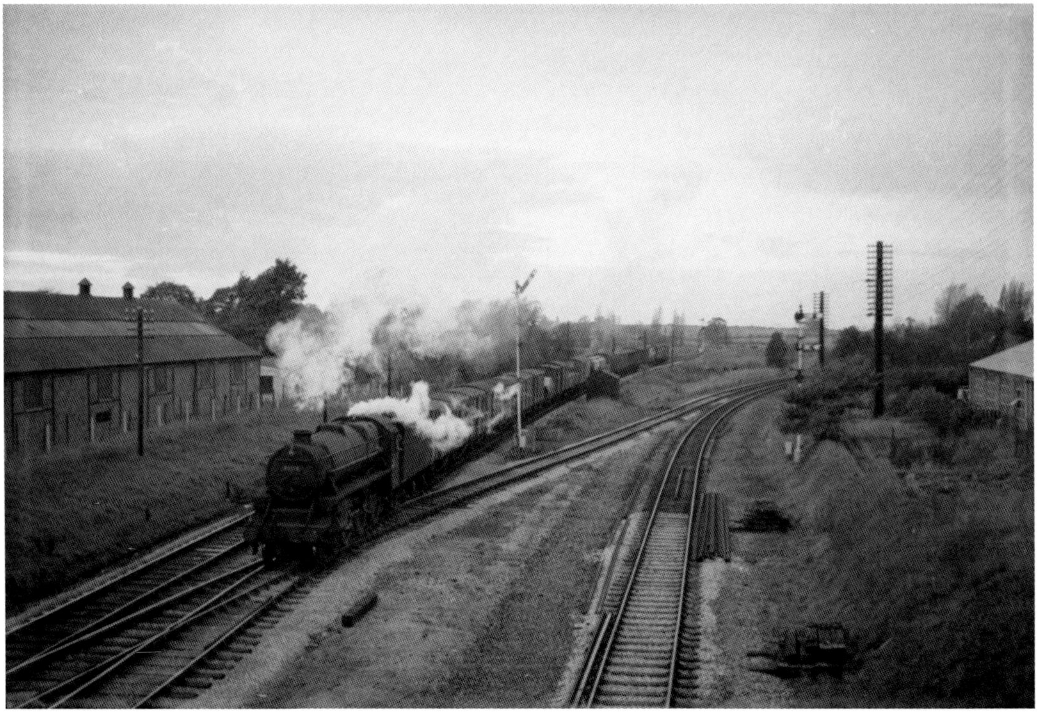

Market Drayton Junction

In 1867, a junction with the main line was made by the GWR's line to Market Drayton, controlled by Wellington signal box No. 4. The junction is shown in this 1967 view looking west (above). The signal box, with the goods yards beyond, is shown in the earlier view (below) looking east. Nothing remains of the junction or the signal box.

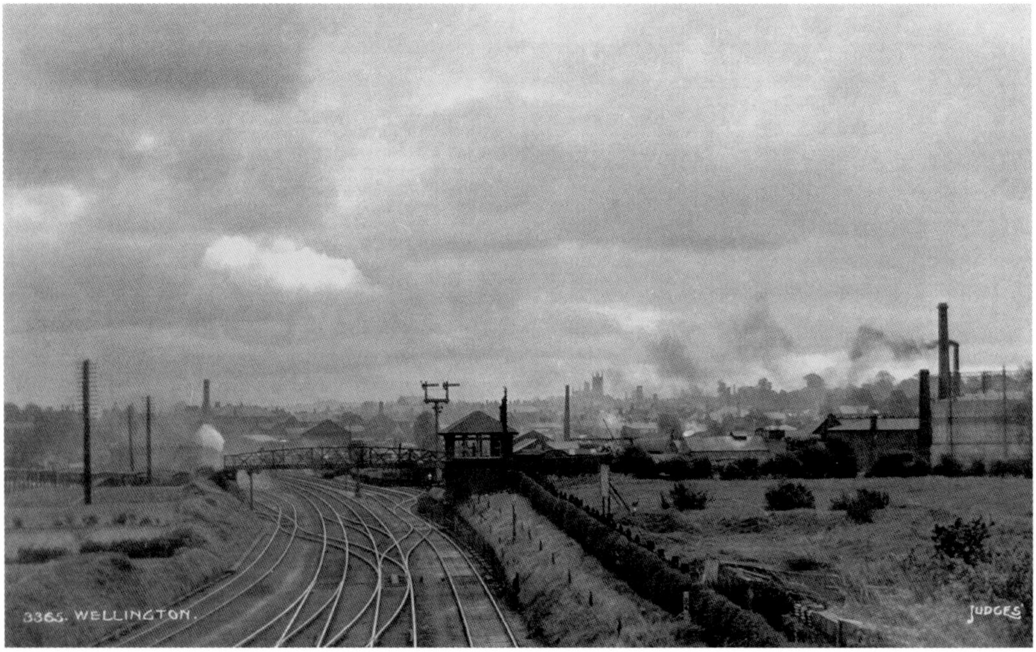

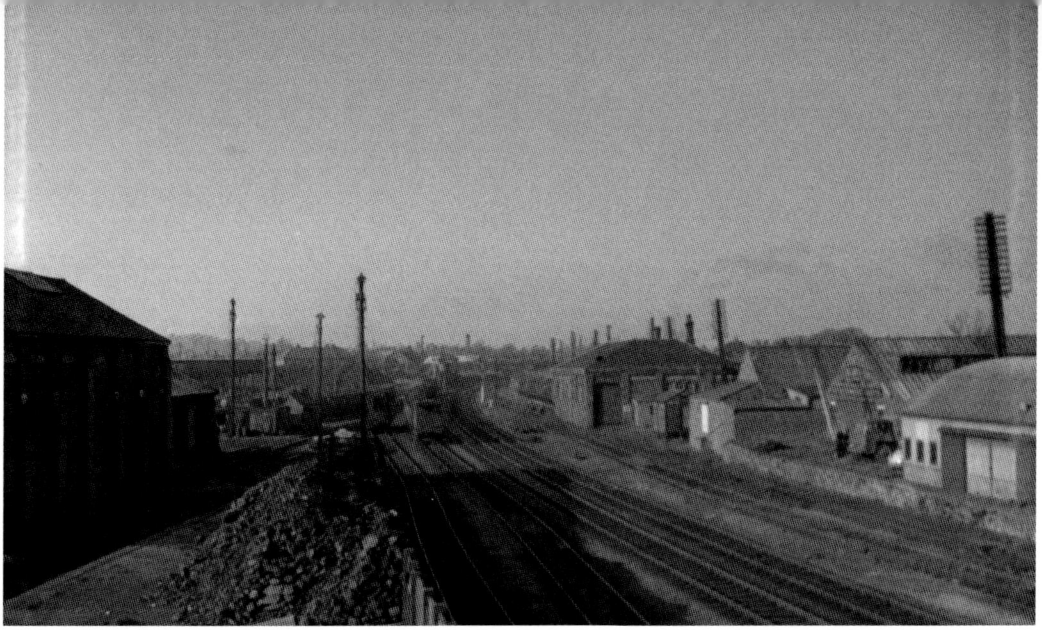

Wellington Goods Yards
Both goods yards (above) handled the livestock of the adjacent Smithfield Market, but while the GWR Town Goods Yard on the Down side (above) received coal supplies for local merchants and the gasworks, the LNWR/LMS Queen Street Yard on the Up side dispatched the products of local manufacturers. A Birmingham-bound train passes the site of the yards, now a supermarket car park and a housing development (below).

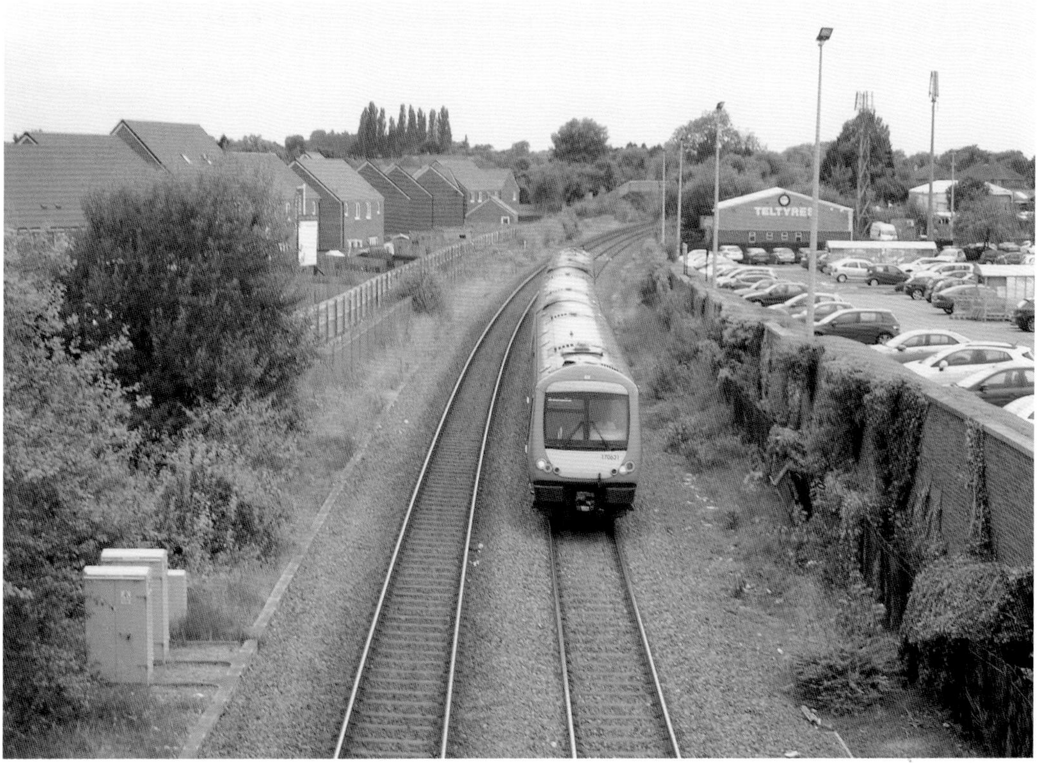

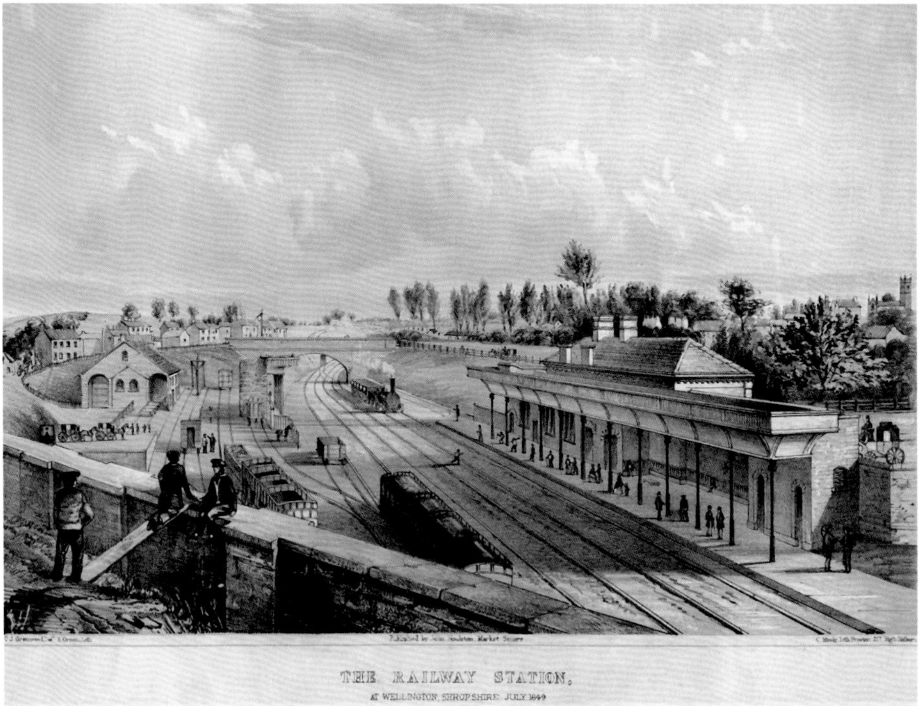

Wellington Station
The lithograph of Wellington station (above) depicts it shortly after opening in 1849, viewed from the wall of the churchyard. The goods shed on the left was purchased by the GWR from the LNWR & GWR Joint Committee in 1867 and utilised as its engine shed, and the up-side platform building was extended in the years following the opening of the station. A similar modern view (below) is from the Church Street overbridge.

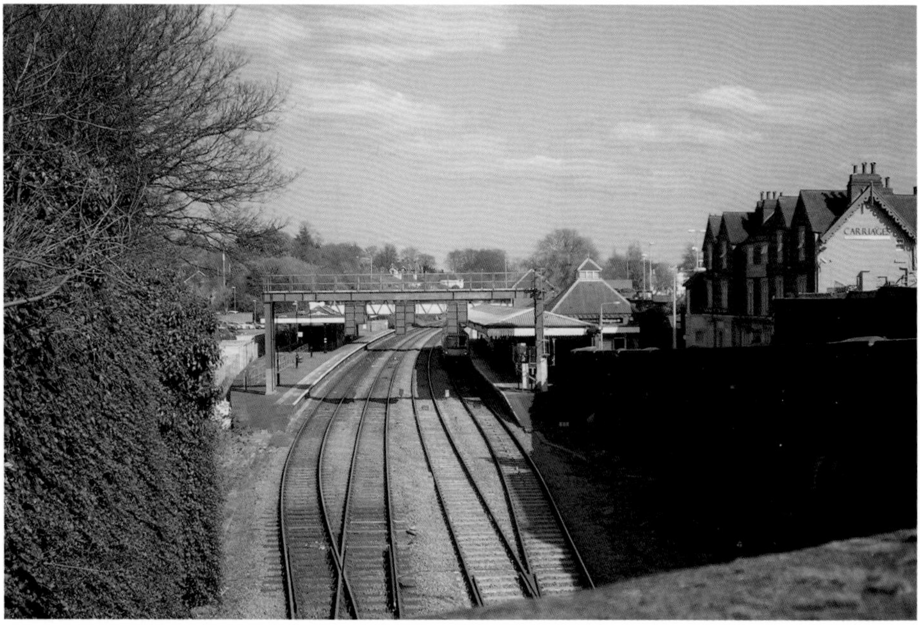

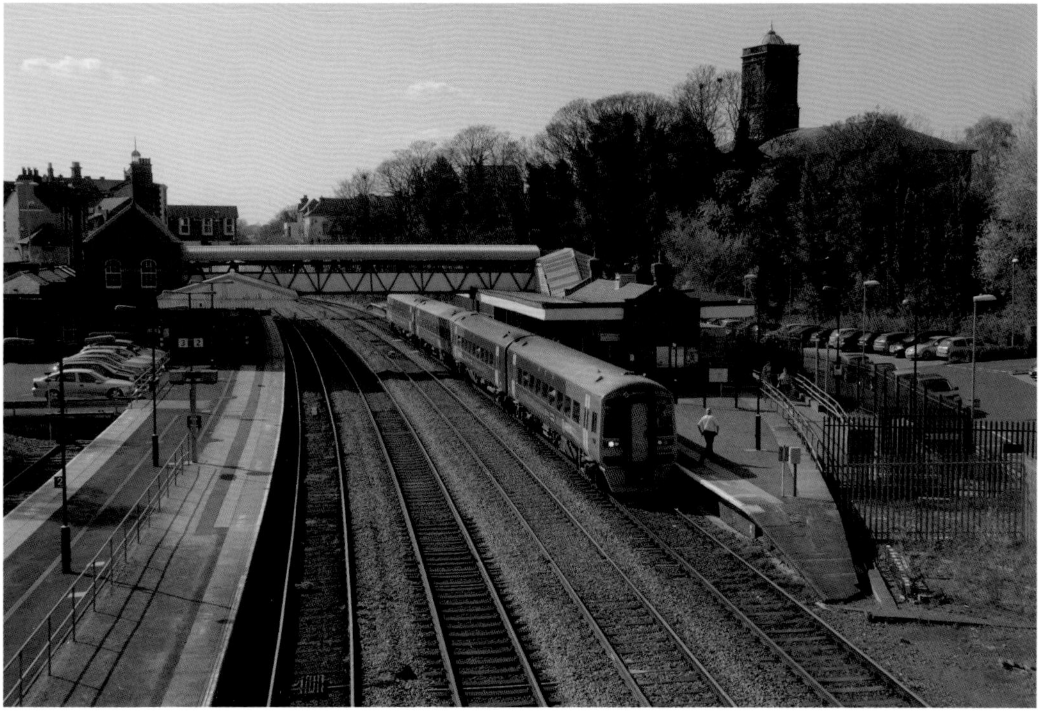

Churchyard and Station

The railway was built in a cutting through the centre of the town (above). Although it is not clear if any graves were disturbed in the adjacent All Saints' churchyard, it is claimed that the two crosses that surmount the main station building (below), reflecting that on the tower of the church, were put there as a mark of respect.

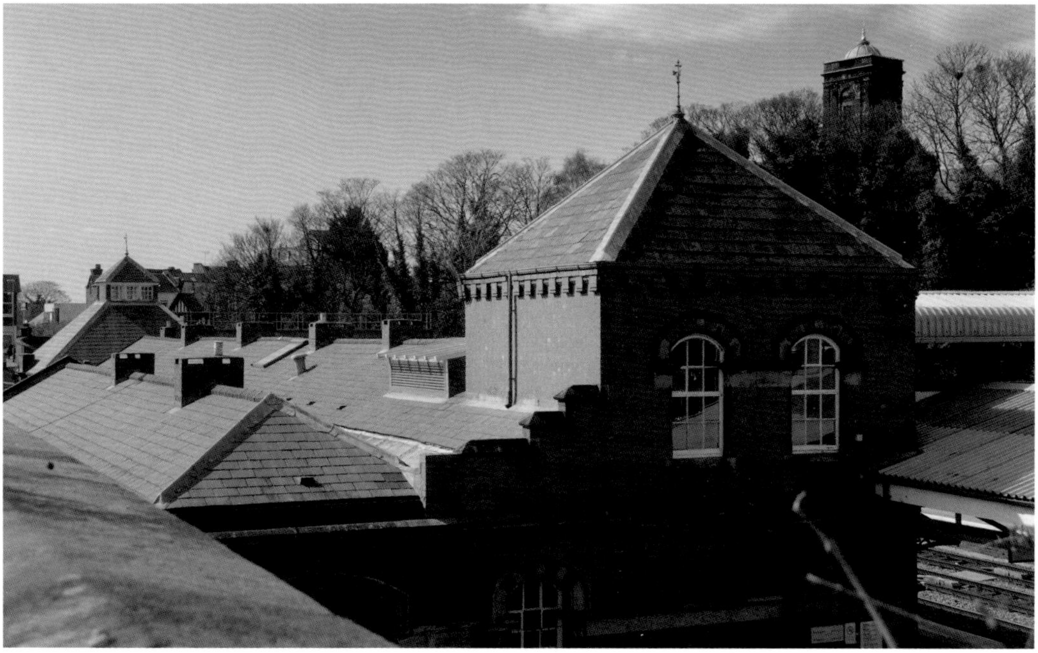

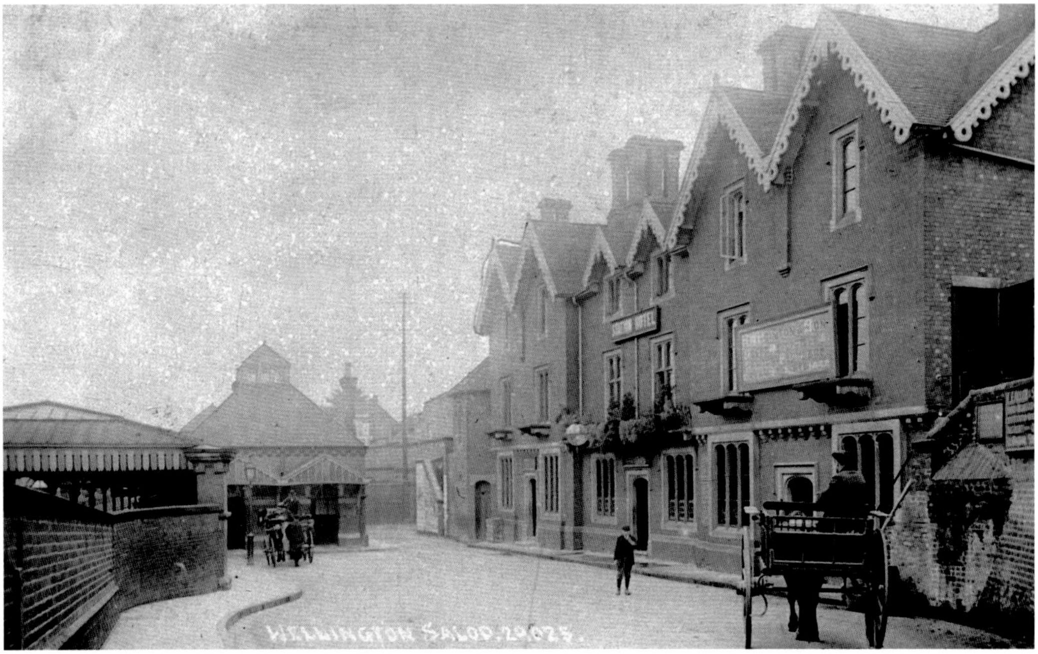

Station Road and Station Hotel

The approach to the station from the centre of Wellington is down Station Road. Adjacent to the station entrance is the Station Hotel, built at the beginning of the twentieth century (above). Apart from cars replacing horse-drawn vehicles, little has changed in the view today (below).

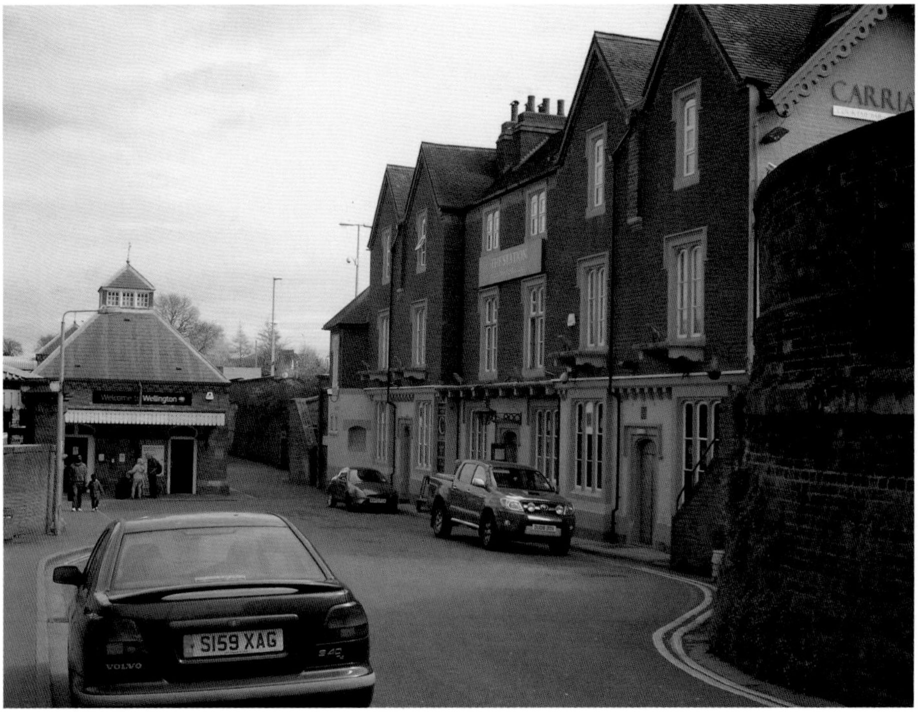

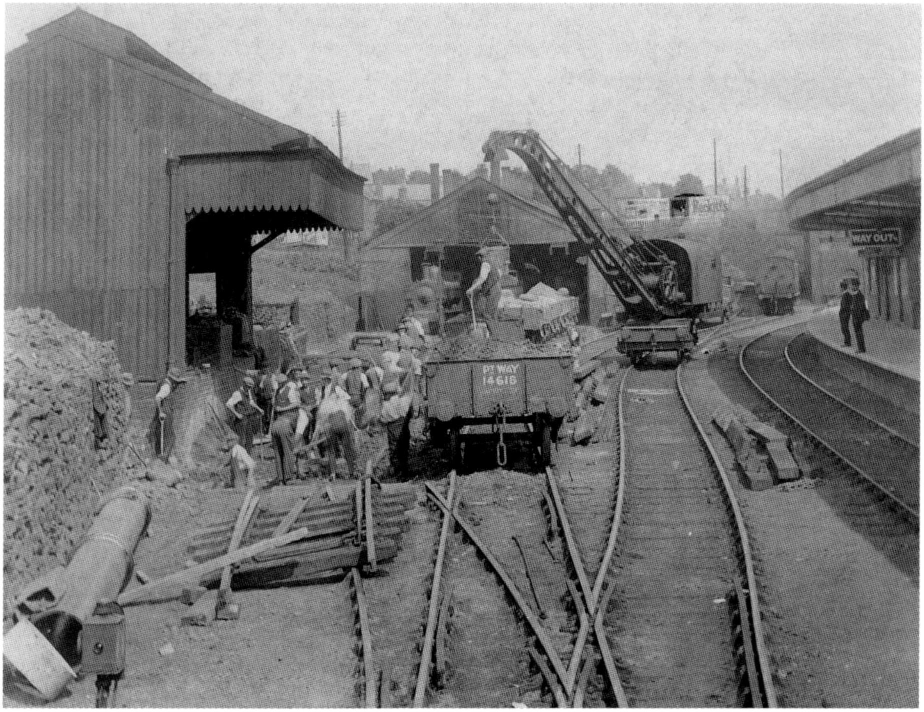

Engine Shed and Yard

Locomotives were needed for local passenger, freight and shunting duties. There were seventeen engines housed at the shed in the 1950s, but this had been reduced to five by the time of closure in 1964. The position of the engine shed and coaling plant in relation to the station is seen in the 1925 photograph (above). The 1960 view (below) is from the other direction.

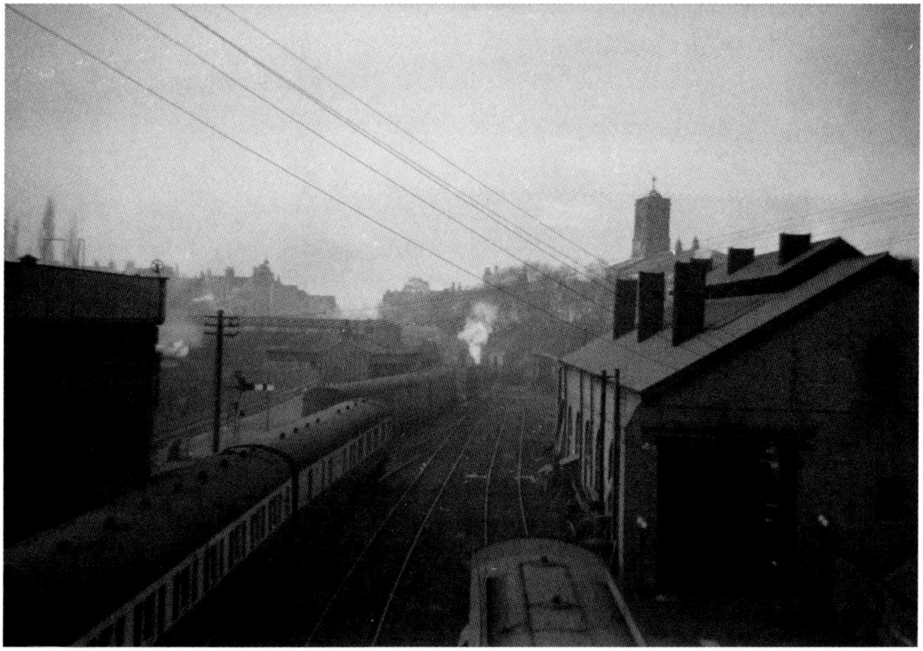

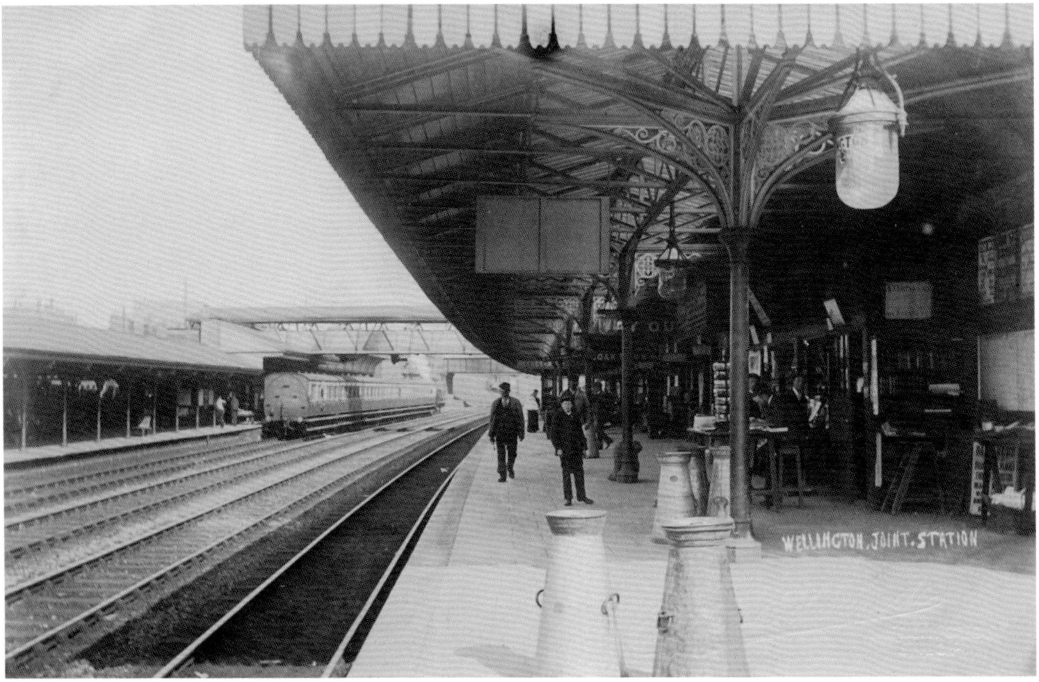

Catching a Train

On Wellington station, a century ago (above), a train leaves for Wolverhampton from Platform 1 and passengers and staff congregate on Platform 2, where a bookstall is open and milk churns await collection. The scene today (below) reveals a departing train for Birmingham on Platform 1 and awaiting passengers on Platform 2, but no staff, no bookstall and no goods for collection.

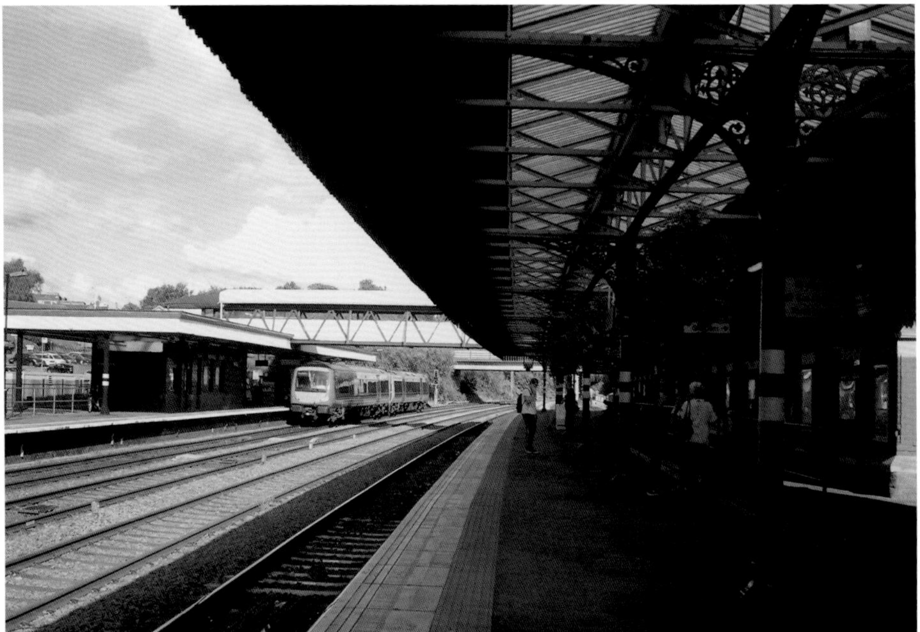

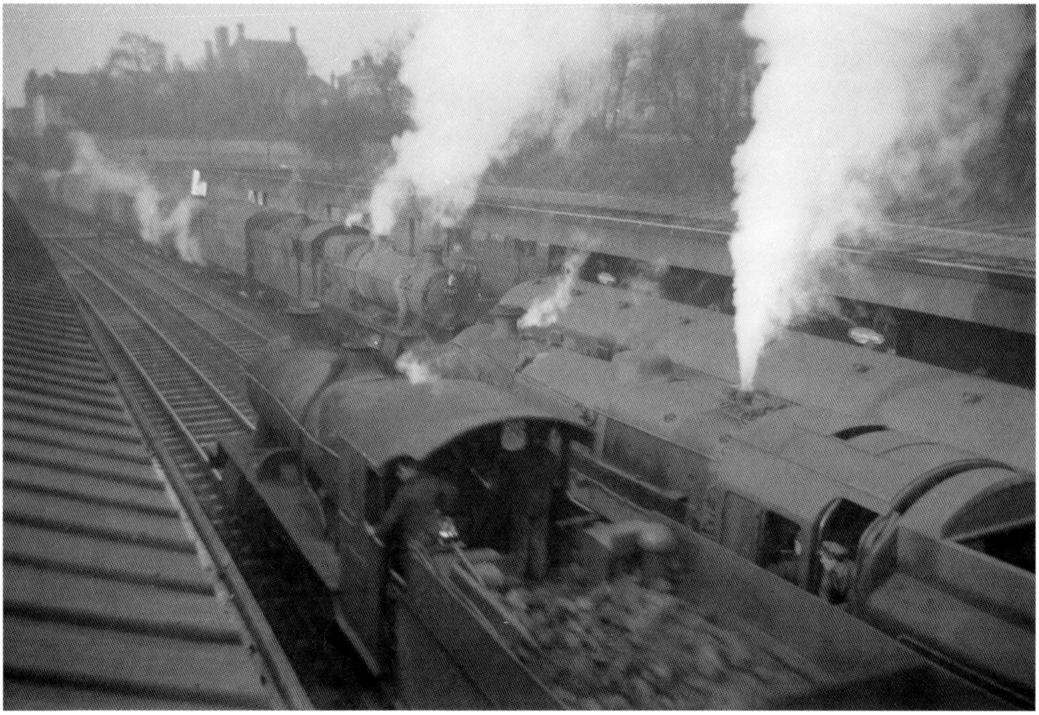

Goods Trains Galore

In the 1950s there was a steady flow of goods trains passing through Wellington, some of which called at the goods yards. This busy scene (above) dates from 1956. Eleven years later (below), it was almost as busy, but by then diesel-motive power had taken over.

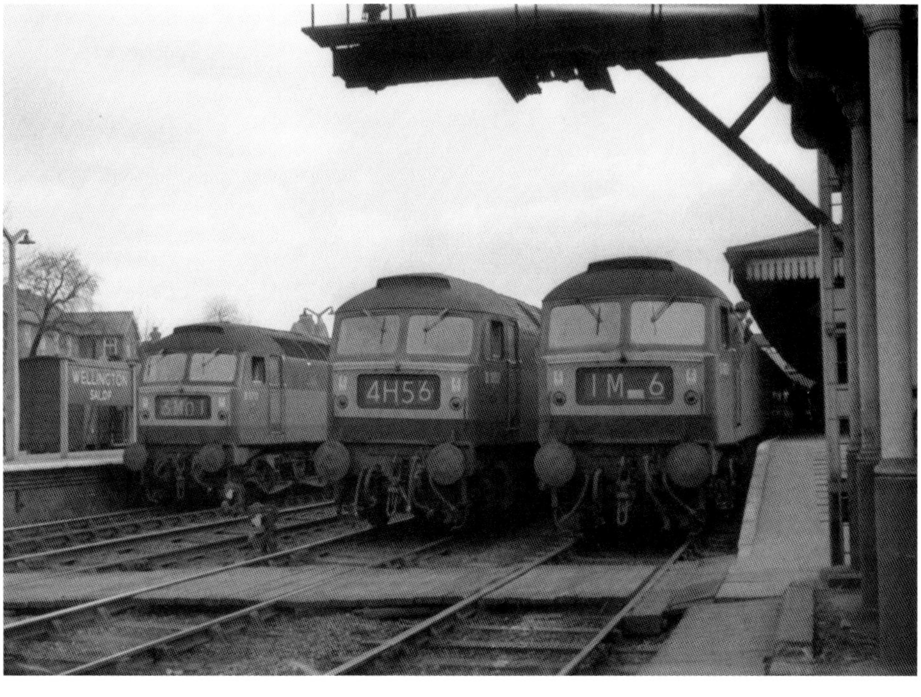

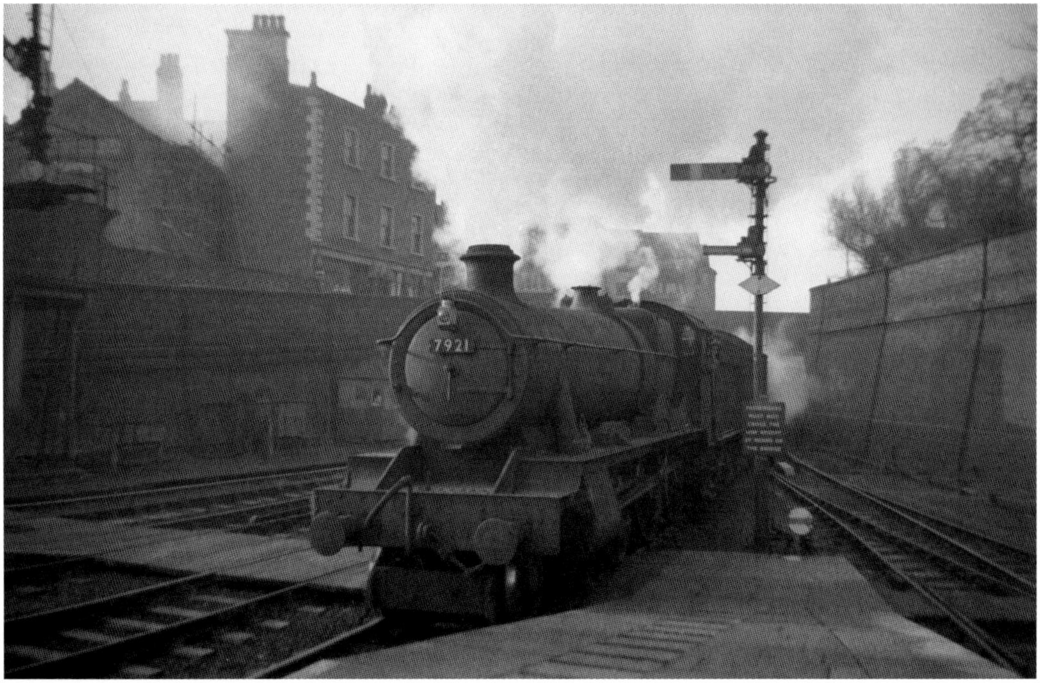

Trains to London

For over a century, most London-bound passengers from Wellington would have travelled on express trains to Paddington (above, 1956). This changed in 1967, when through trains arrived in London at Euston. When this service was removed, the Wrexham & Shropshire Company provided trains to Marylebone between 2008 and 2011 (below).

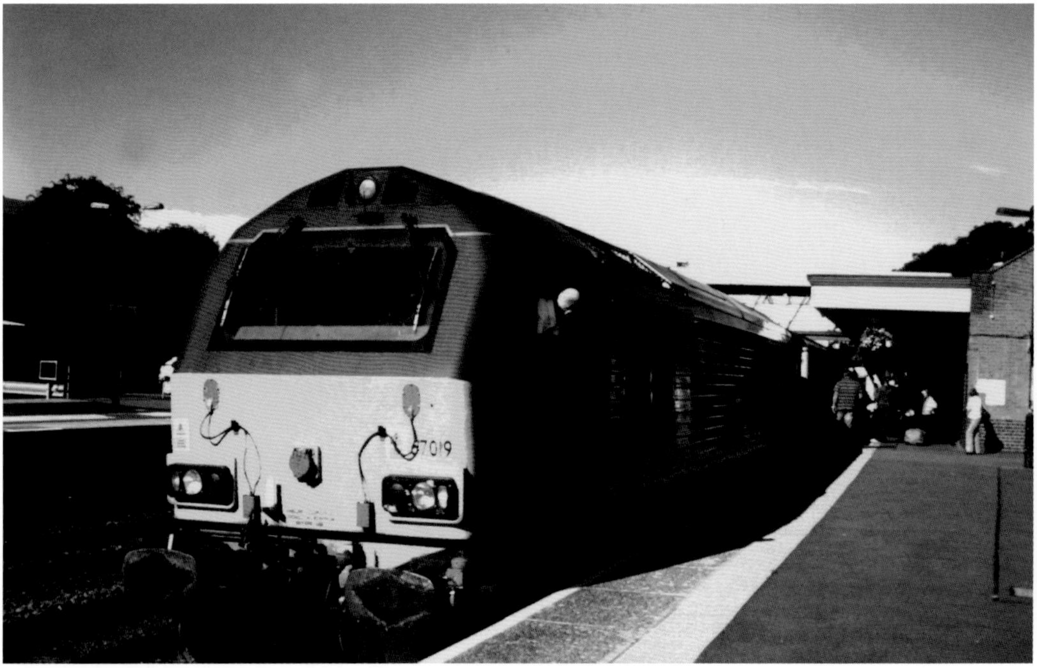

Special Trains
To mark the last weekend of services on the Paddington-Birkenhead route, ex-GWR 4-6-0 *Pendennis Castle* heads 'The Birkenhead Flyer' on the down fast line through Wellington on 4 March 1967 (right). Relief trains from the Welsh Coast passed non-stop through Wellington on the up fast line (below, 1964).

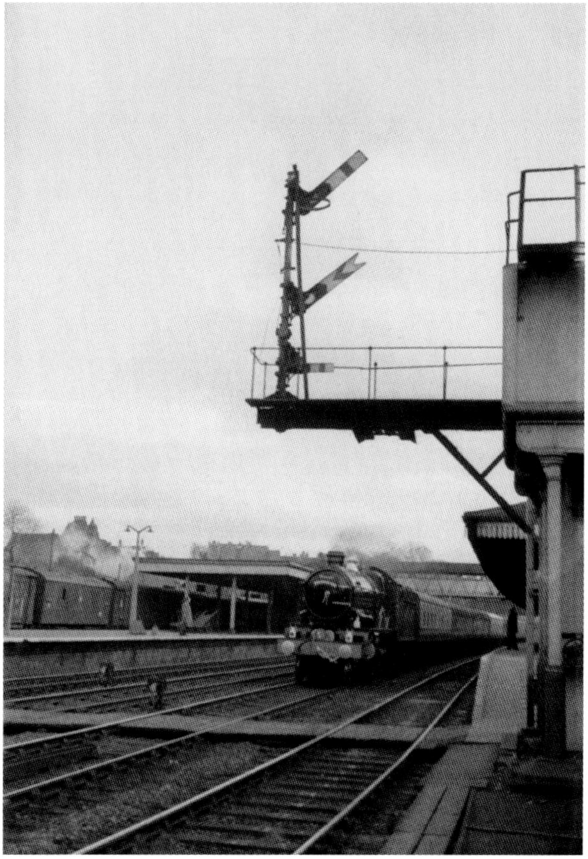

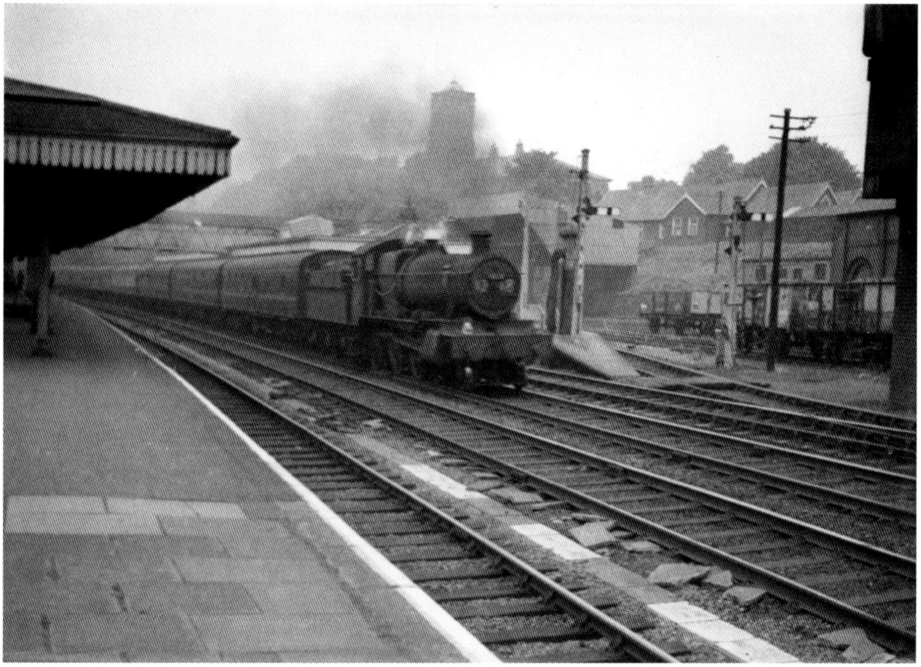

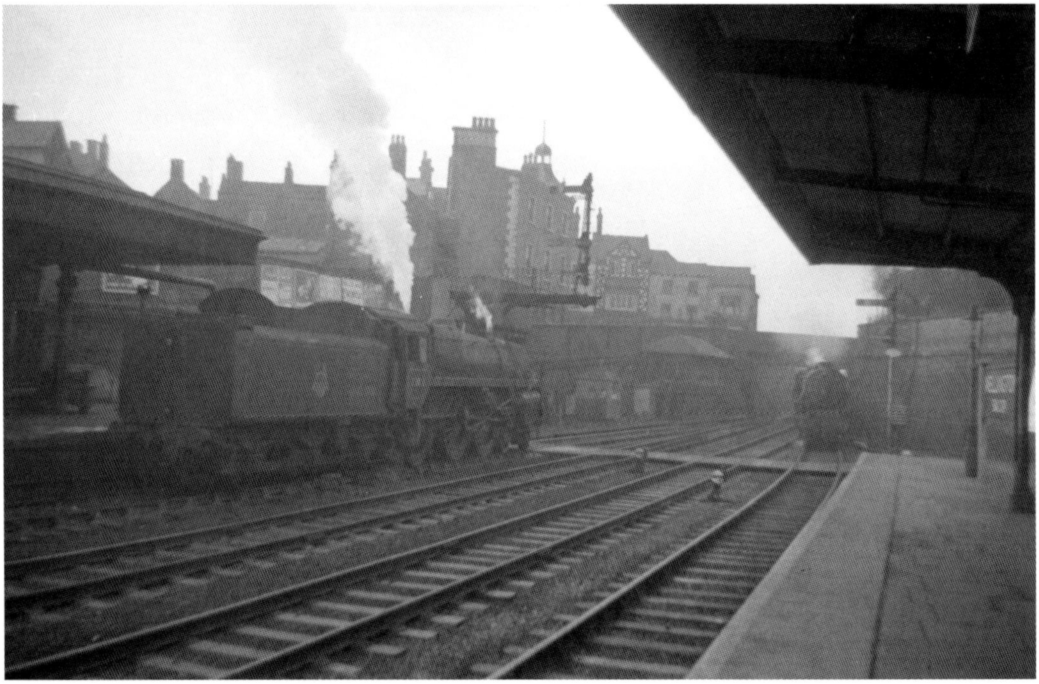

Wellington's Signal Boxes

Railway movements around Wellington were controlled by four signal boxes, two at the junctions beyond the station and two at either end of the station's platforms. No. 3 box was situated below the Church Street bridge (above, 1956); a train of oil tanks passes No. 2 box in 1967 (below).

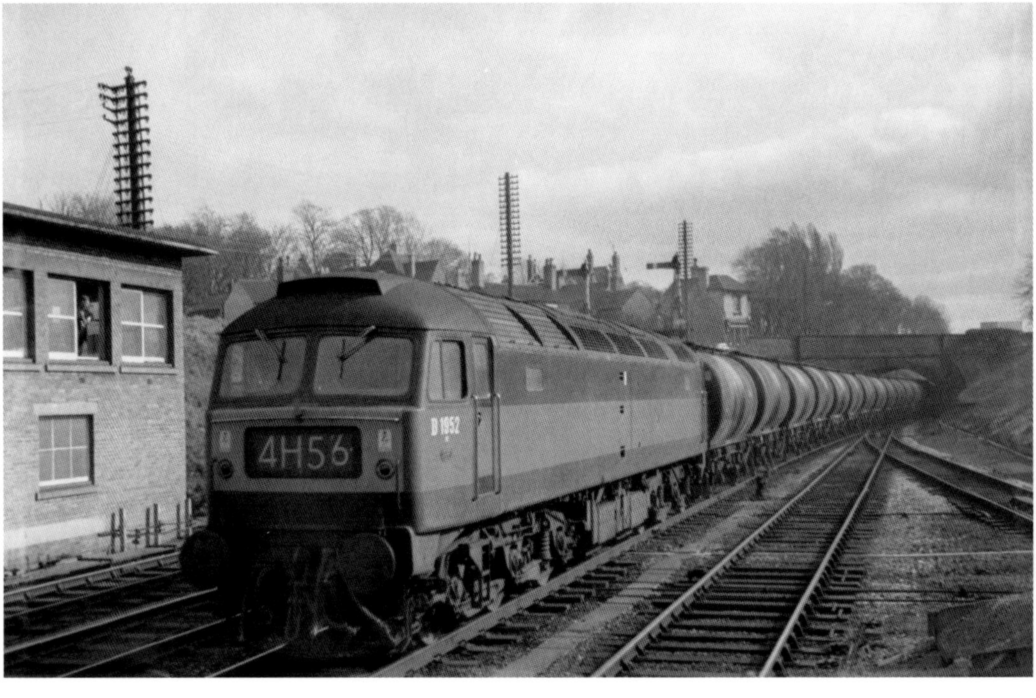

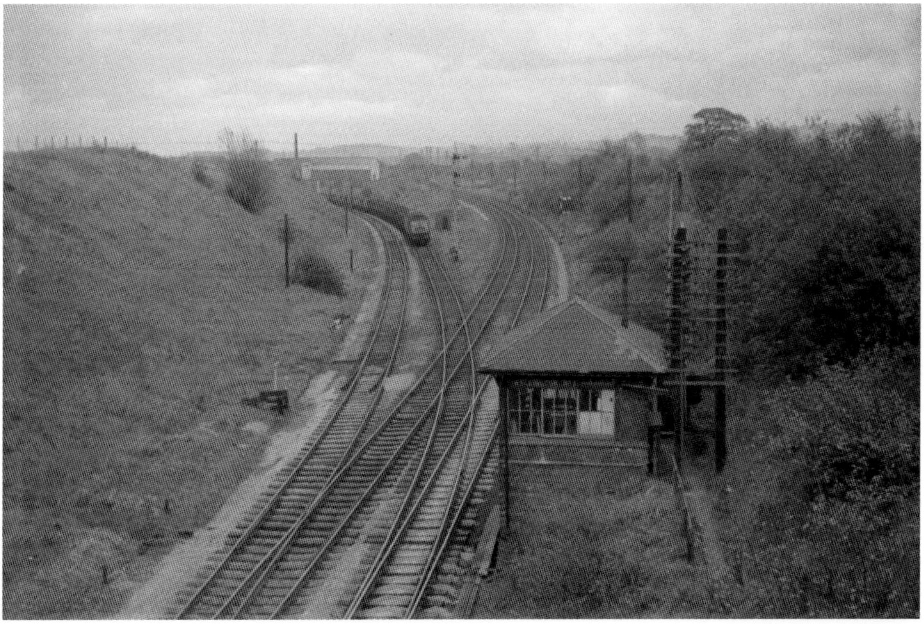

Stafford Junction
The junction for the Stafford line was controlled by Wellington No. 1 signal box (above). This was demolished after closure of the line; but the junction was restored and renamed Donnington Junction in 2008 (right), with the single track serving a new freight depot.

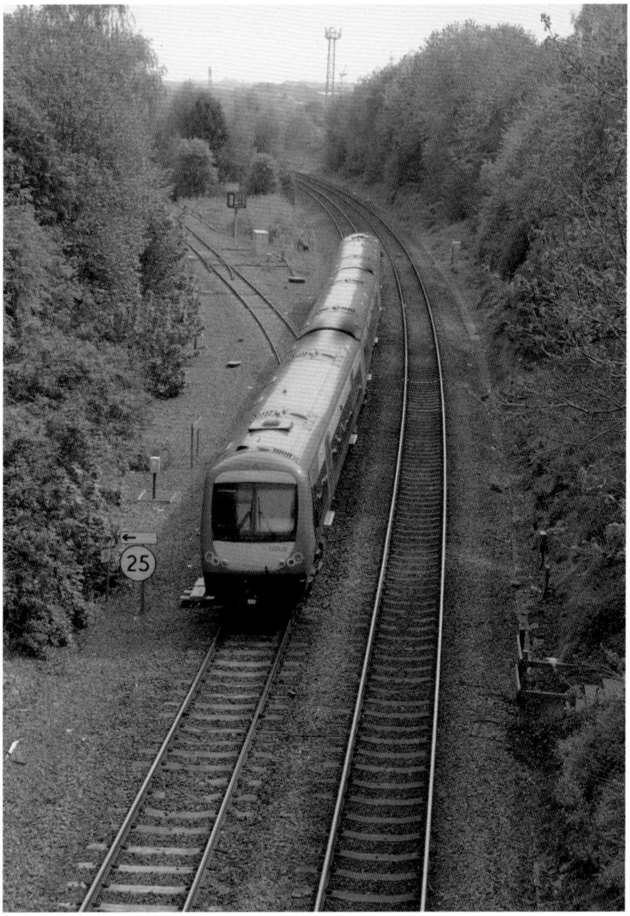

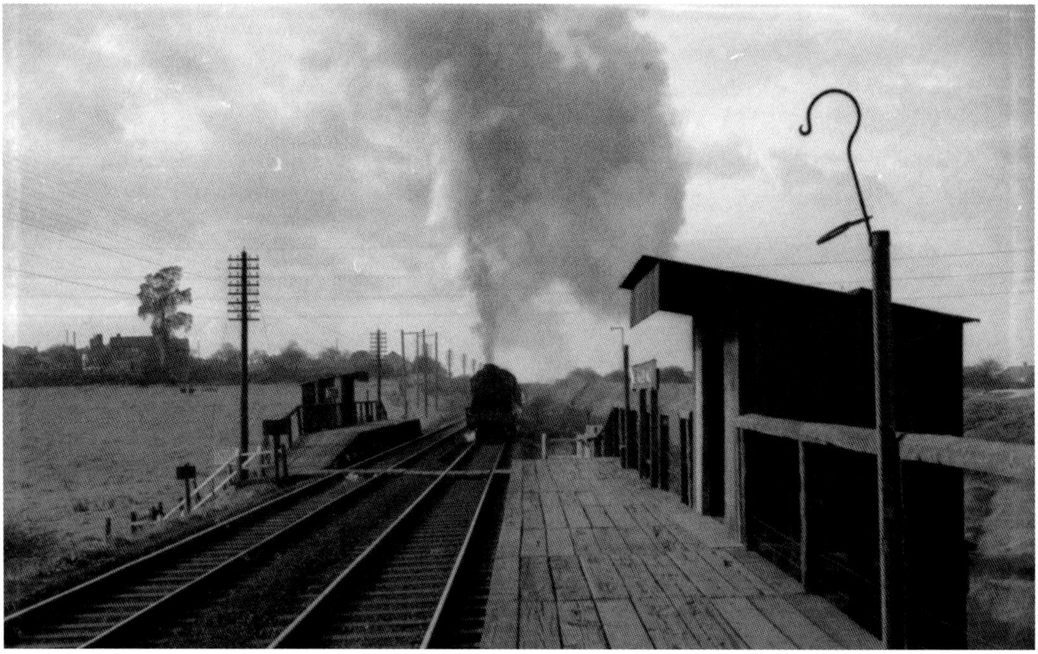

New Hadley Halt

Between Wellington and Oakengates, a half-mile beyond the junction for the Wenlock Branch, was New Hadley Halt. This opened in November 1934 and had staggered platforms (above), approached by an up goods train in 1965. Before its closure in May 1985, boys from the local comprehensive school's railway club start their annual rail excursion from the neglected halt (below).

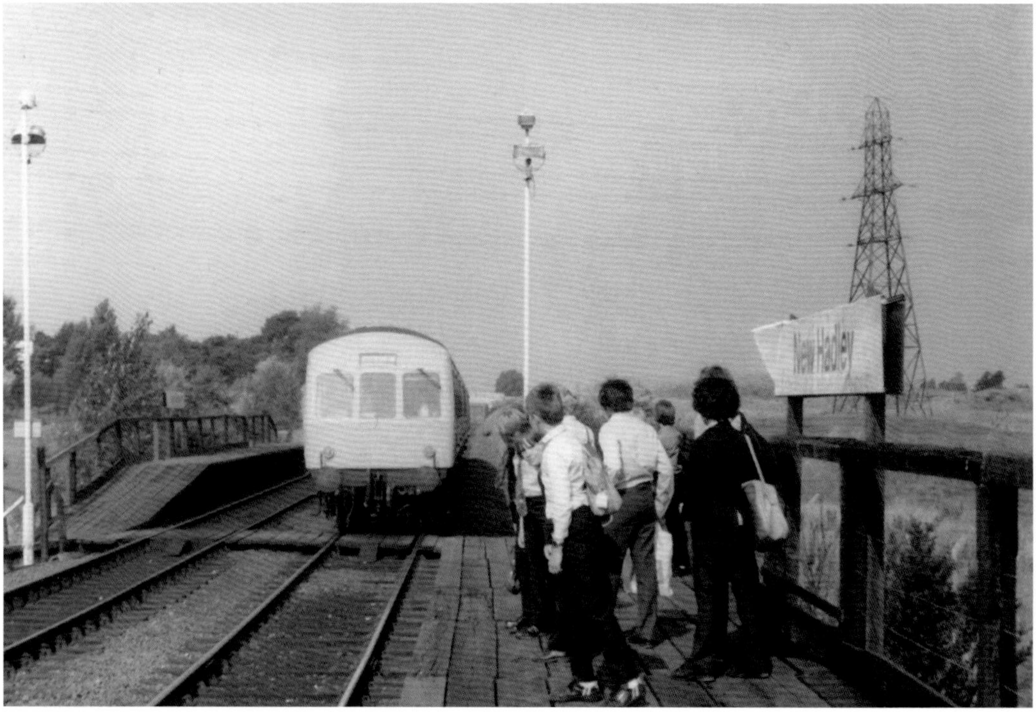

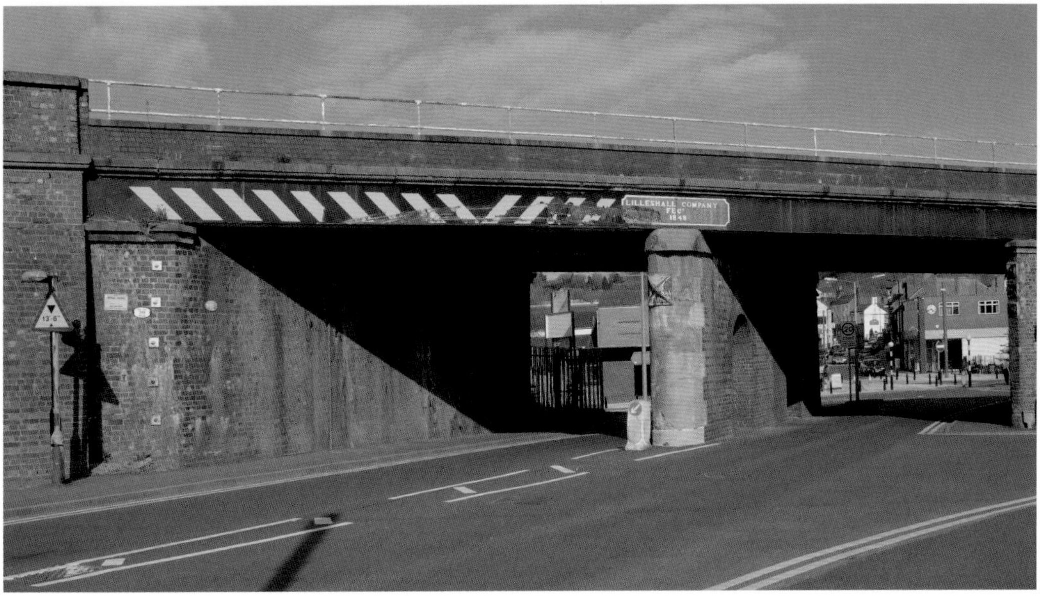

Oakengates Bridge

Oops – someone didn't see the sign! In 2013, a high-sided vehicle caused superficial damage to the bridge, built by the Lilleshall Company in 1848, which carries the railway over the town's main street (above). The view from the other side (below), some fifty-or-so years previous, shows a down goods train crossing the bridge, beneath which is a busy street scene.

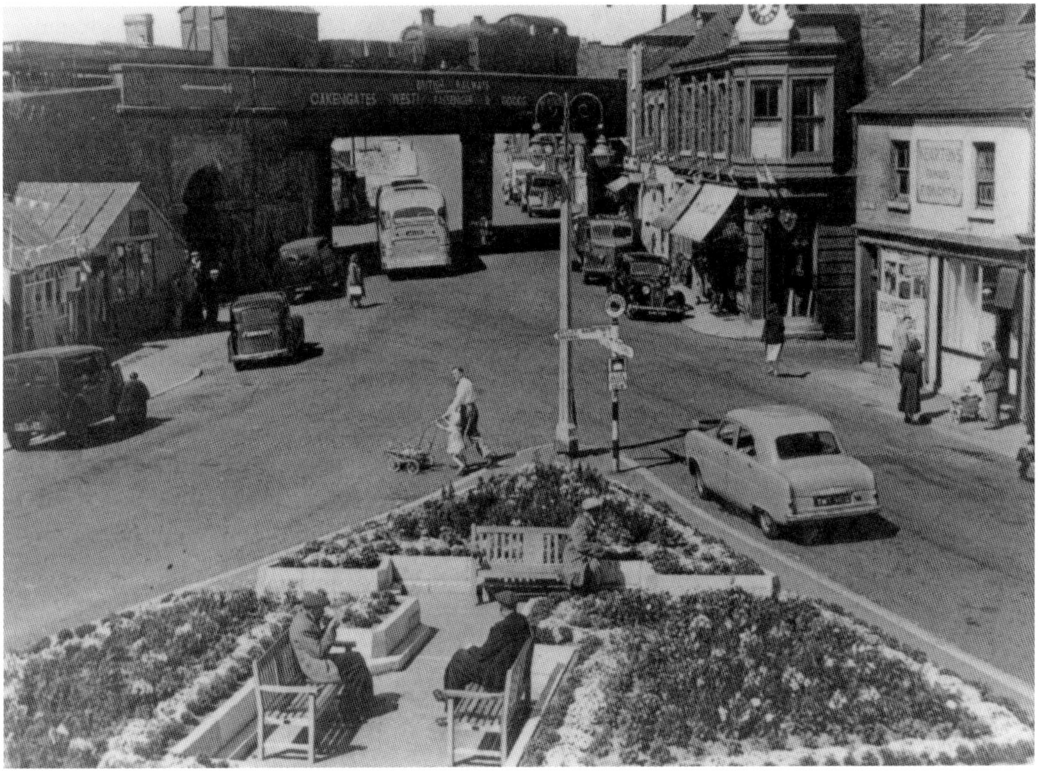

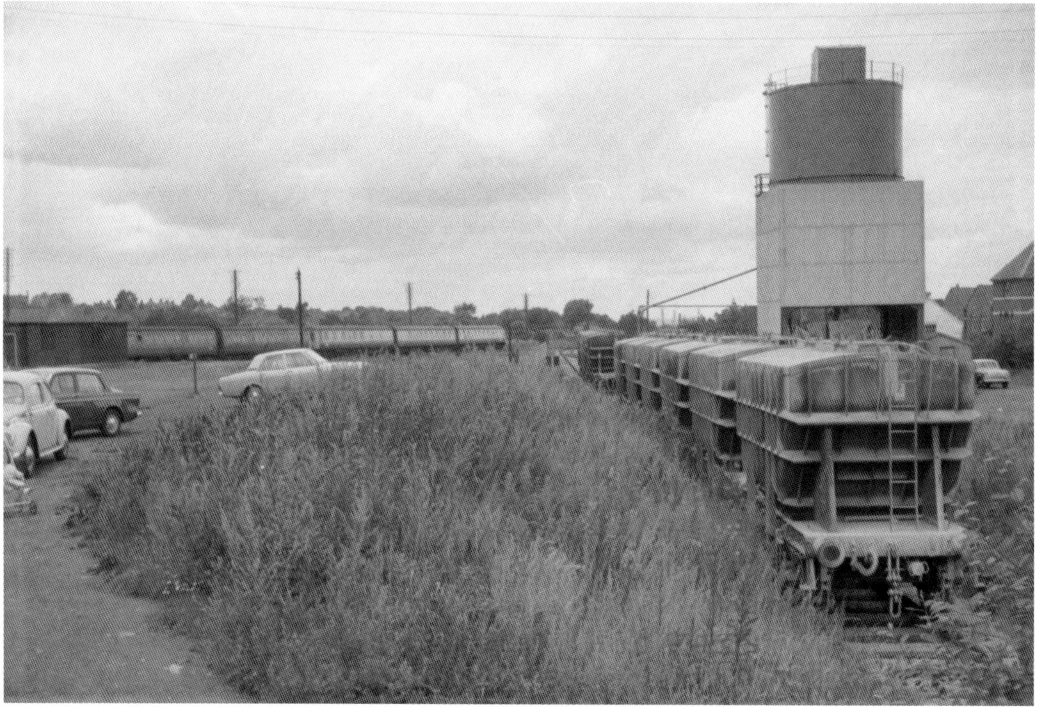

Oakengates Goods Yard

The goods yard, signposted on the bridge, closed in 1965. Replacement sidings handled cement traffic required by the development of Telford New Town until 1991 (above). Subsequently, the area was converted to a car park, offices and a small housing development (below).

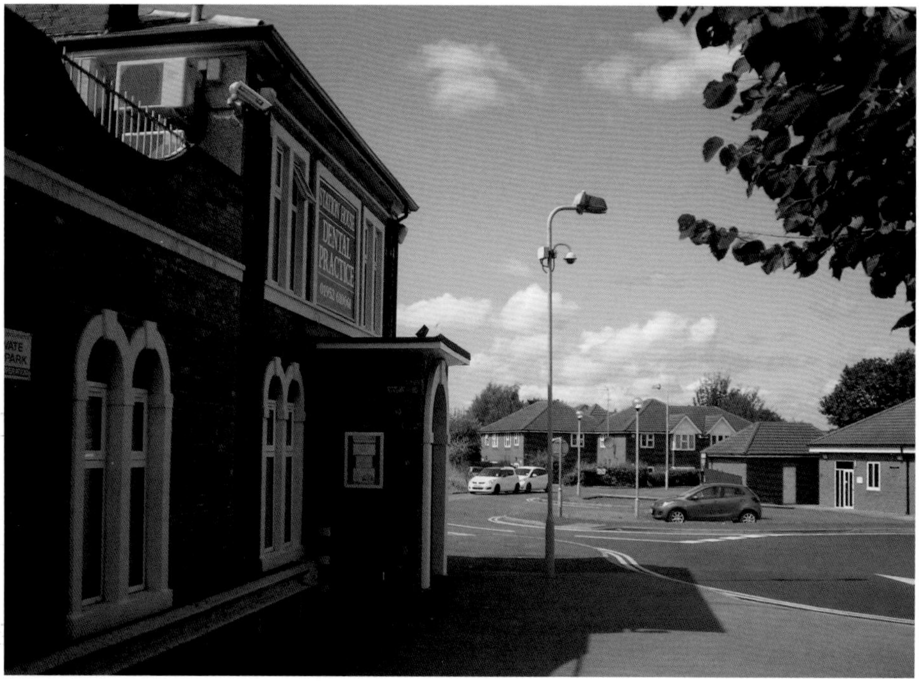

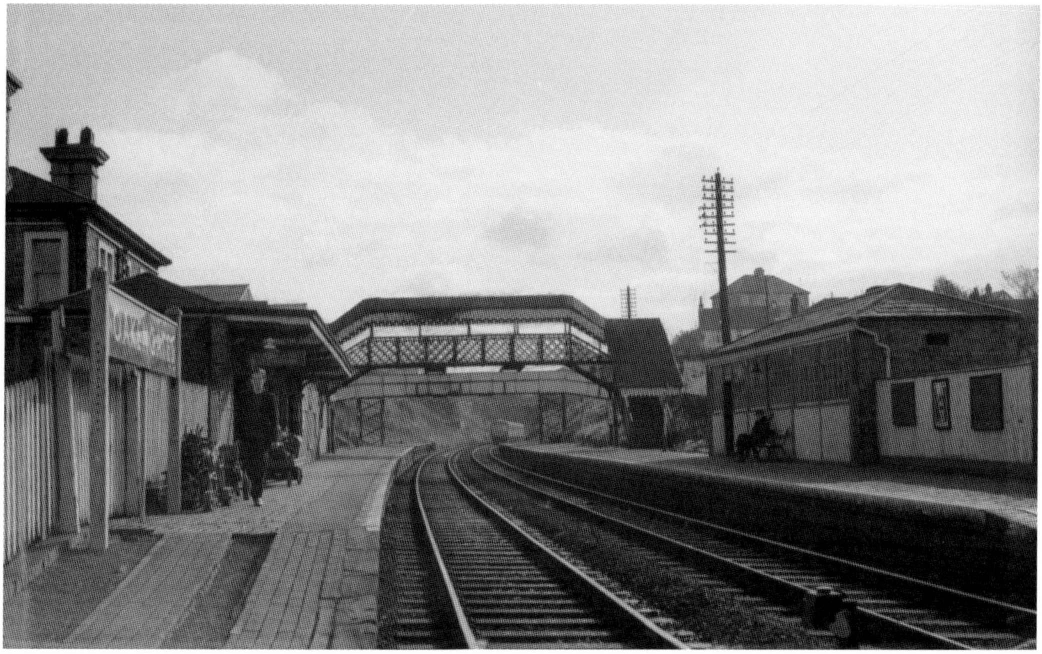

Oakengates Station

Opened in June 1849, this was the eastern terminus of the SBR for five months. Some main line expresses stopped at Oakengates West, as it was briefly renamed in the 1950s (above). Now unstaffed, it is served by hourly Shrewsbury–Birmingham trains (below). The neat, Italianate station building is now a dental practice.

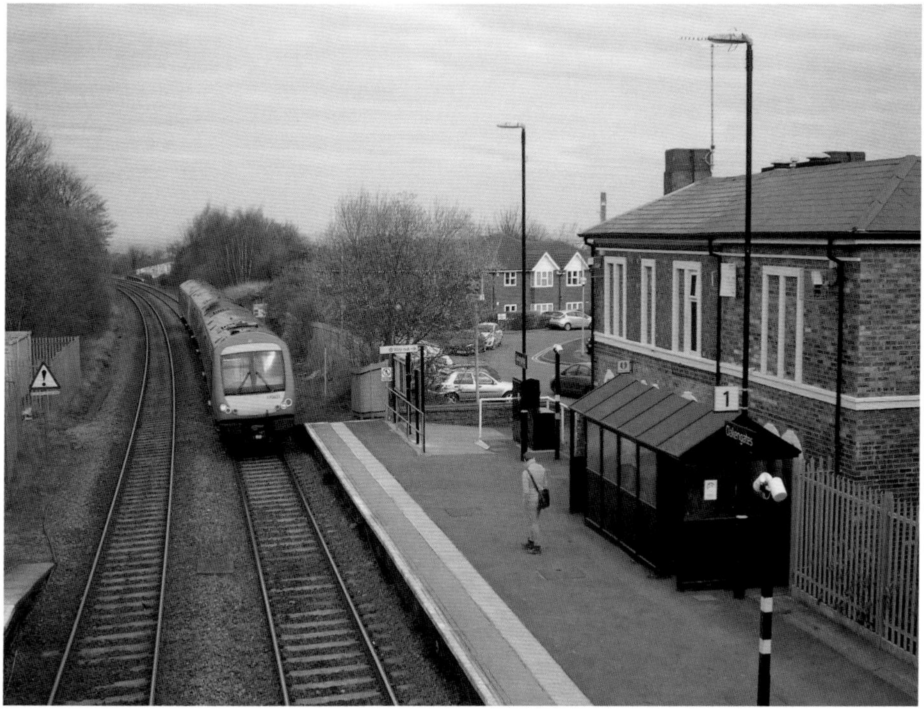

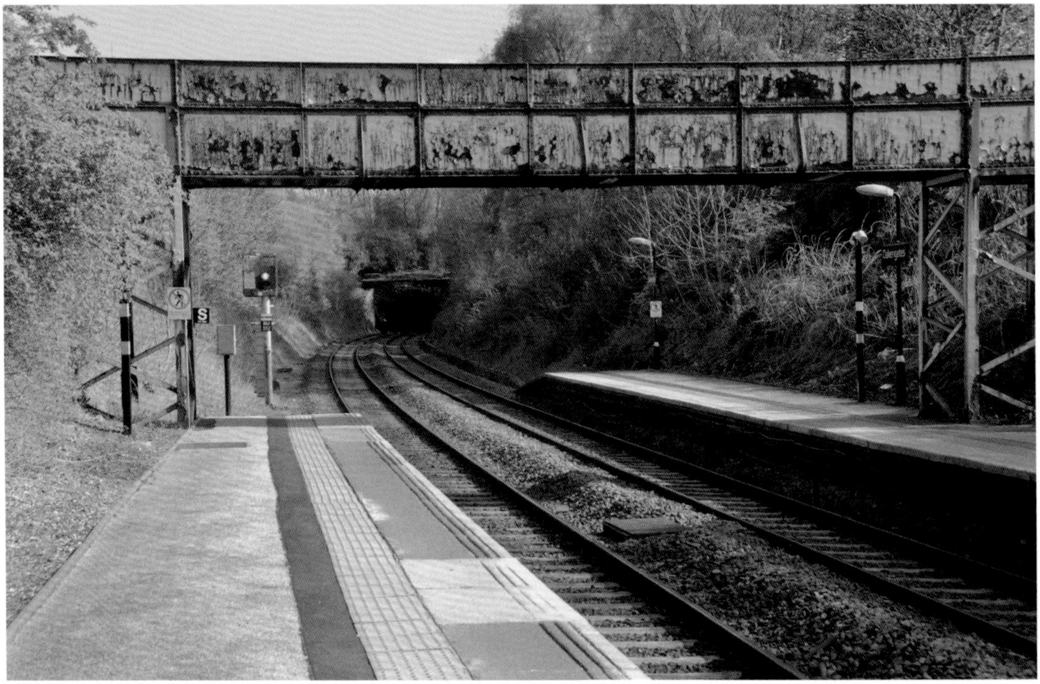

Oakengates Tunnel

The delay in the opening of the SBR through to Wolverhampton was caused by drainage problems in the 471-yard tunnel at Oakengates, the western portal of which is just beyond the station (above). The first passenger train through the tunnel was on 12 November 1849. A train is shown emerging from the eastern portal in 1965 (below).

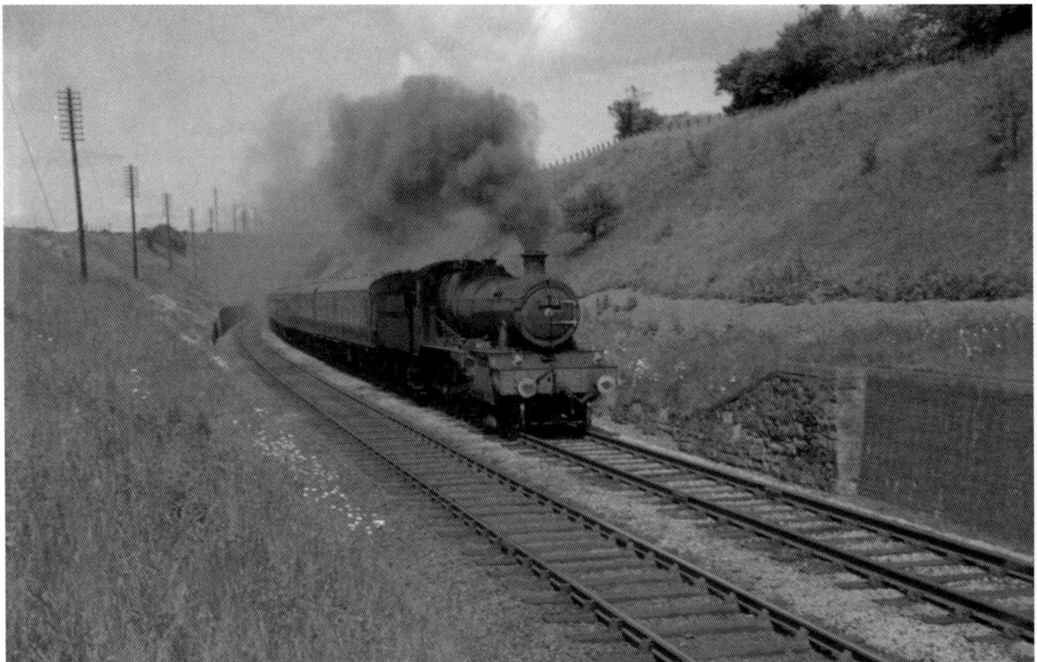

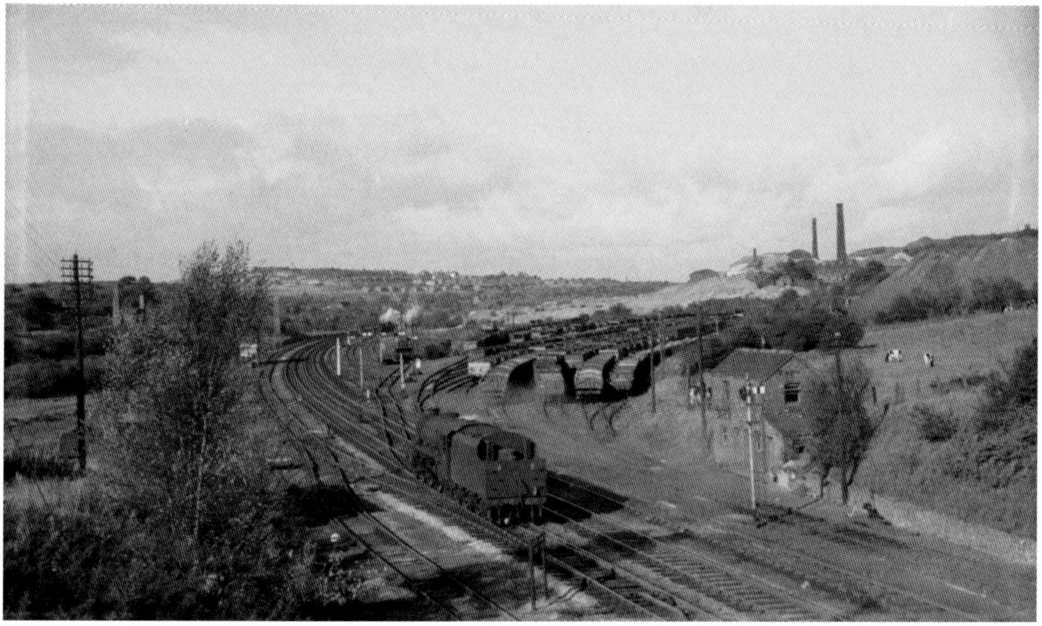

Telford Central

To serve the growing complex of administrative offices, shopping centre and residential development of the new town, this station was opened in May 1986. Telford Central was built on the site of Hollinswood Sidings (above), which served local industry, including the Lilleshall Company, until 1965. The station (below) has recently been refurbished.

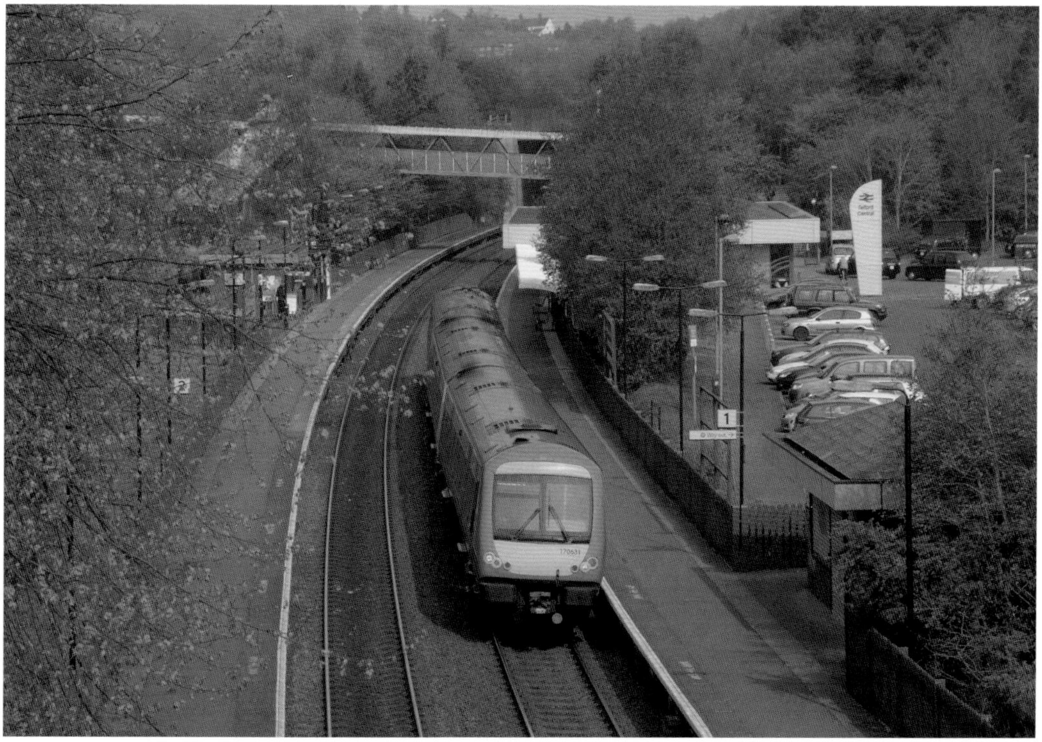

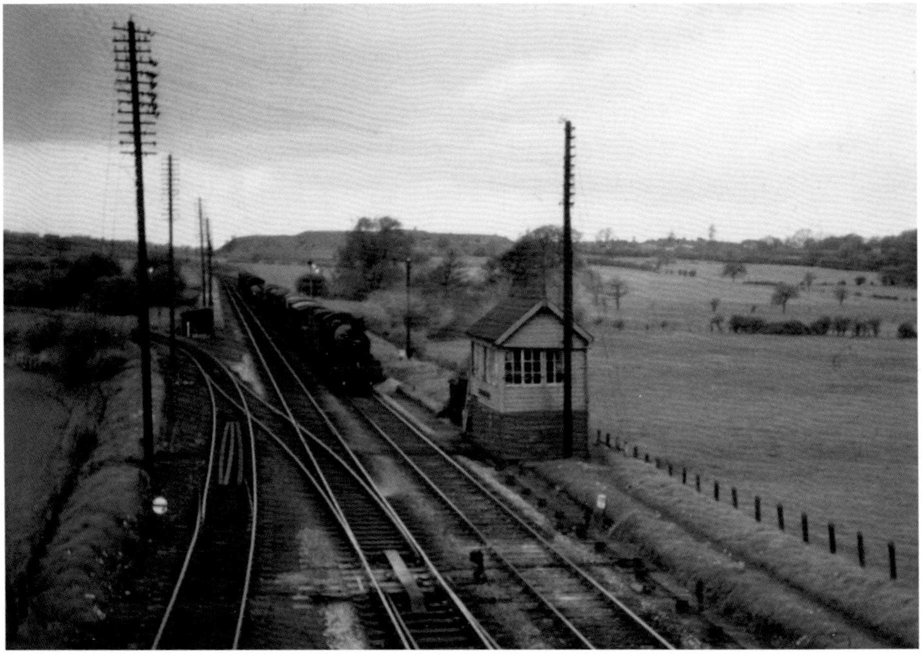

Madeley Junction (1)

The only branch of the SBR left the main line two miles west of Shifnal. The original location of the junction signal box can be seen as an Up goods train approaches on the main line in 1964 (above). A new signal box, which opened in 1969 in the angle between the main line and the branch line, is approached by a train of coal empties from Ironbridge power station (below).

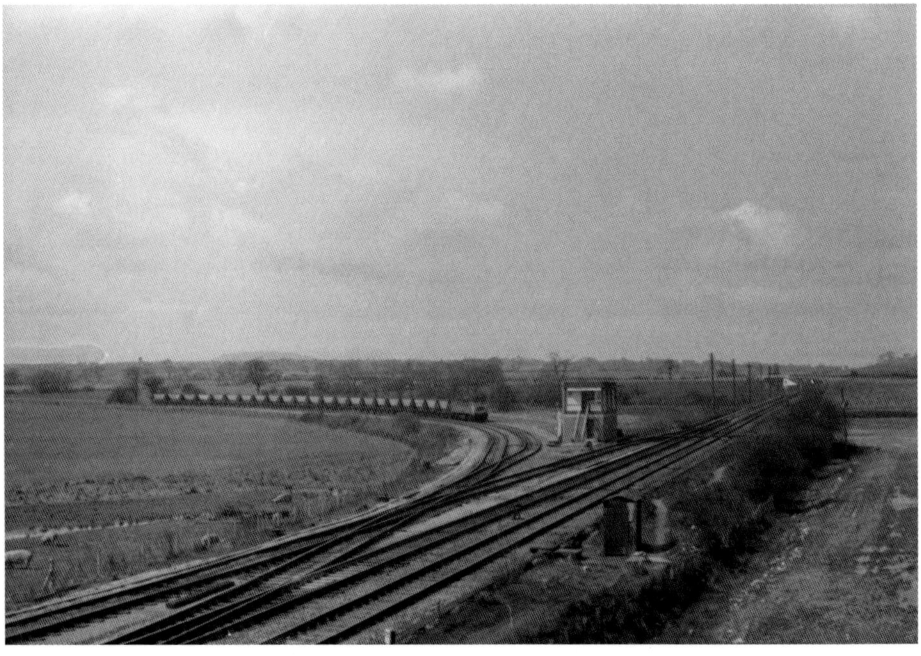

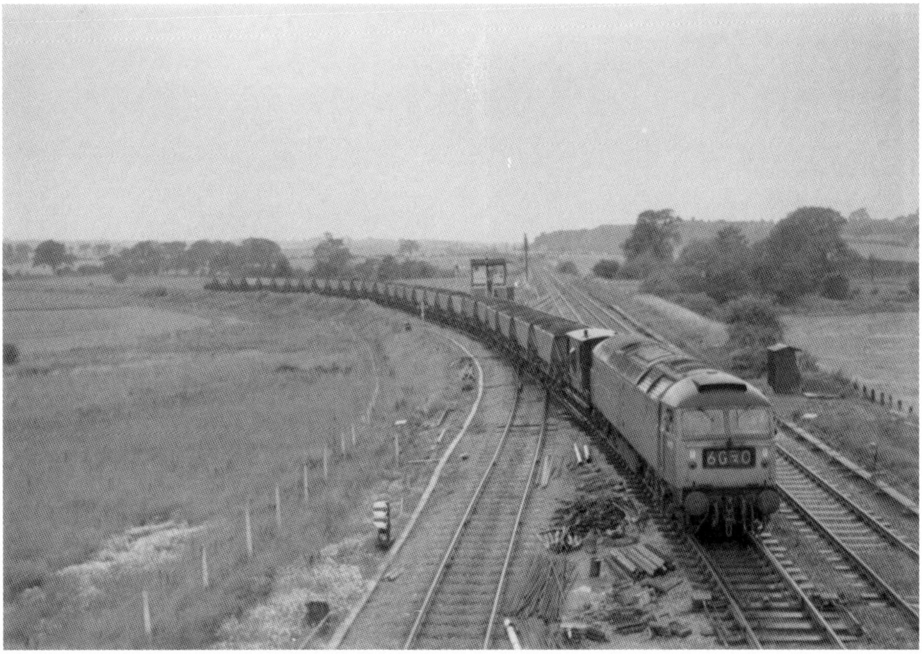

Madeley Junction (2)
A coal train from Granville Colliery to Ironbridge power station reverses past the new signal box onto the Madeley branch in July 1970 (above), prior to the locomotive running around the train. With the closure and demolition of this box in 2012, the Madeley branch is now controlled from Saltley (Birmingham). This is the scene at the junction today (below).

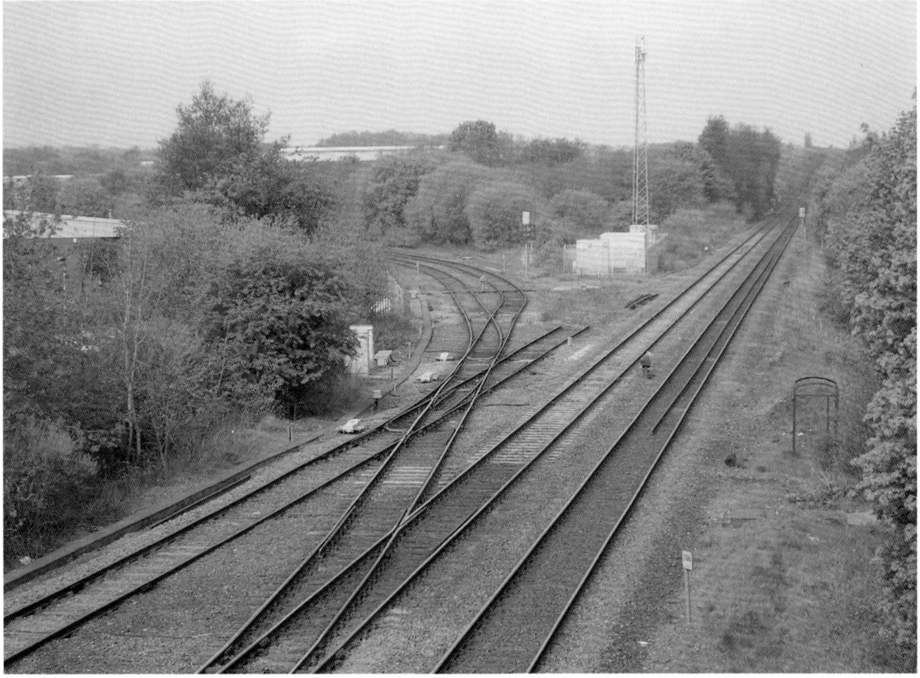

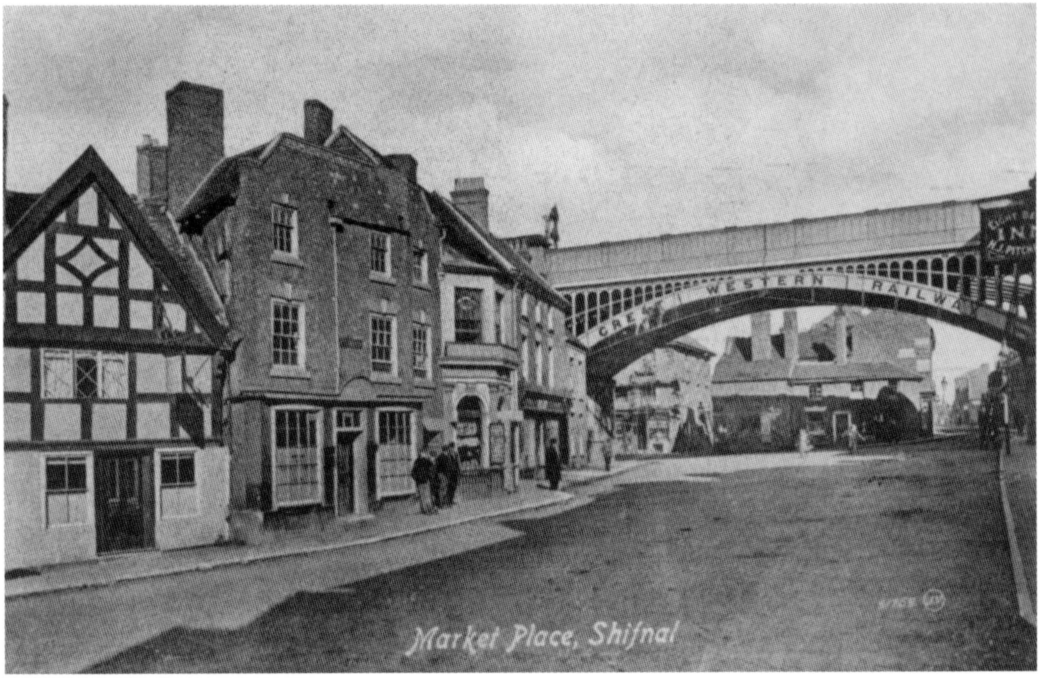

Shifnal Embankment and Bridge

Building the line on an embankment and brick arches through Shifnal was a considerable undertaking. The original railway bridge carrying the line over the town's main street (above) was a single-span cast-iron arch, built by the Horseley Ironworks, Tipton. It was replaced by the present girder structure (below), built by the Horsehay Company in 1953.

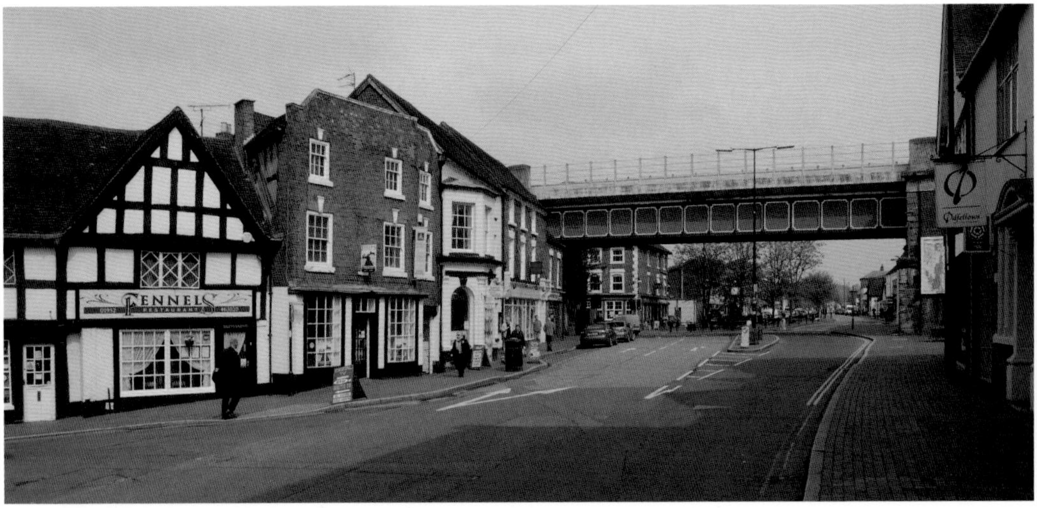

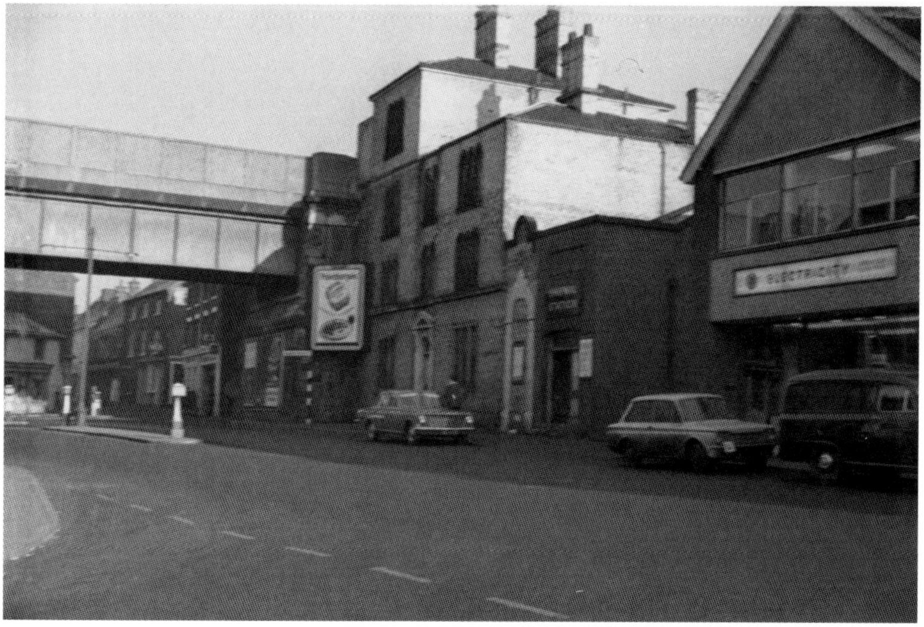

Shifnal Station Entrance

The original street entrance to Shifnal station, at ground level in a three-storey building (above), was demolished in around 1970. The present entrance, through an attractive metal gateway and beneath one of the imposing brick arches, is alongside the town's public conveniences (below).

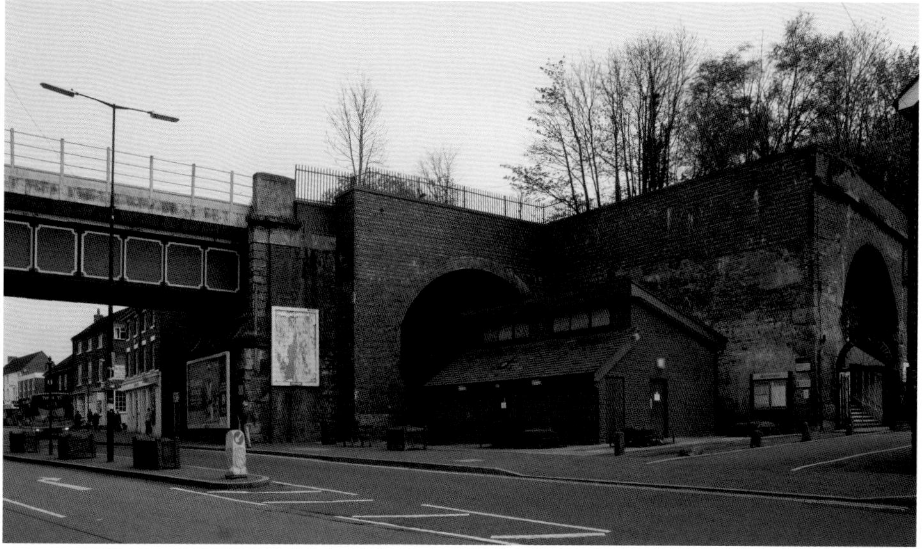

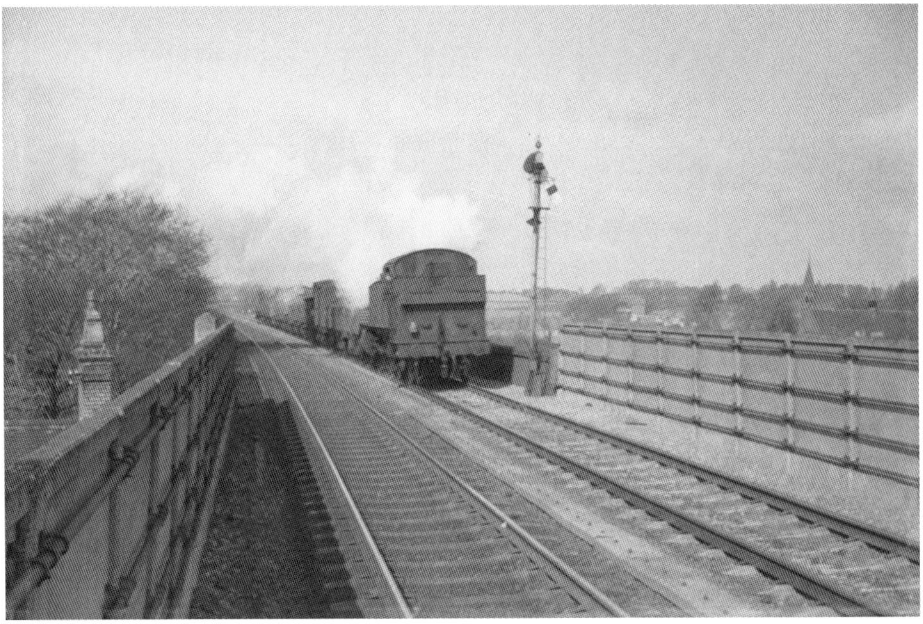

Shifnal Station

In April 1965, an Up goods train is crossing the bridge on the approach to Shifnal station (above). An hourly Birmingham–Shrewsbury train pulls into the station (below), where basic shelters now serve waiting passengers, leaving only the boarded-up, red-brick block as a reminder of former glory.

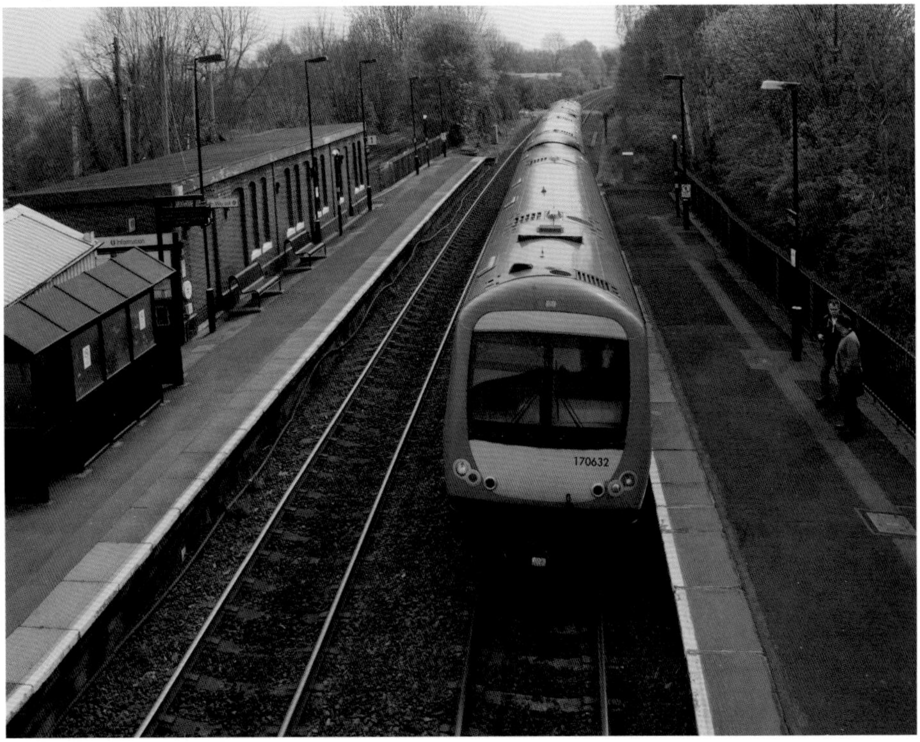

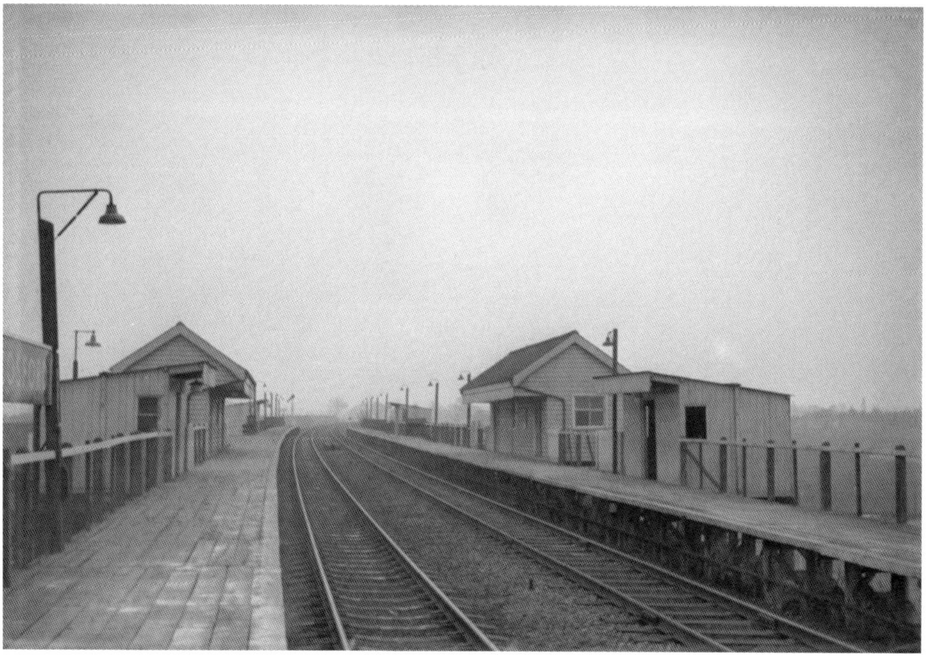

Cosford

RAF Cosford opened in 1938 as a joint aircraft maintenance, storage and technical training unit. The station, first known as Cosford Aerodrome Halt, opened in January of that year for construction workers and in March for the public. Wartime security led to it simply becoming 'Cosford' in 1940. The original wooden structure, shown above in 1968, was completely rebuilt in 2012 (below).

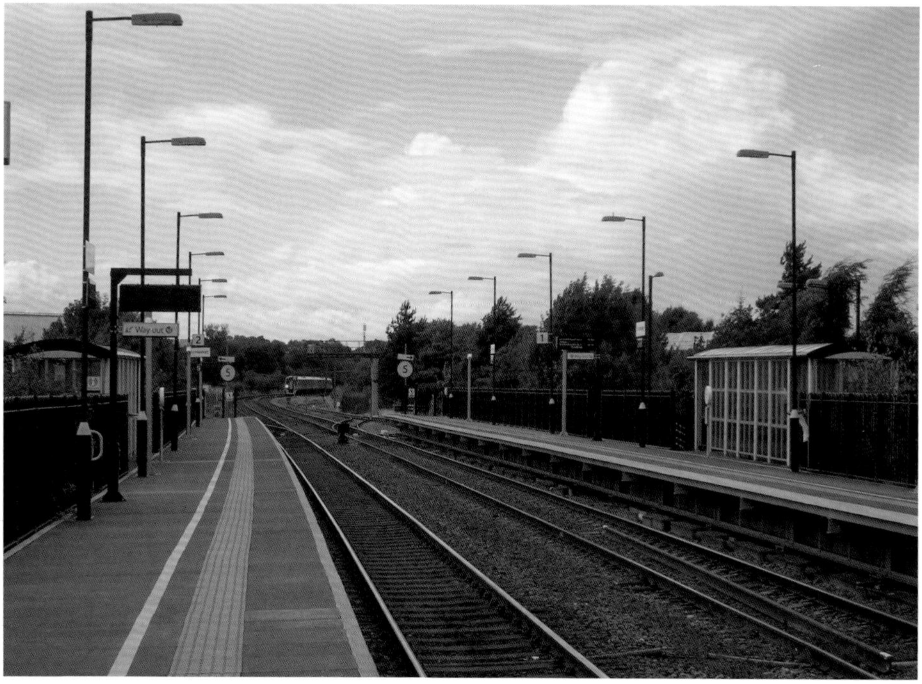

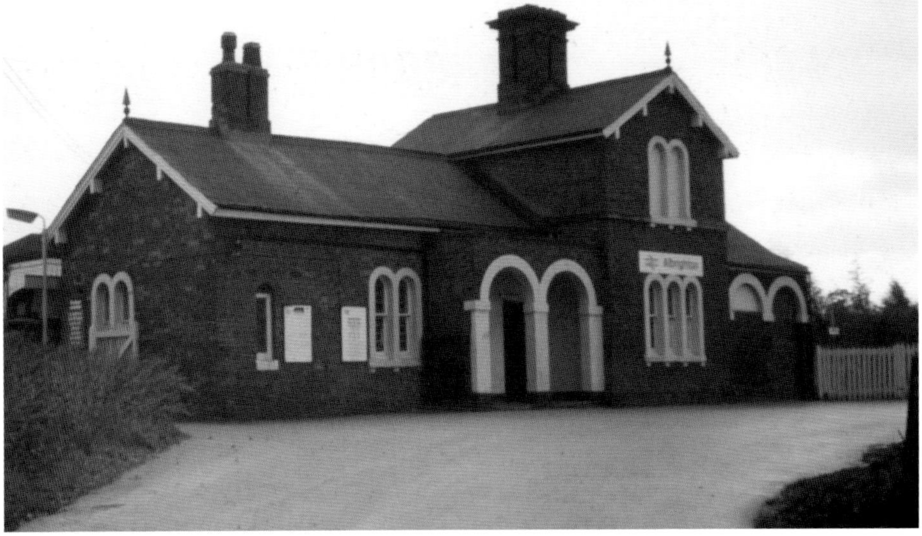

Albrighton

The attractive station described by Revd Priestley over a hundred years ago has seen little change in these 1983 views, but the busy goods yard, like others along the line, had closed twenty years previously. The station is now unstaffed and the main building privately owned, but recently the platforms and footbridge were refurbished and there are plans to purchase the station master's house for community use.

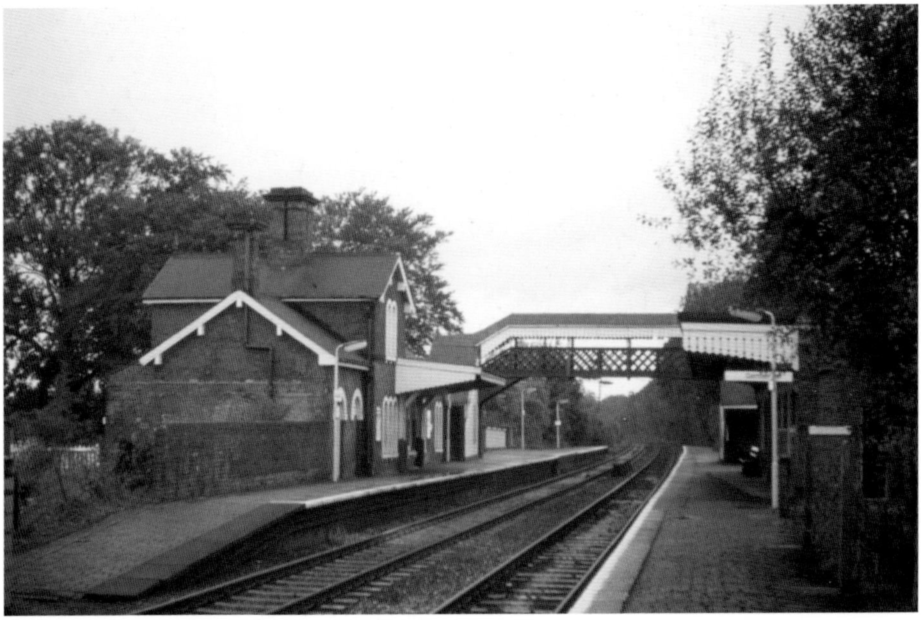

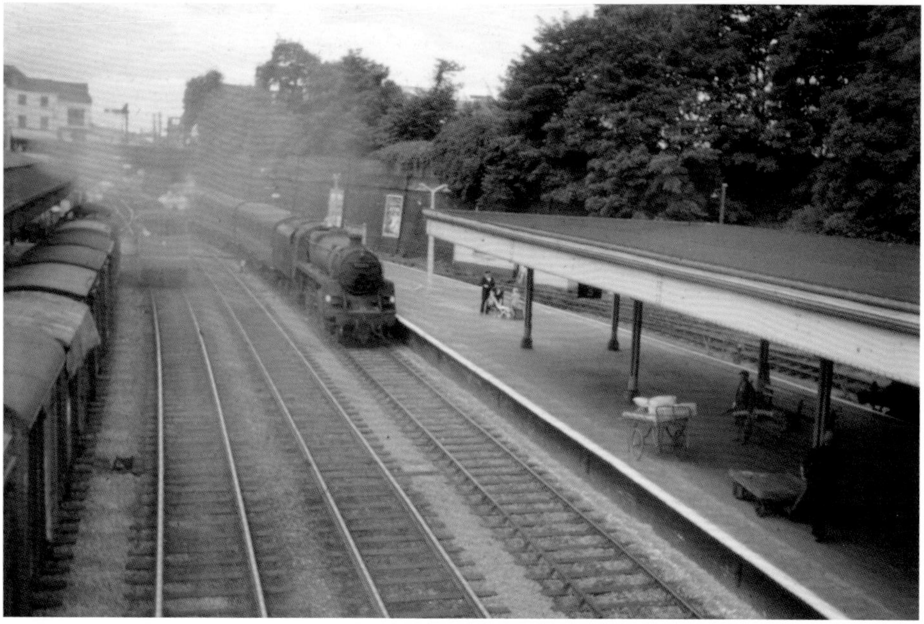

The Line to Stafford

A Shrewsbury–Stafford train enters Wellington station in January 1964 (above), the last year of the service. The SURCC built a 19-mile double track from the junction with the SBR at Wellington to the LNWR main line at Stafford. The junction, originally named Stafford Junction, was closed in 1991, but reopened in 2008 and renamed Donnington Junction (below), with the single three-mile track serving a new freight depot.

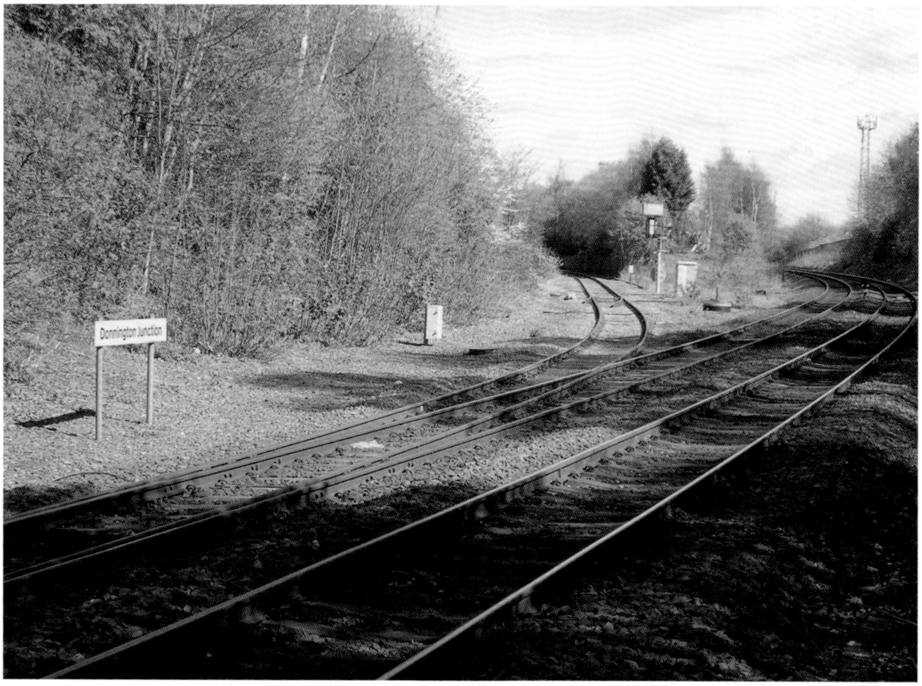

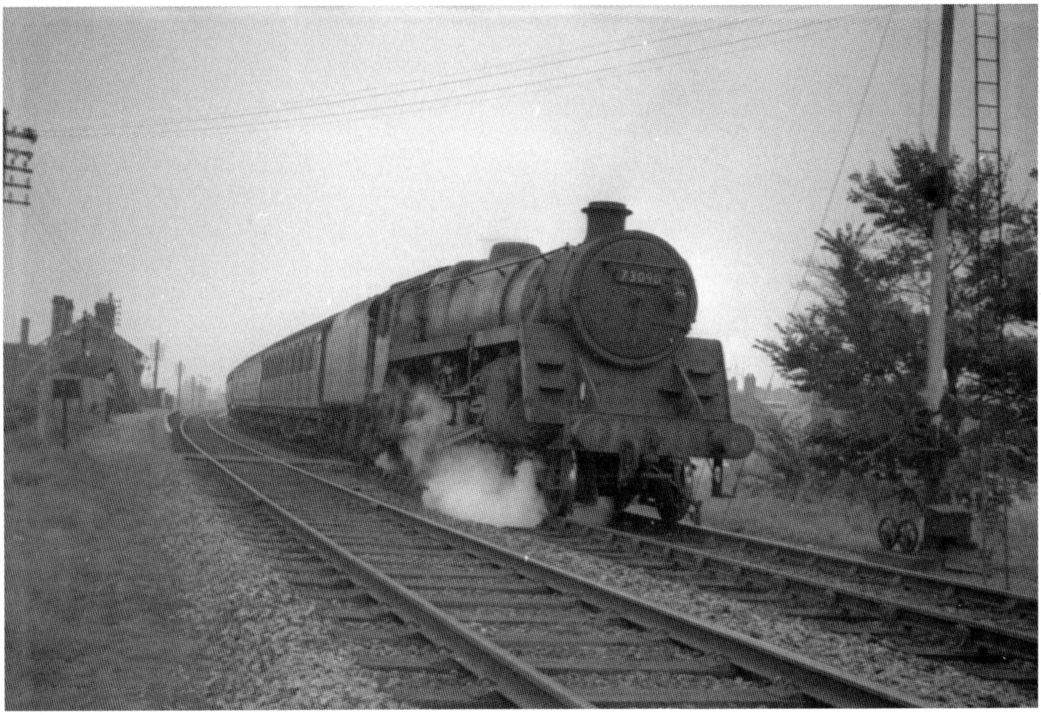

Hadley

In the last week of passenger services on the line, a Stafford–Shrewsbury train leaves Hadley station (above). The station was also served by trains on the Coalport branch, the junction for which was half-a-mile further east. Hadley Junction signal box also controlled the sidings of the Castle Works. The railway, sidings, signal box and station can be seen in this early depiction of the Castle Works, looking towards Wellington and the Wrekin (below).

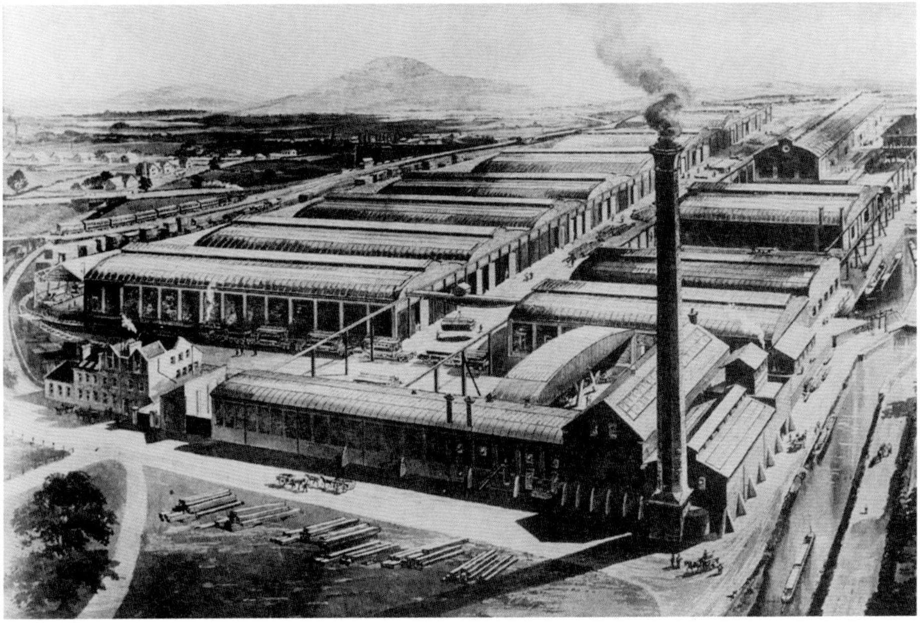

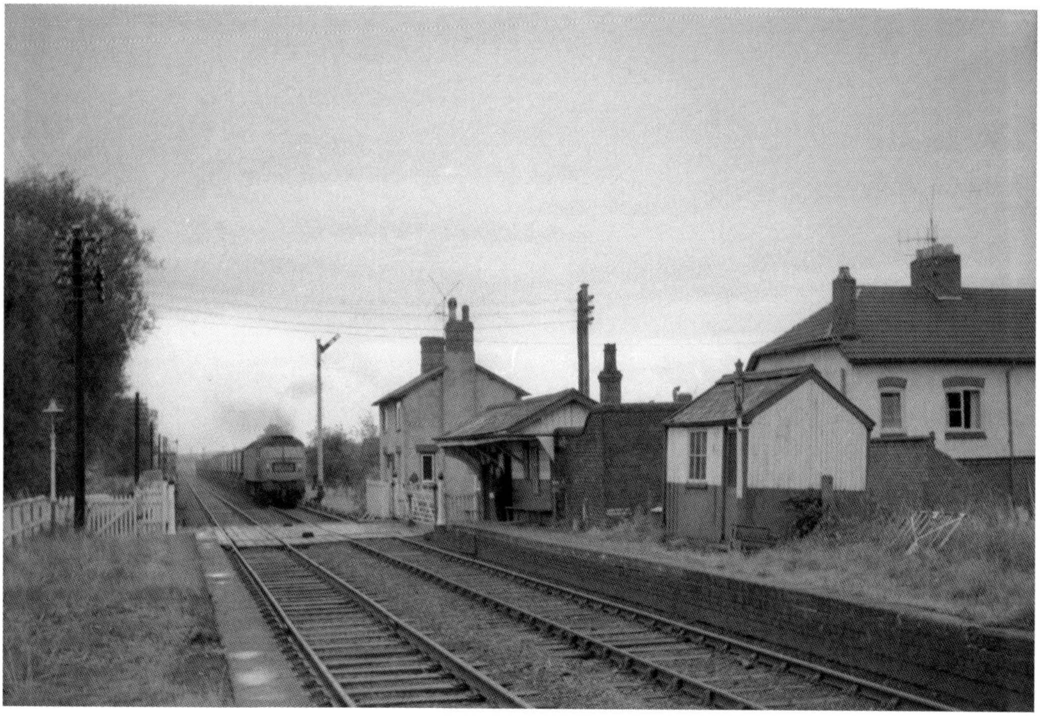

Trench Crossing

Unlike other stations on the line, Trench Crossing opened in January 1855. Following closure of passenger services in 1964, both tracks on this section of line were still *in situ* when a train carrying coal from Granville Colliery passed through in 1970 (above), but the line had been singled by the time of the view below, seven years later.

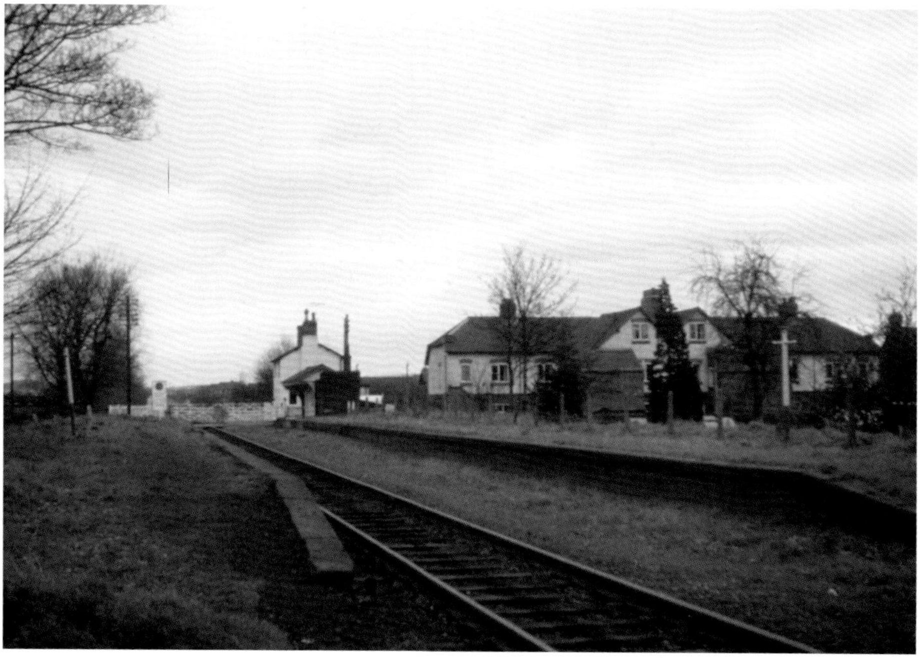

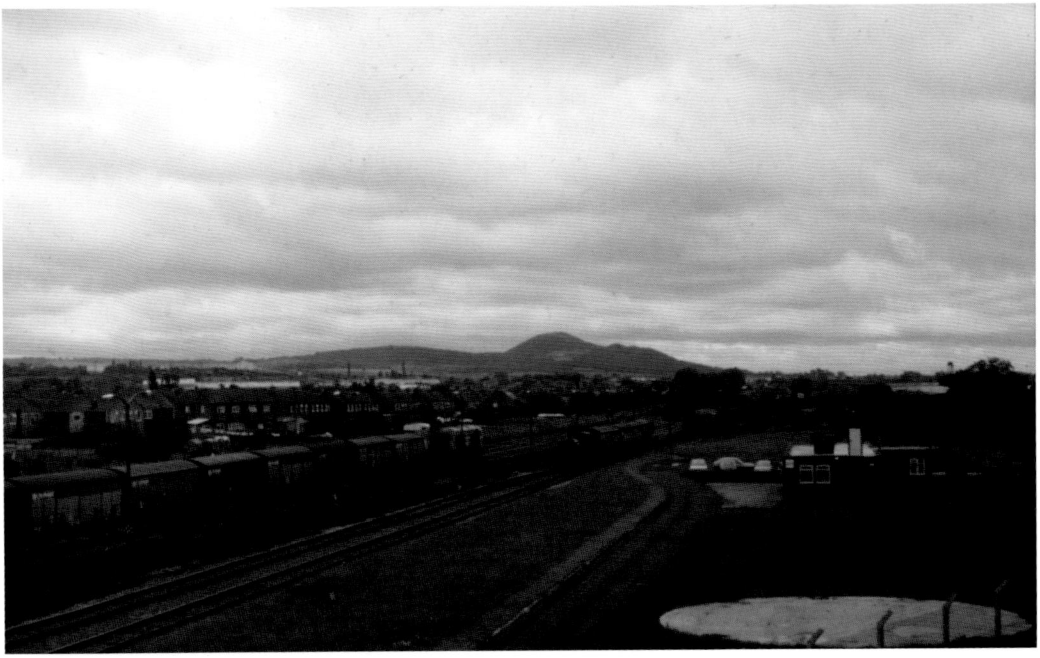

Donnington Sidings

After 1979, the truncated branch line terminated in a goods yard which served the Army's Central Ordnance Depot at Donnington until 1991. A train is about to leave the yard in 1985 (above). Re-laid in 2008, the track was in place for the opening of Telford International Freight Terminal the following year. Traffic to date has been sparse (below).

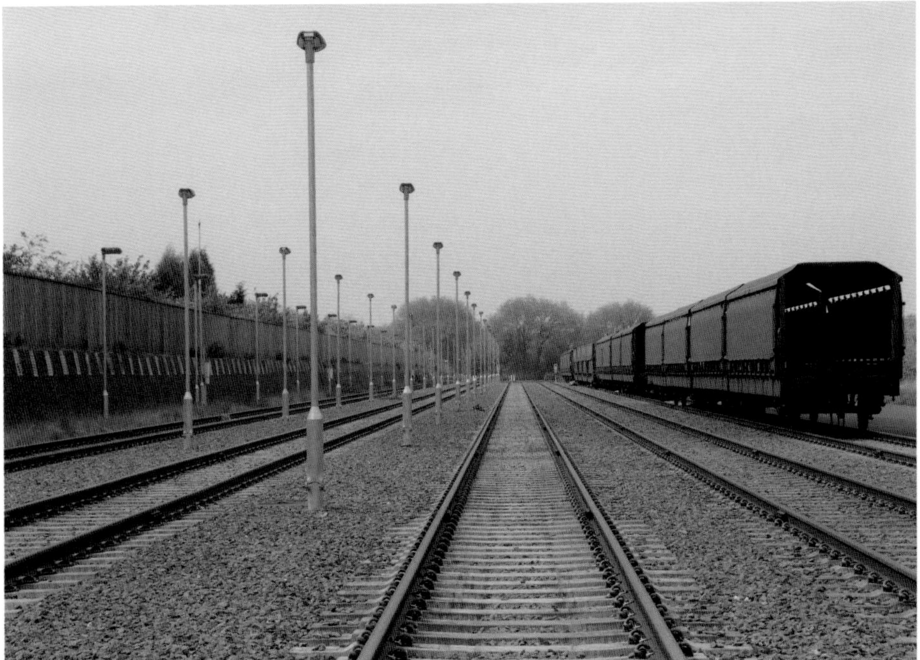

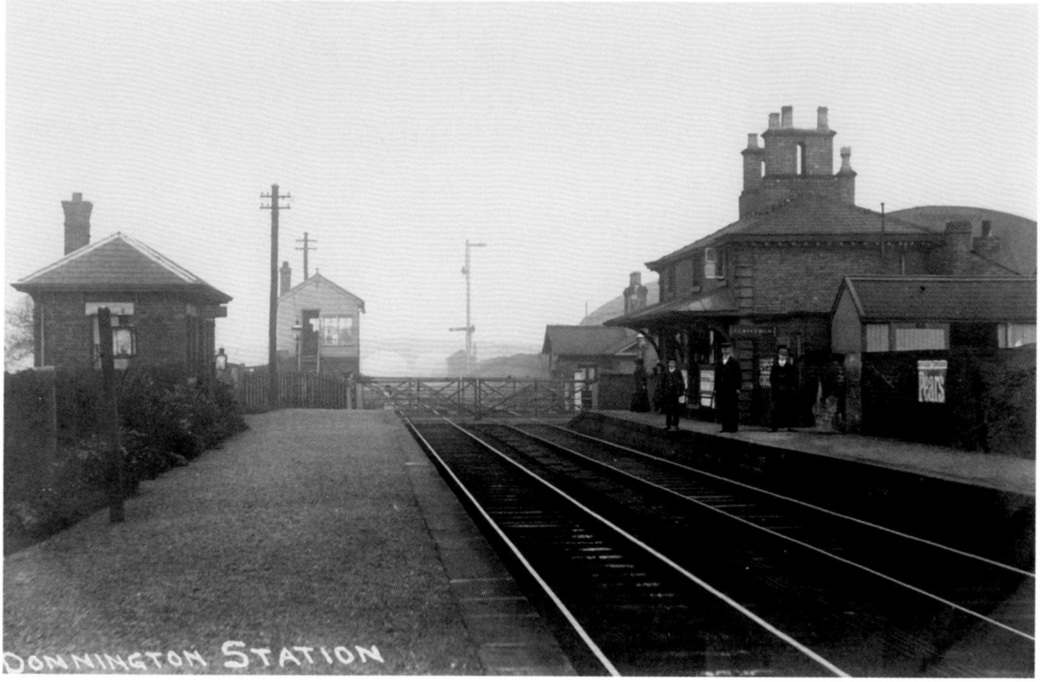

Donnington

The station and level crossing, shown in this early twentieth-century view (above), remained intact for a few years after closure, but the site was derelict by 1977 (below). The buffers marked the end of the remaining line in use, the exchange sidings beyond handling coal traffic from Granville Colliery for two more years. Soon after, the former line of track through and beyond Donnington was converted to a realigned section of the A518 road.

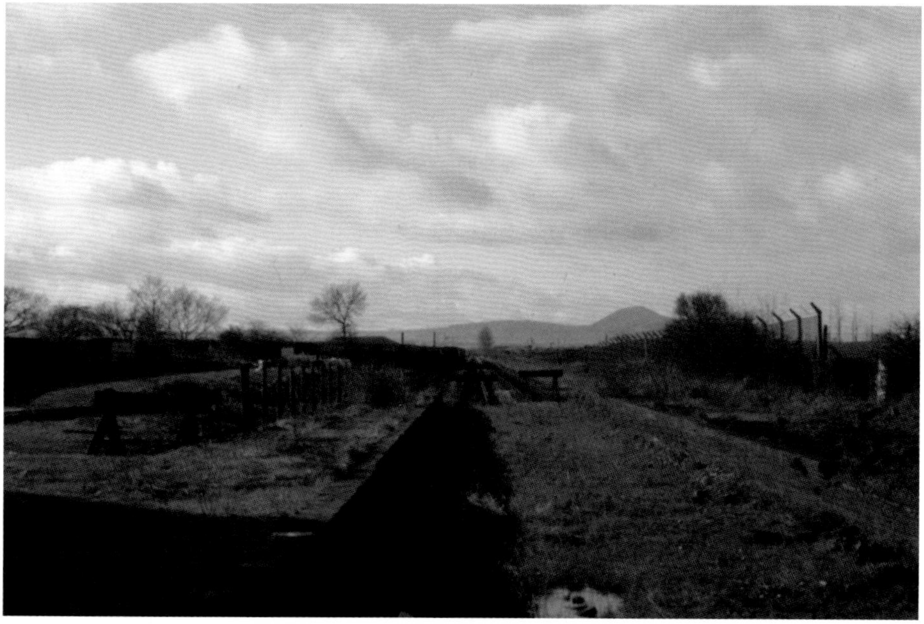

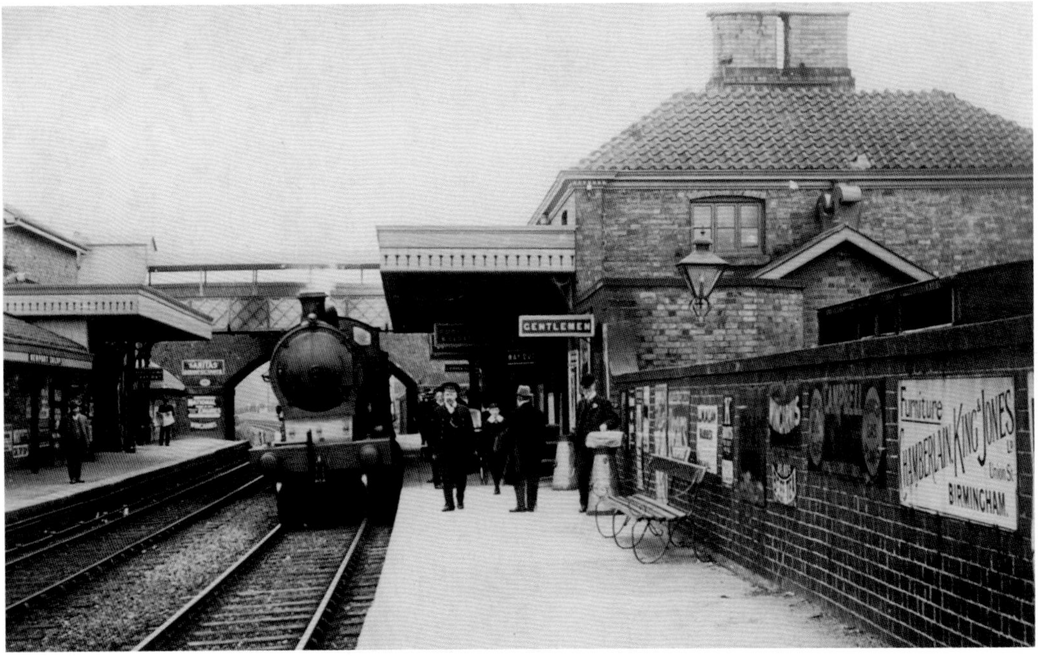

Newport (1)

Over fifty years separate these views of Stafford-bound trains in Newport station. Entering a busy station in around 1910 is a LNWR train (above), and below an ex-LMS 4-6-0 Jubilee class locomotive in charge of a three-coach train calls at the station a month before closure in September 1964.

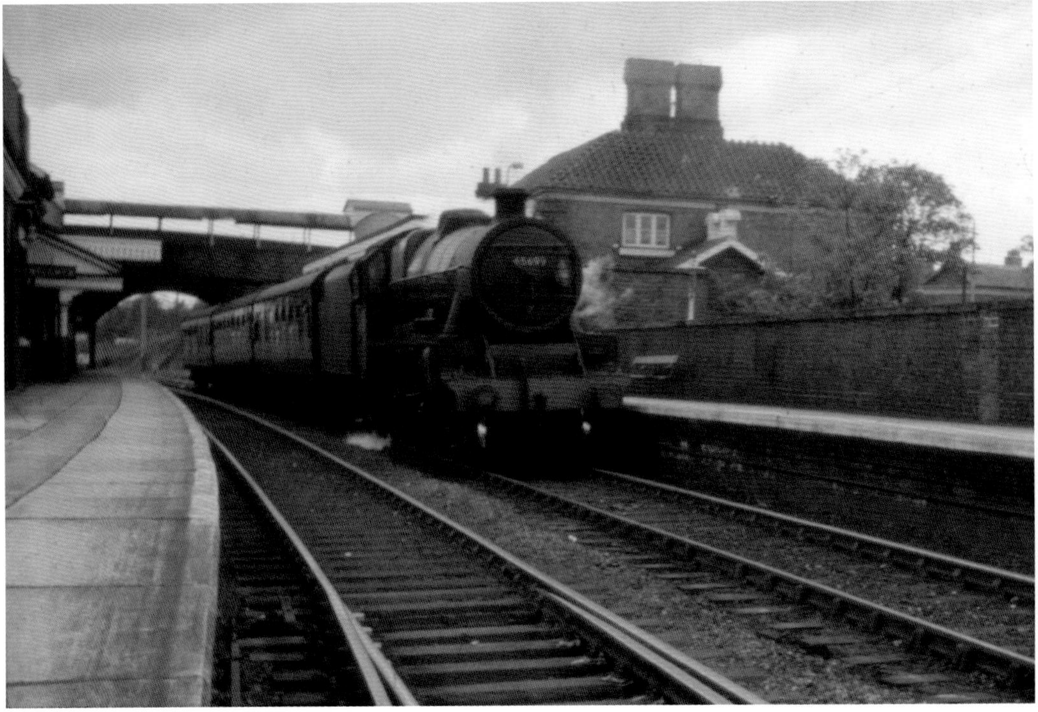

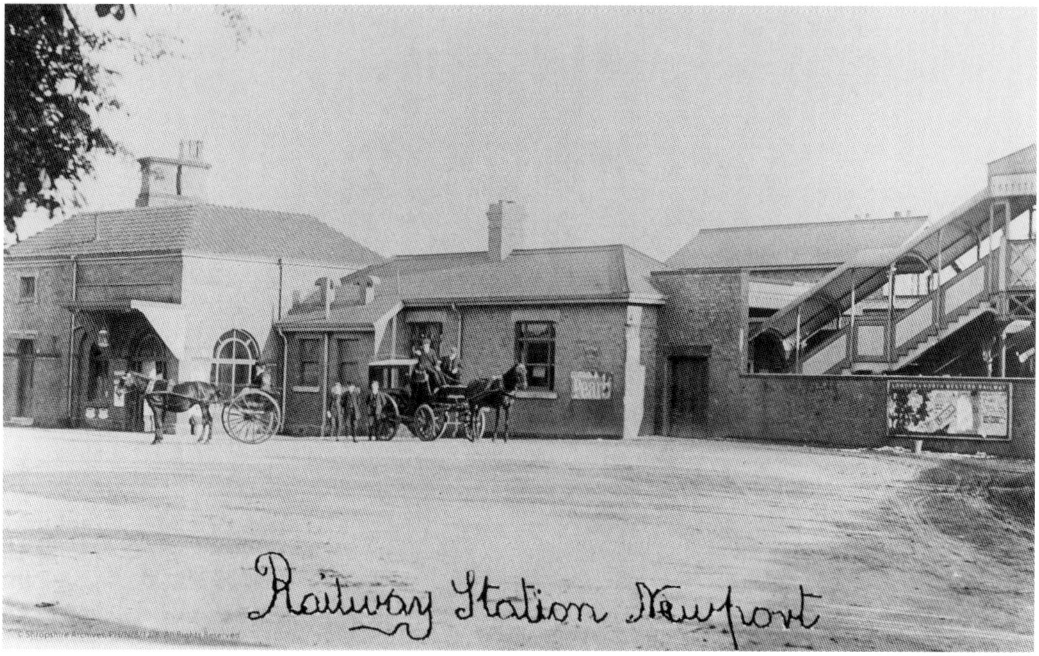

Newport (2)

At least a hundred years separate these views of the entrance to Newport station. The top image shows the station frontage in around 1900. Following the closure of the railway and the demolition of the station, the area became a housing development approached along the appropriately named Station Court (below).

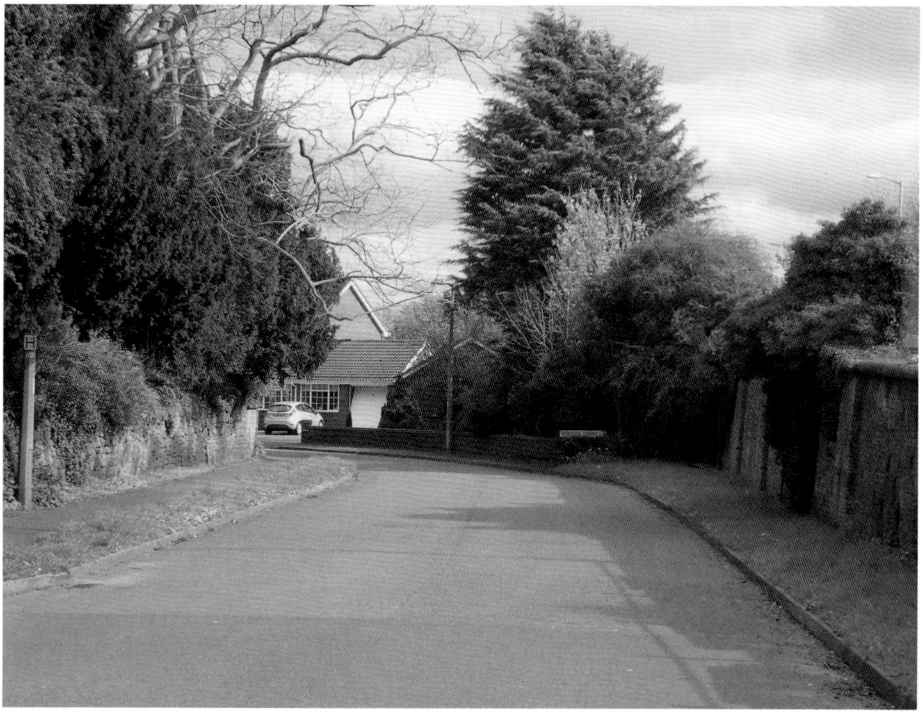

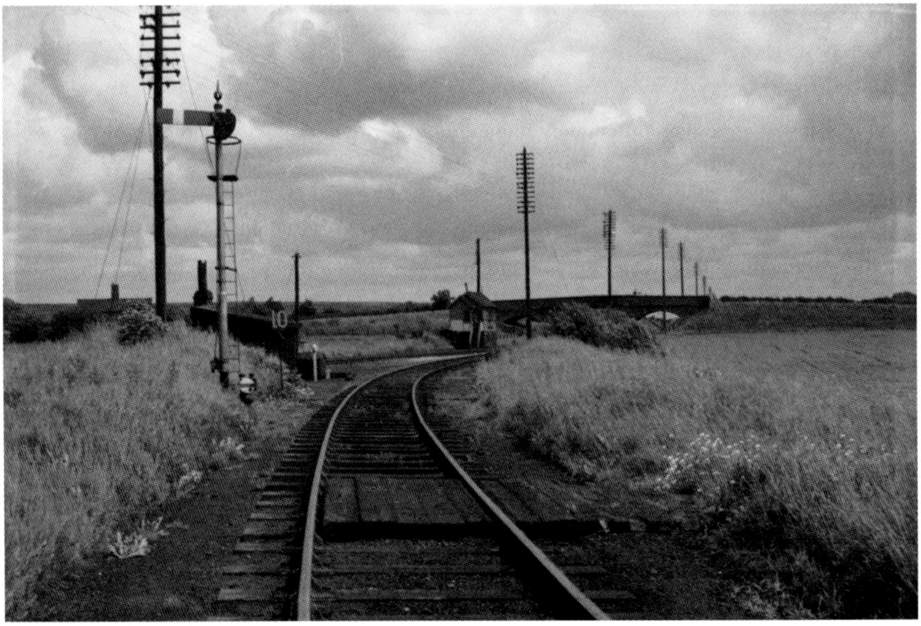

The Madeley Branch
The four-mile branch line from Madeley Junction (above, 1965) to Lightmoor was opened by the SBR in 1854. Built to tap the output of local ironworks, the single line connected at Lightmoor with the Coalbrookdale Company's tramway system (below) and in 1858 with the Wellington & Severn Junction line (WSJR).

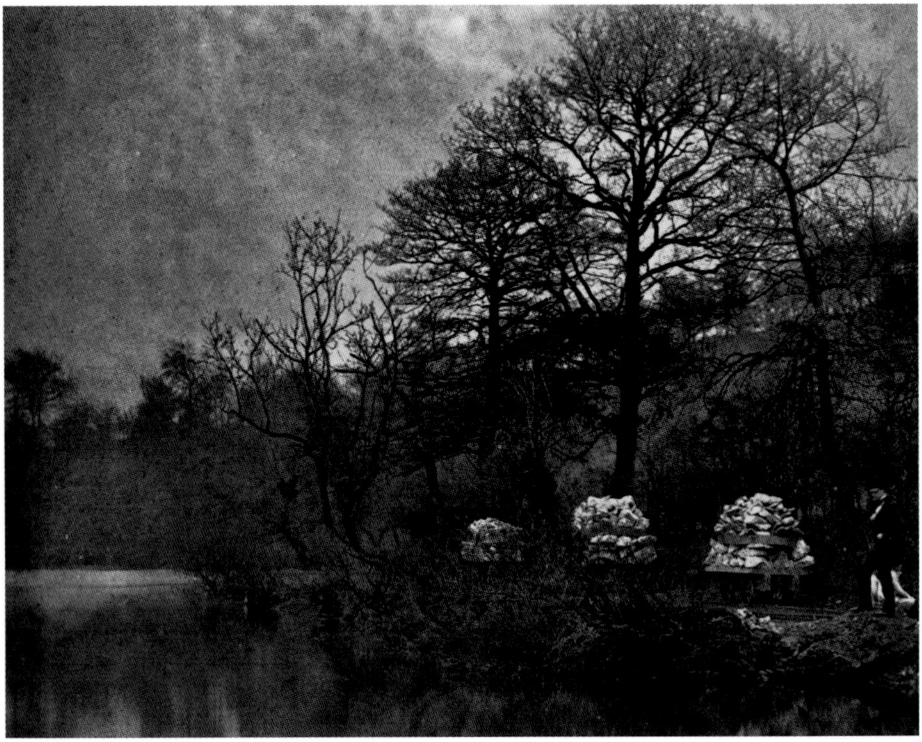

Kemberton Siding

Two miles south of Madeley Junction, a siding served the Halesfield and Kemberton pits of the Madeley Wood Company. The colliery's rope-worked tramway system (right, around 1900) supplied coal to a screen, beneath which standard-gauge wagons were loaded. These wagons, which were moved by horses, rope-haulage and gravity, were returned to four sidings, where they were marshalled into trains and hauled by a locomotive onto the branch line. Some coal was for land sale (below). Kemberton pit closed in 1967.

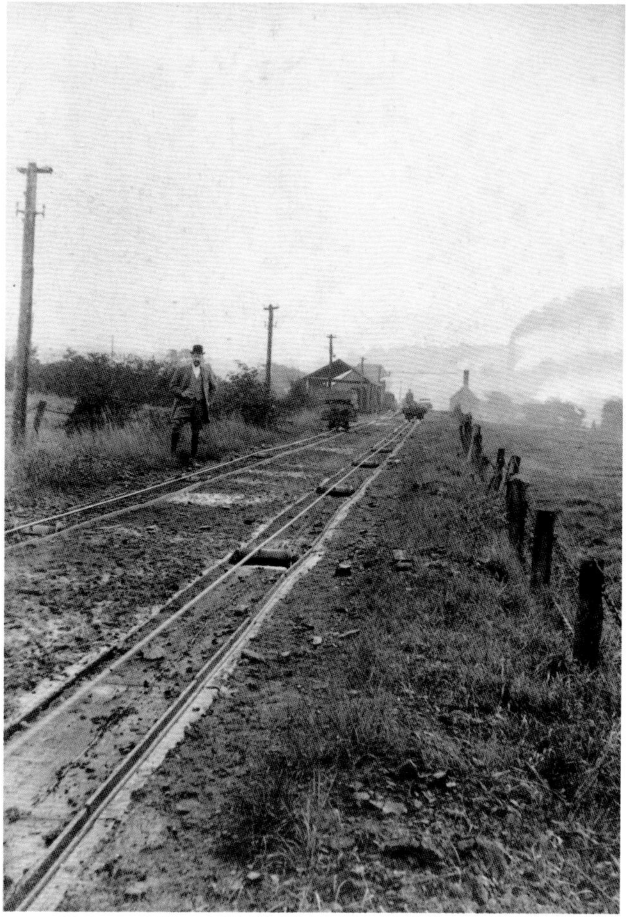

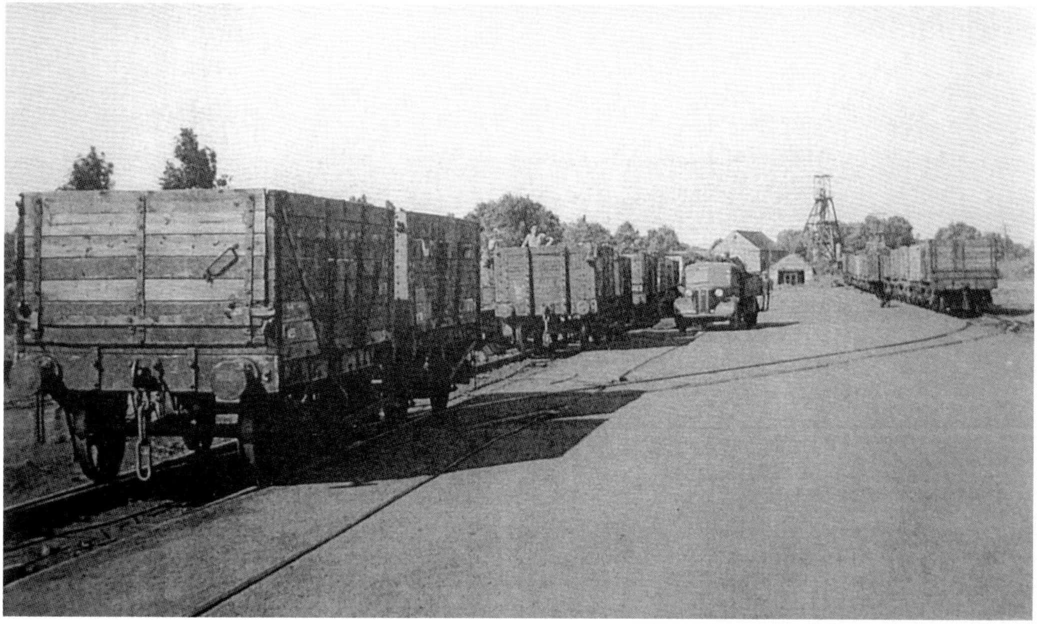

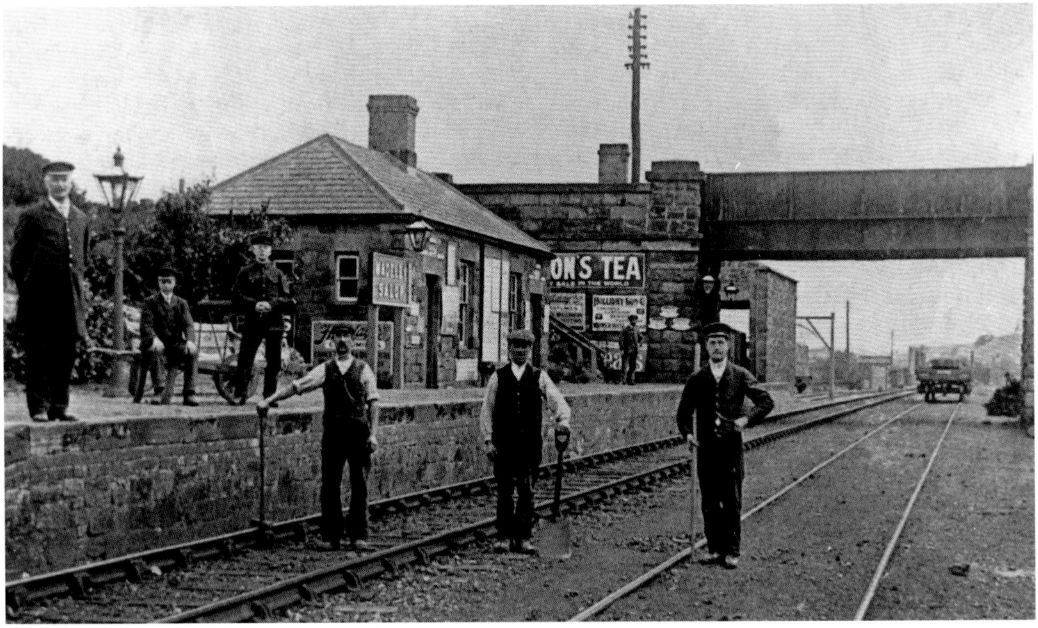

Madeley Station

Originally known simply as 'Madeley' when opened in 1859, it became Madeley Court in 1880 and Madeley Salop in 1897. It was the only station on the branch and was served by trains from Shifnal to Wellington, via Lightmoor. Closed due to wartime conditions in 1915, the station (always referred to locally as Madeley Court) was reinstated in response to local demand in July 1925, but finally closed after only two months.

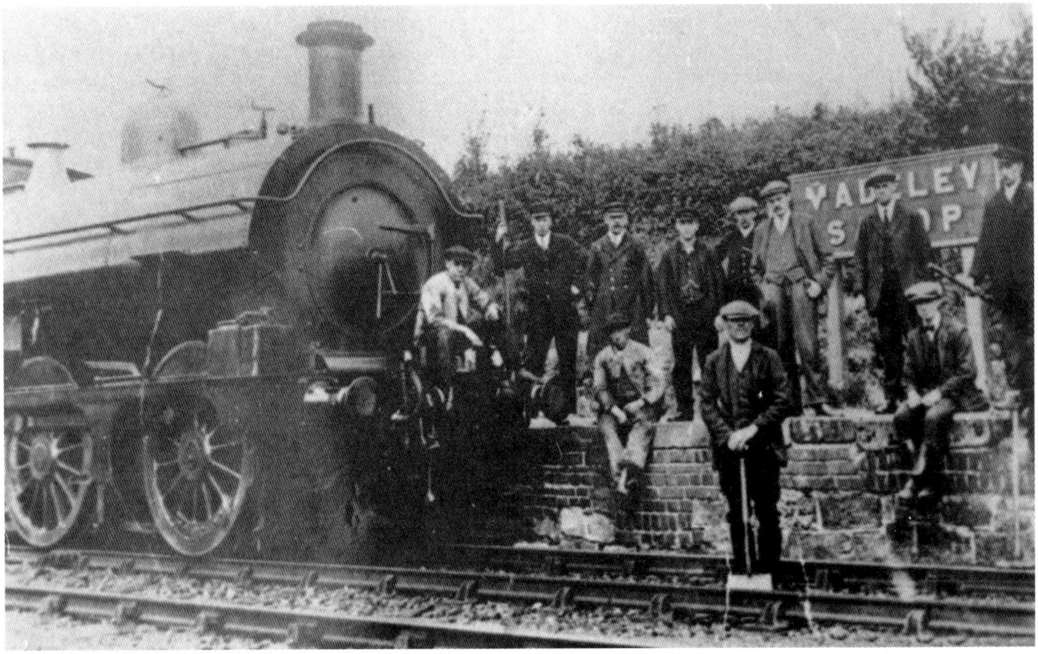

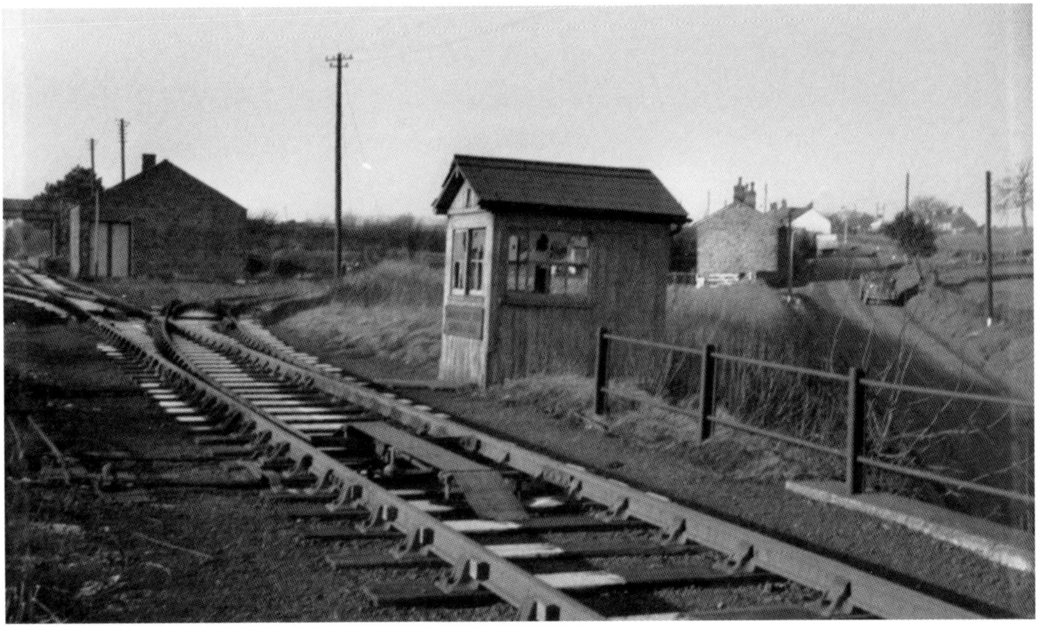

Madeley Goods

The sidings into the goods yard and the adjacent Court Works foundry were controlled by a five-lever ground frame, seen here at the time of closure in 1963 (above). By 1971, the goods shed and former station master's house were in a semi-derelict state (below) and were demolished soon afterwards.

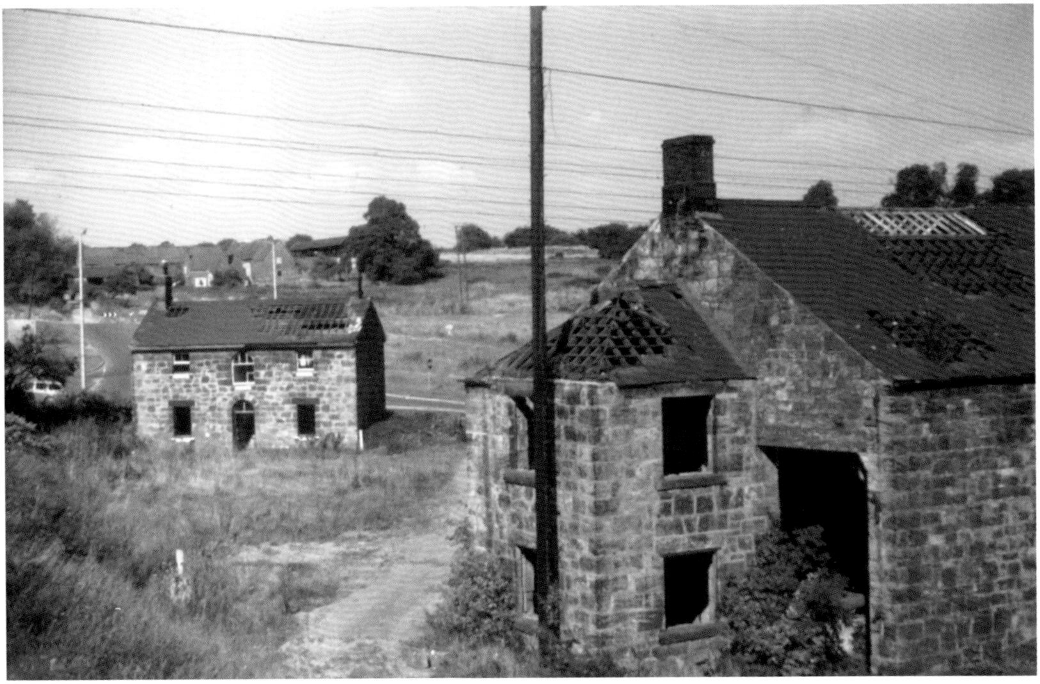

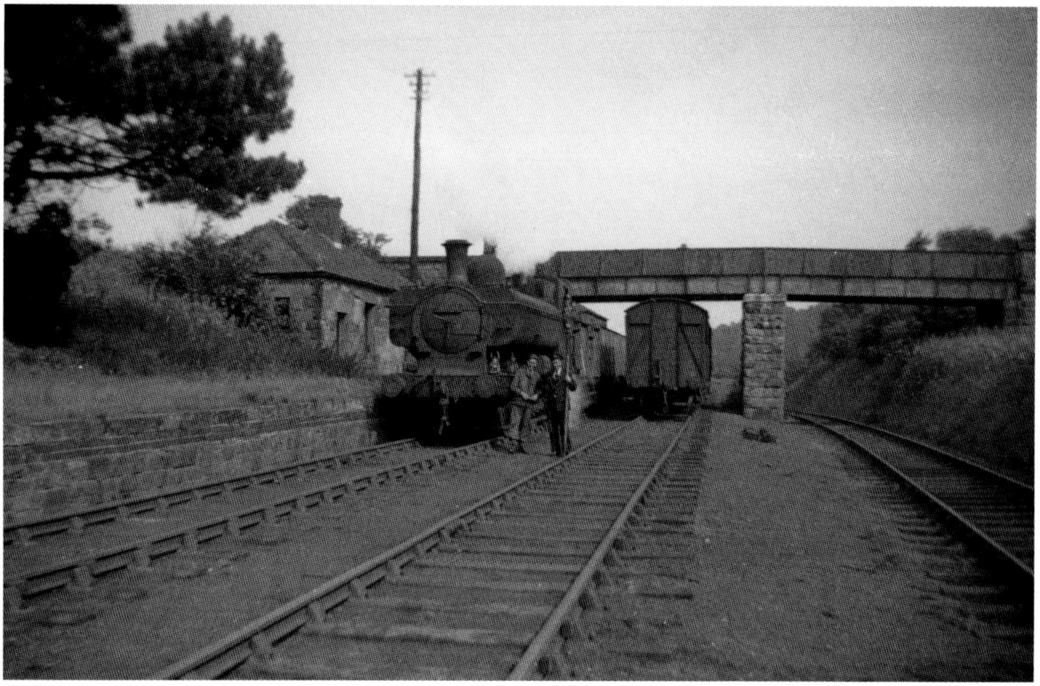

Coal Traffic

Opened in 1932, the power station at Buildwas (which later became 'Ironbridge A') was supplied with coal from local pits by rail. A train carrying coal from Kemberton colliery pauses at Madeley Court in 1956 (above). From the 1960s, coal was also supplied from mines in Staffordshire and beyond – the train approaching Lightmoor Junction in 1967 (below) is carrying coal from Silverdale, North Staffordshire.

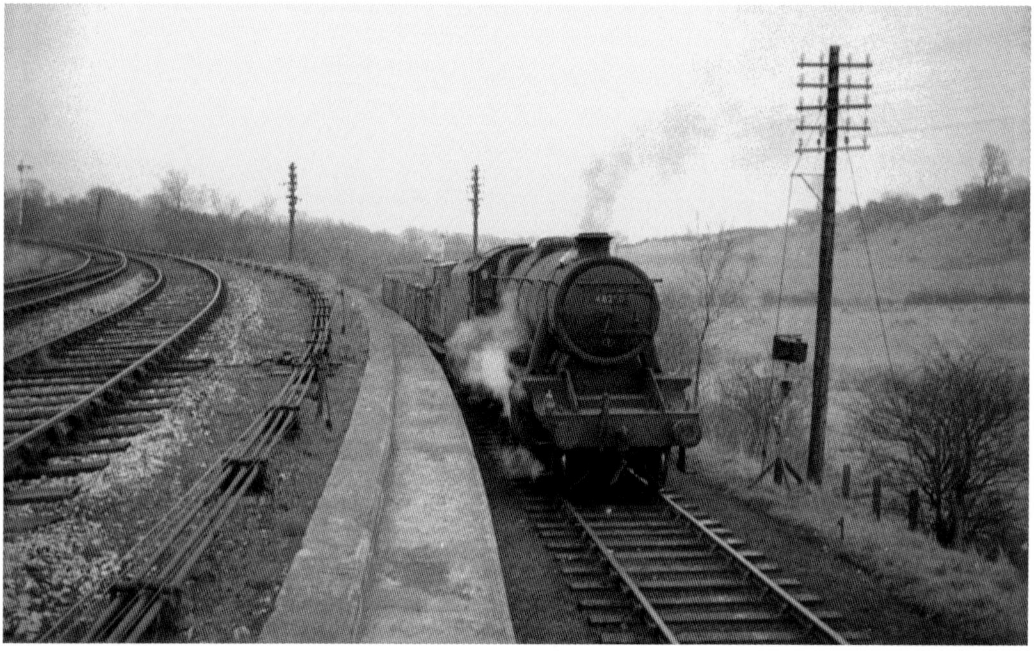

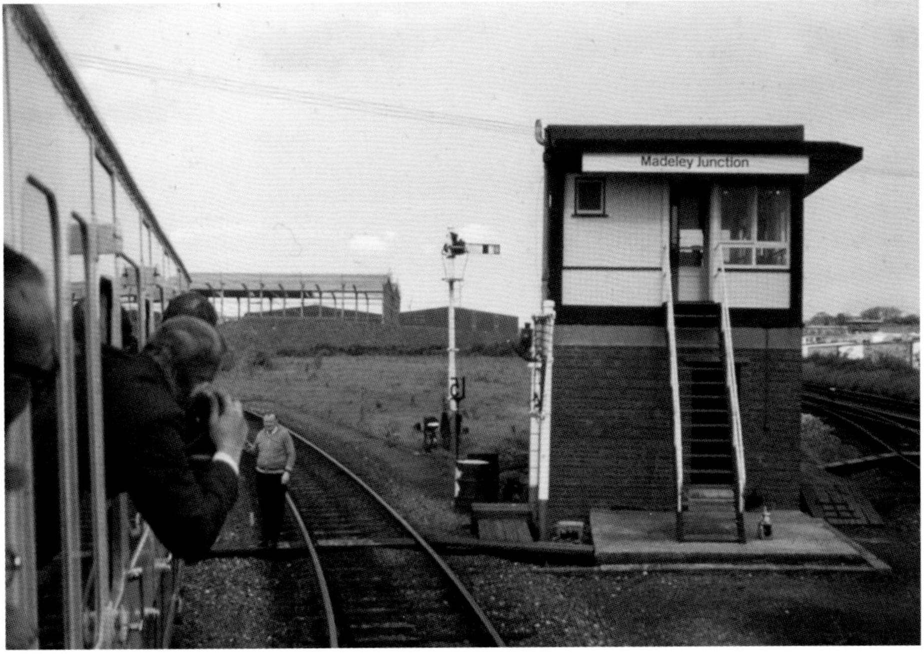

Museum Specials

On several summers between 1979 and 1990, the Madeley branch carried Sunday trains from Birmingham to a temporary station at Coalbrookdale for visitors to the Ironbridge Gorge Museum. Above, beyond an enthusiast's head (!), the driver of the inaugural train collects the token from the Madeley Junction signalman to gain access to the branch; below, a return train awaits access to the main line.

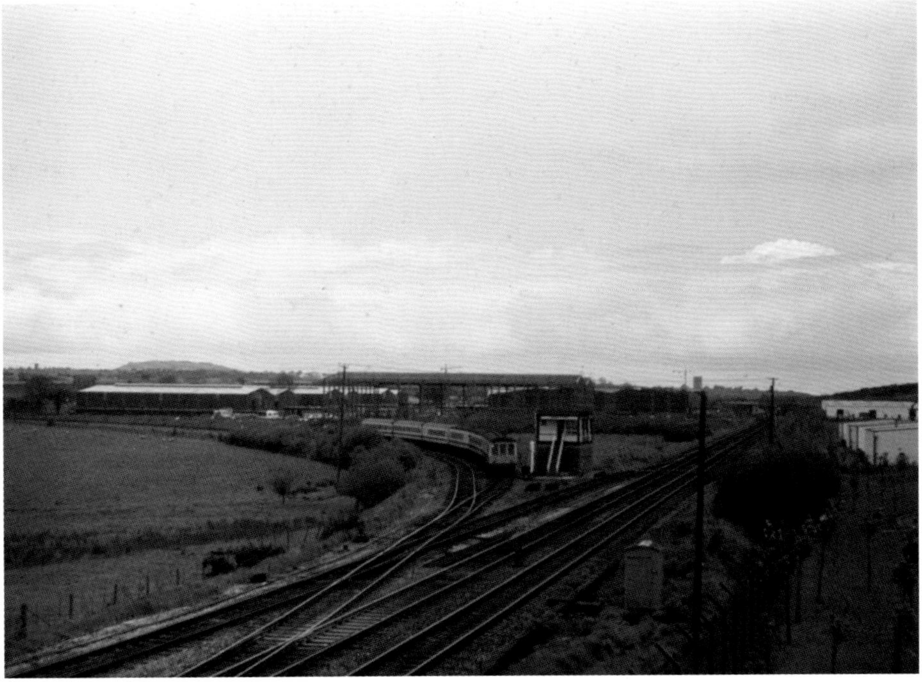

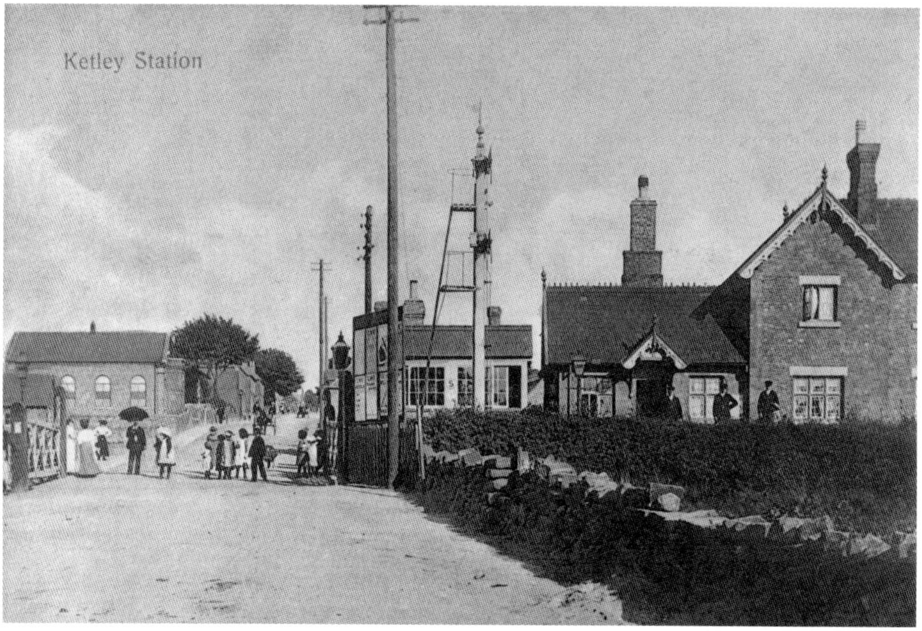

The Wenlock Branch

The WSJR opened in stages from Ketley Junction (Wellington) to Lightmoor between 1857 and 1858. The line crossed the Holyhead Road before entering its first station at Ketley (above). Halts were later opened at Ketley Town and New Dale on the section before the next station at Lawley Bank (below). The crossing gate here was manned for many years before closure by the ever-present Mrs Cottam.

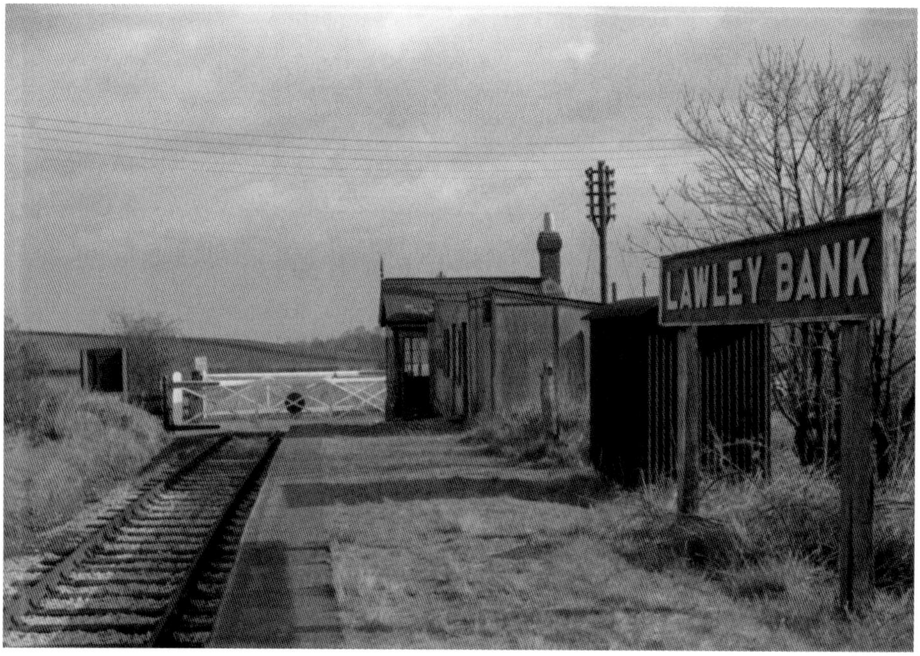

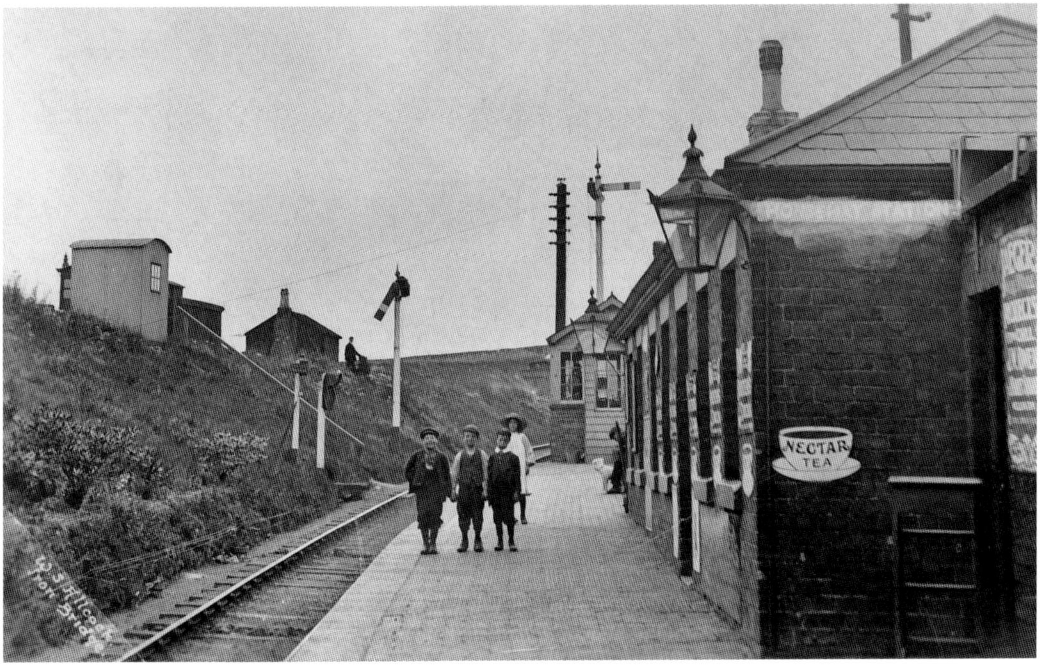

Horsehay

The summit of the railway was reached through the short Heath Hill tunnel before the line dropped to Horsehay & Dawley station. A group of children pose on the platform in around 1900 (above). The view in the opposite direction (below) was subsequent to closure of passenger services in 1962.

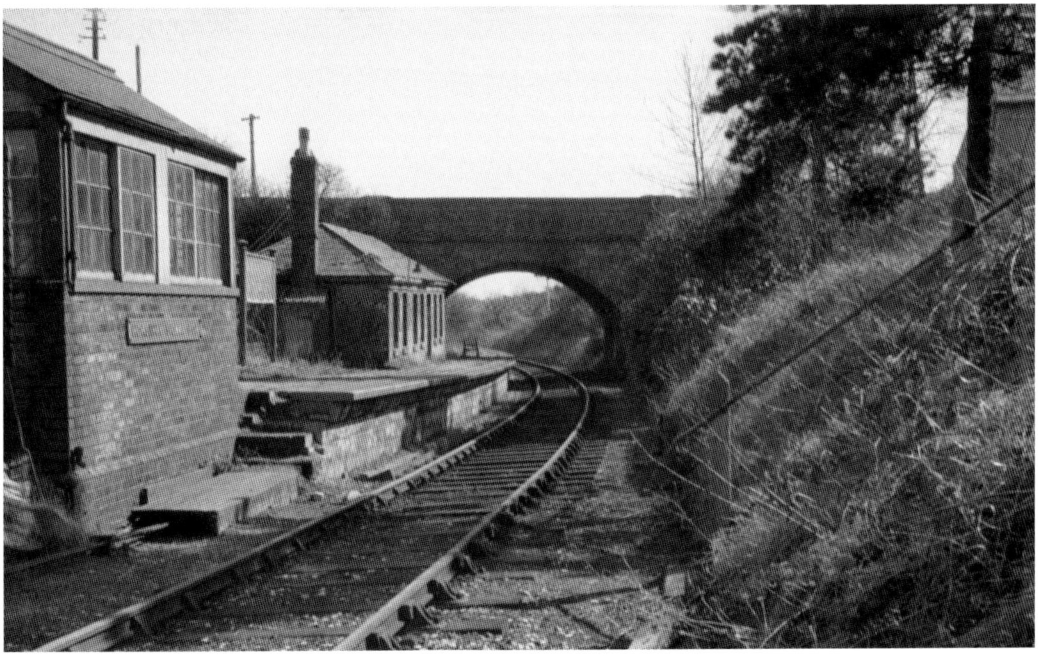

Horsehay Goods Yard

There were ten sidings in the goods yard at Horsehay, one of which led into Horsehay Ironworks. Many of the large girders made at the ironworks were carried by rail, and the section of the WSJR between Horsehay and Lightmoor was kept open for this traffic until 1979. This very early morning departure from the Adamson Butterley works (above) was in 1972, and below, the train reaches the main line at Madeley Junction.

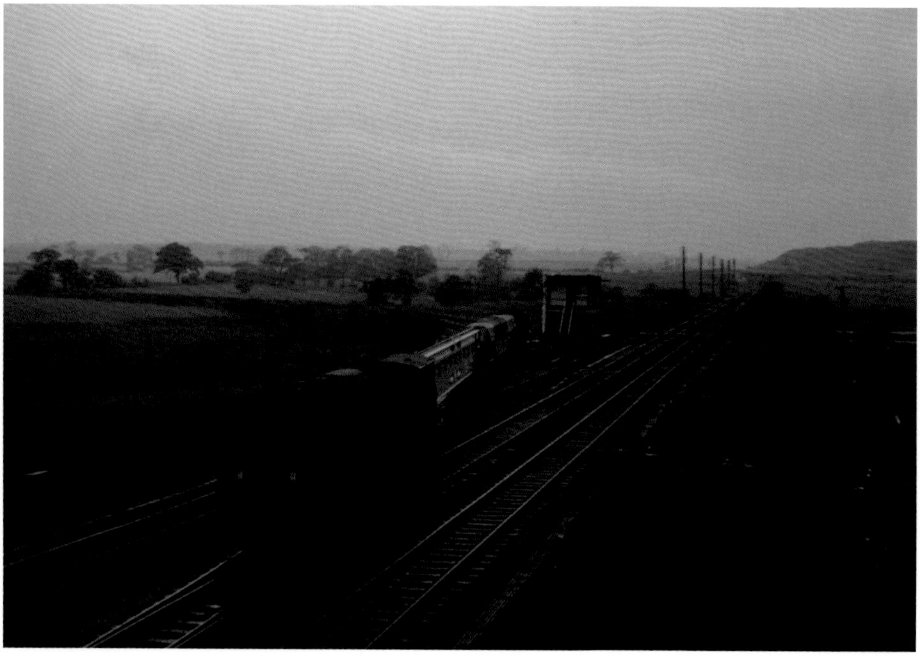

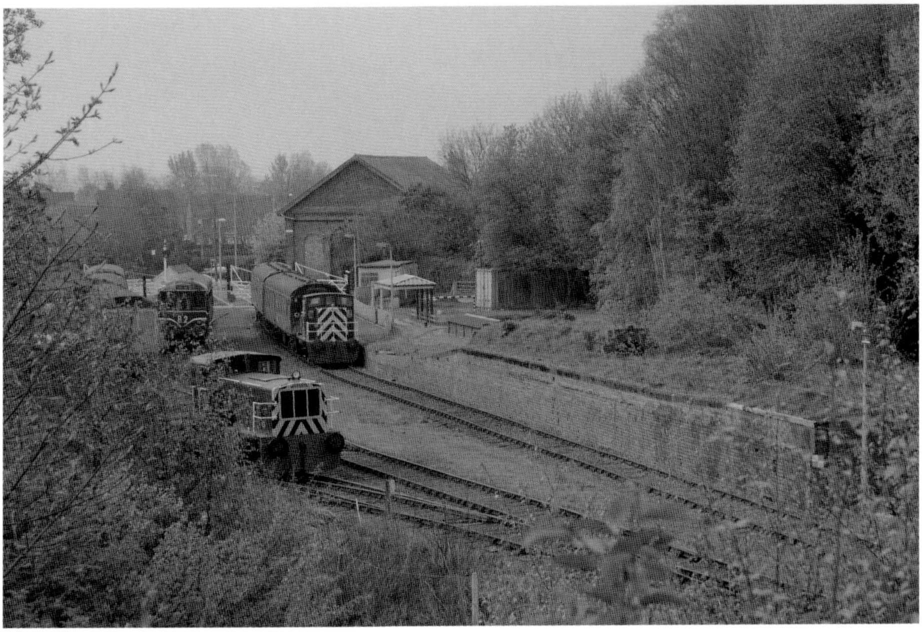

Telford Horsehay Steam Trust
Formed in 1976, the heritage Telford Steam Railway, based at the former Horsehay goods yard (above), operates a small section of line on Sundays and bank holidays from Easter to September, and during the Christmas period. The goods shed is now the Trust's workshop. A visiting locomotive in 2006 (below) was a Beattie 2-4-0 'Well Tank' from the National Collection.

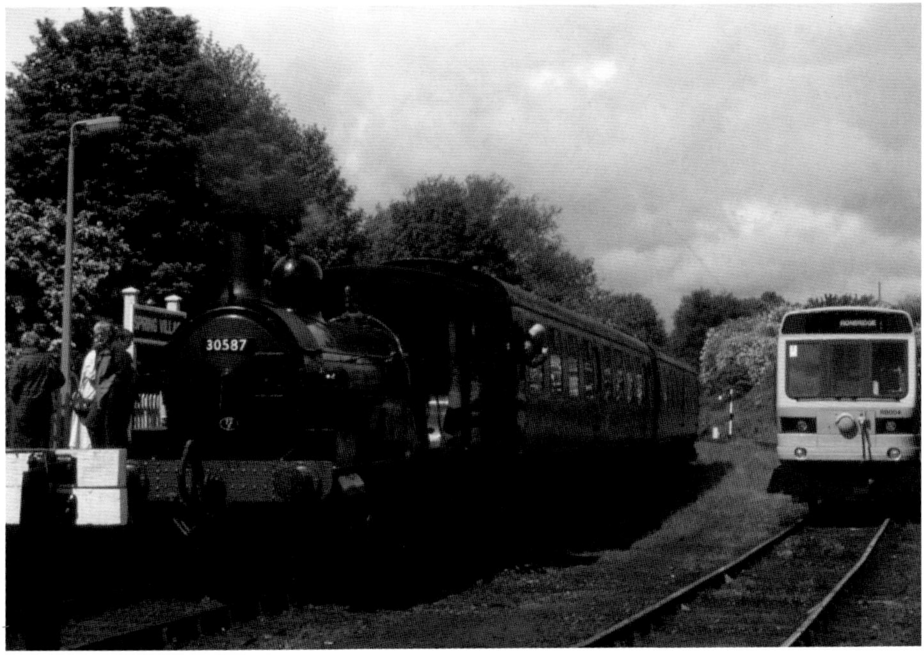

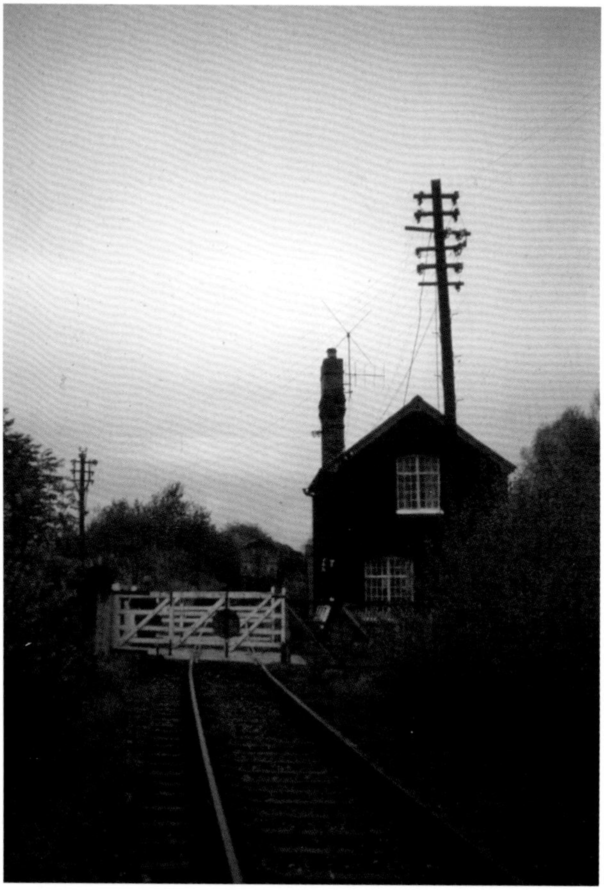

Level Crossings
Between Horsehay and Lightmoor were two level crossings. At Doseley, a halt was opened in 1932 next to the crossing and crossing keeper's house (above). Immediately below the crossing gates at Dawley Parva, the ground frame, which until the 1880s had controlled the sidings into the former Lightmoor furnaces, still survived in this 1967 view, together with a GWR cast-iron warning notice (below).

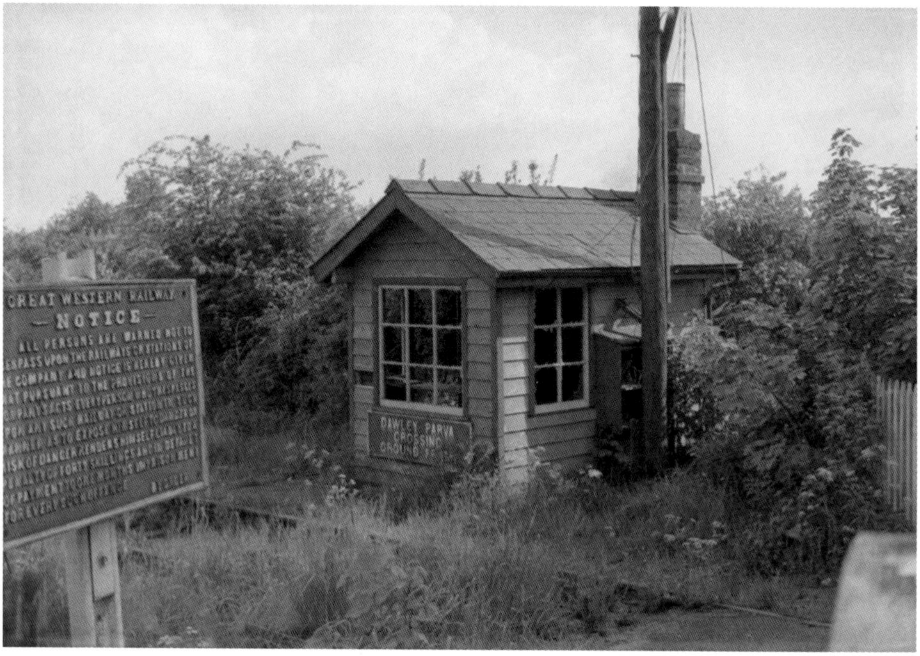

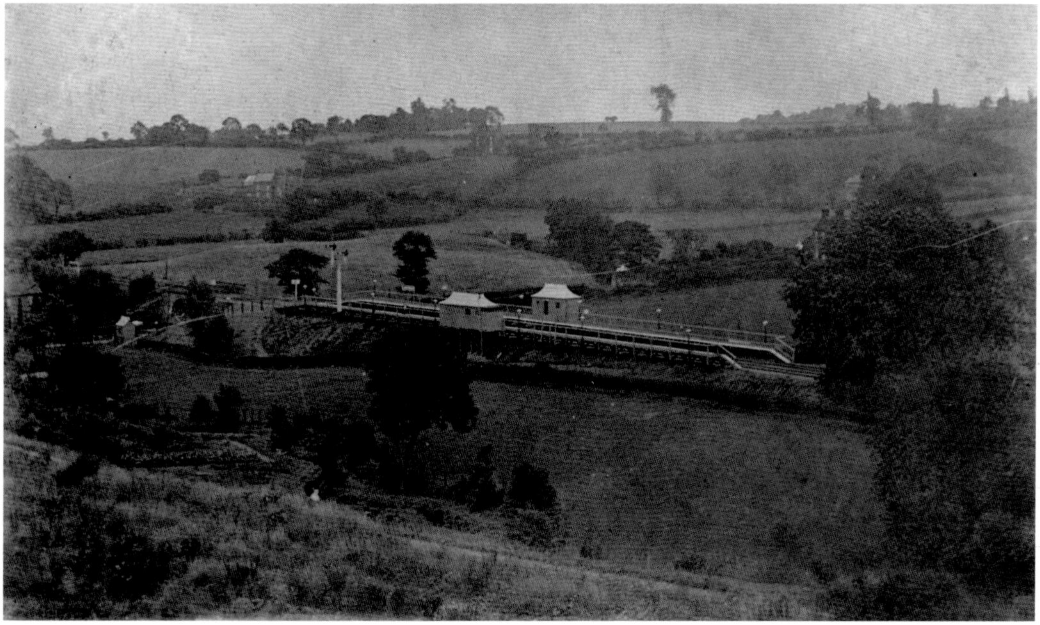

Lightmoor

Just beyond the junction of the Madeley branch and the WSJR, the first station at Lightmoor operated between 1859 and 1864. It closed following the extension of the railway to Coalbrookdale, but opened again as Lightmoor Platform in 1907, with its distinctive pagoda-style shelters (above), and served the area until the closure of passenger services in 1962. Six years later, the former station's notice board at road level (below) was the worse for wear.

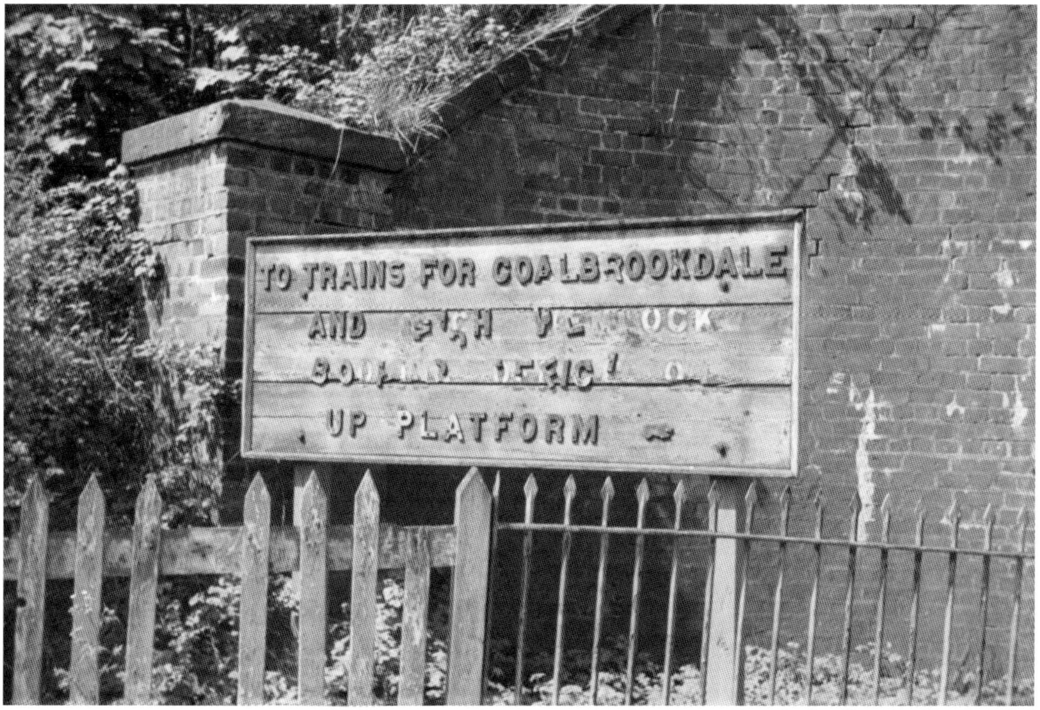

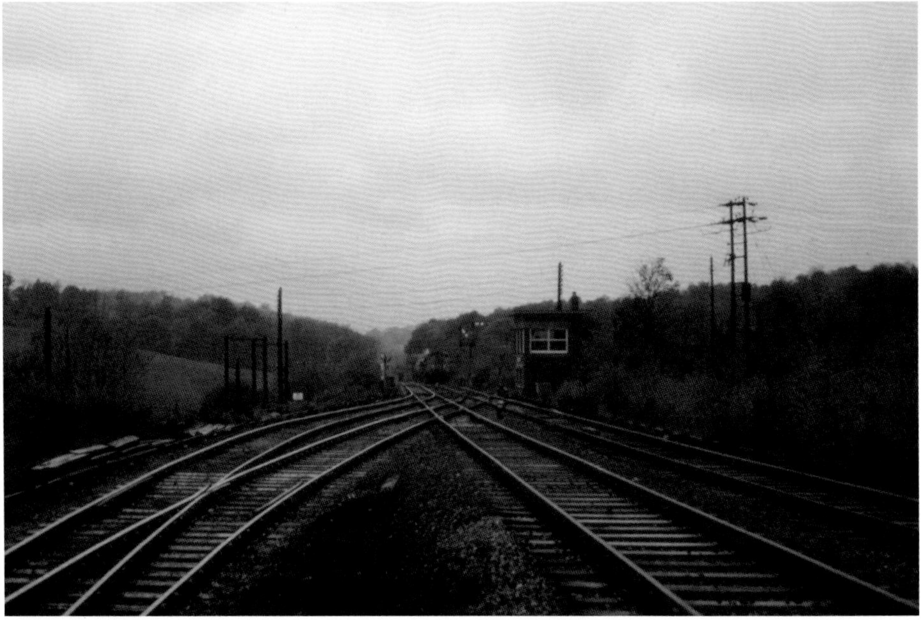

Lightmoor Junction

The signal box at Lightmoor controlled the junction of the single lines of the Madeley branch and the WSJR, and also the double-track extension to Coalbrookdale and Buildwas Junction (above). A train of coal empties picks up the single-line token for the Madeley Branch from the Lightmoor signalman (below). The signal box closed in 2006 when the entire line to Ironbridge power station was reduced to single-line working.

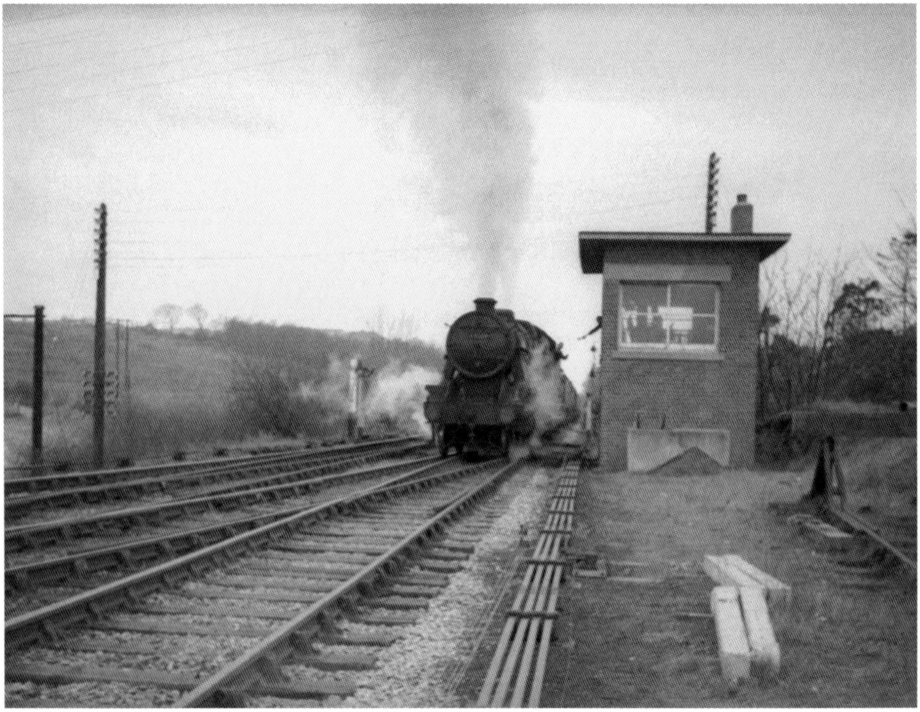

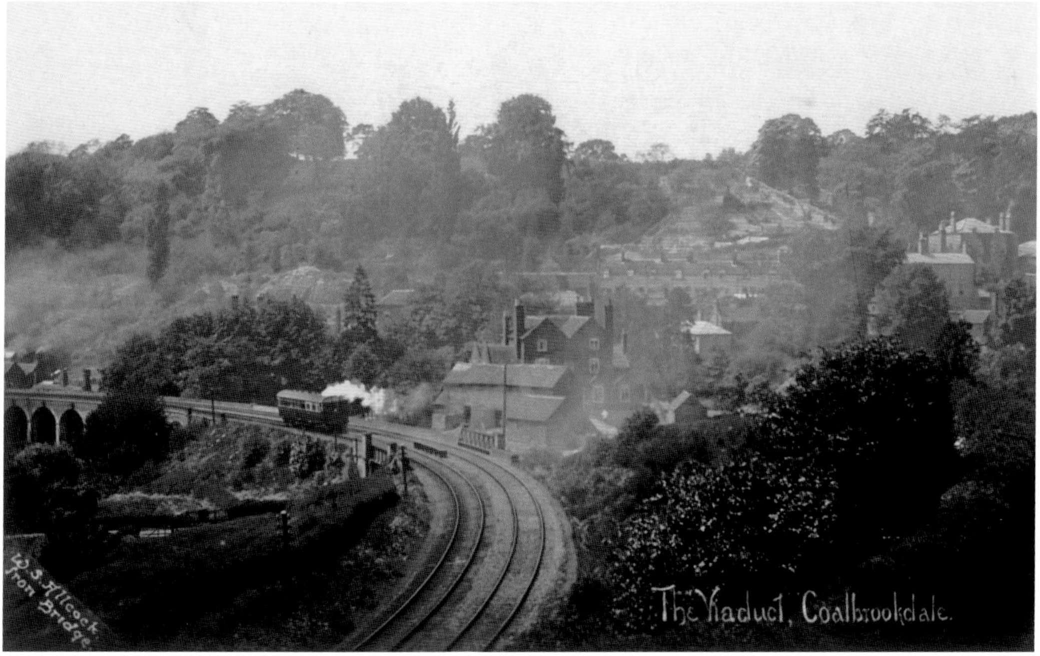

Coalbrookdale

In 1864, the GWR extended the railway from Lightmoor on a falling 1 in 50 gradient and over a 26-arch viaduct to Coalbrookdale, where a connection was made with the Wenlock Railway's line from Buildwas Junction. In 1906, a steam railmotor is about to cross the viaduct at Coalbrookdale (above). On the sharp curve in the foreground of the picture, the GWR opened Green Bank Halt in 1934 (below).

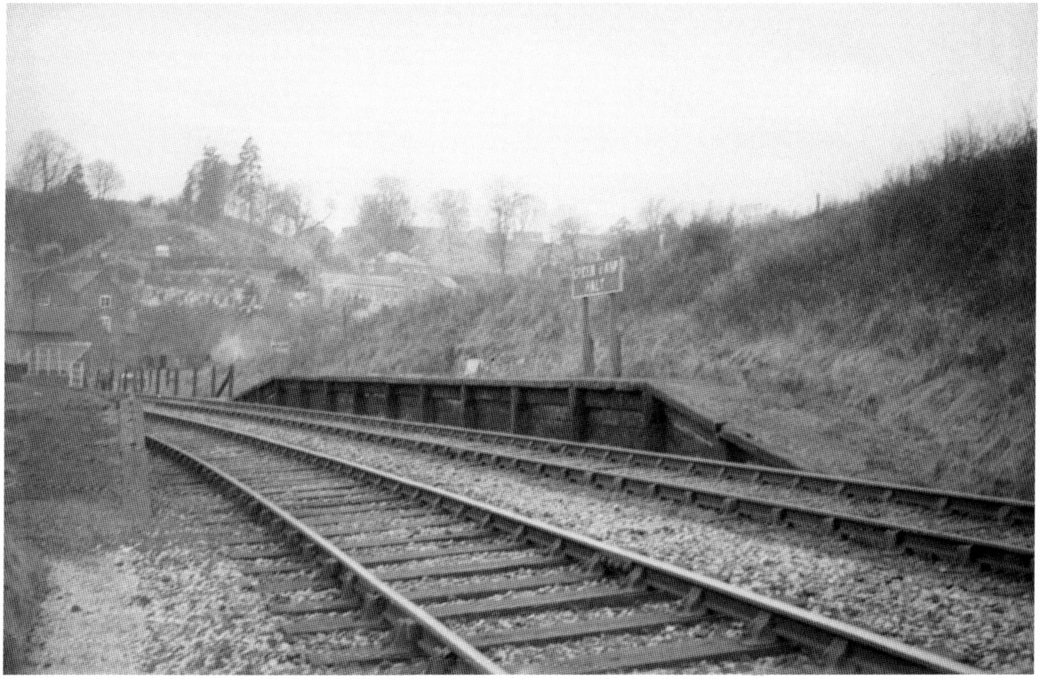

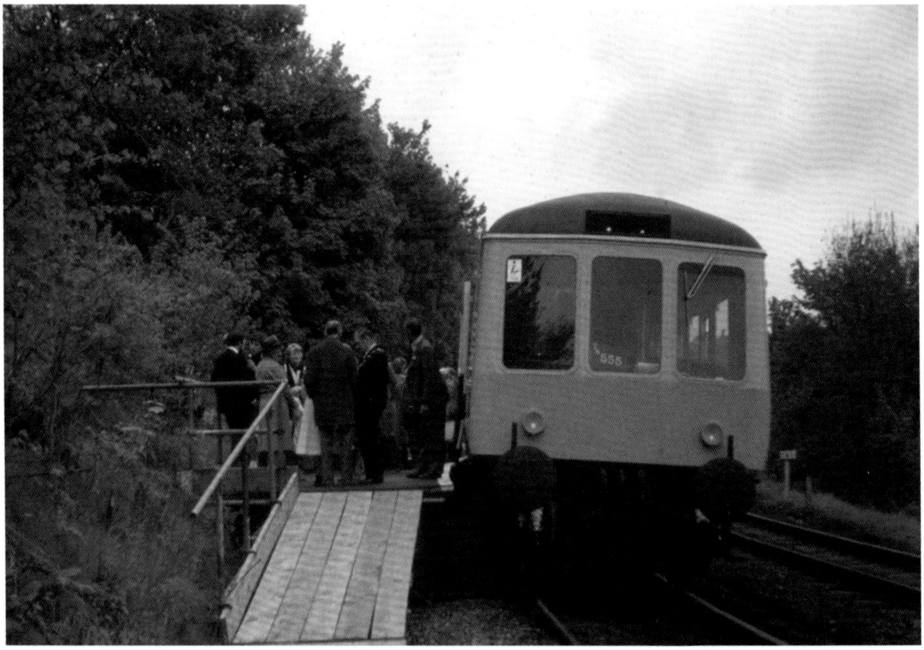

Museum Station

In 1979, in connection with the bicentenary of the building of the world's first iron bridge, British Rail opened a platform beyond the south side of the viaduct at Coalbrookdale to enable visitors on summer Sundays to travel by rail to the Ironbridge Gorge Museum. Local dignitaries meet the first train (above), and a train leaves for Wolverhampton and Birmingham (below).

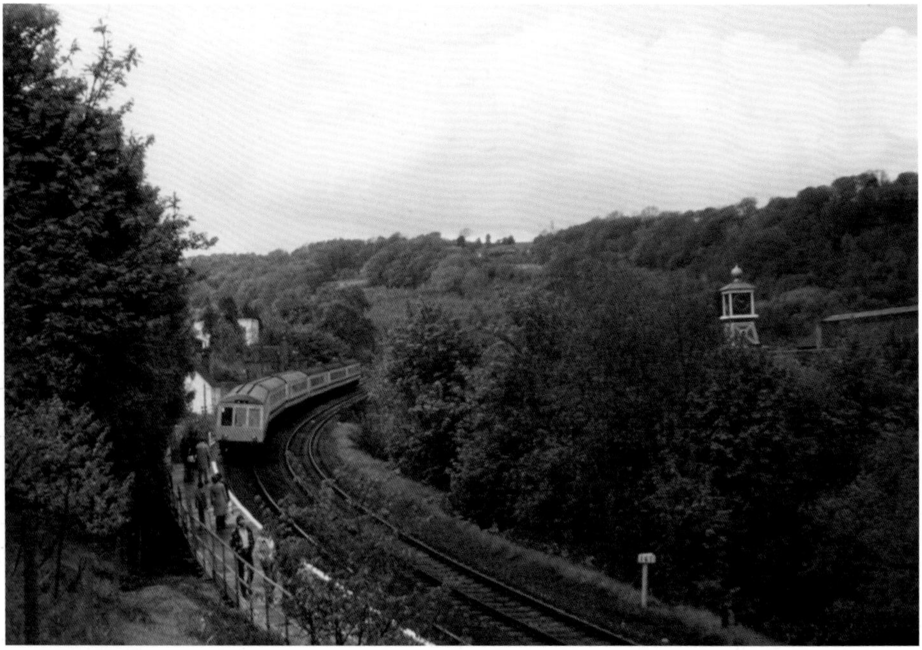

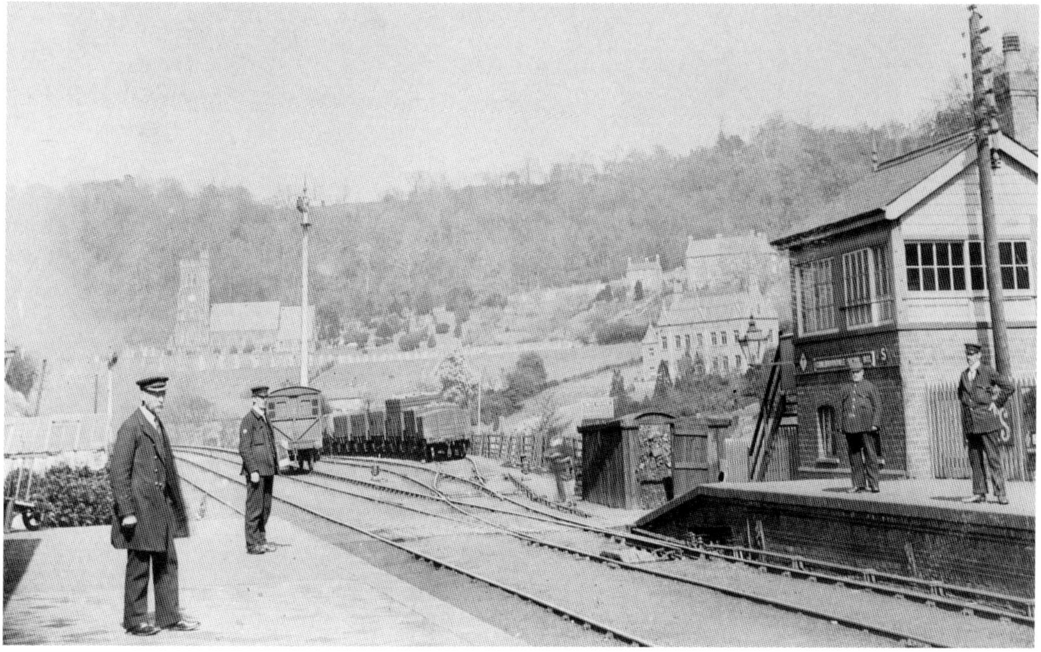

Coalbrookdale Goods

At Coalbrookdale, there were steep sidings into the works, controlled from the signal box at the end of the down platform of Coalbrookdale station (above). The goods agent's office in Wellington Road, indicated by a board on the side of the building at the entrance to Allied Ironfounders' Coalbrookdale Works (below), was some way from the station.

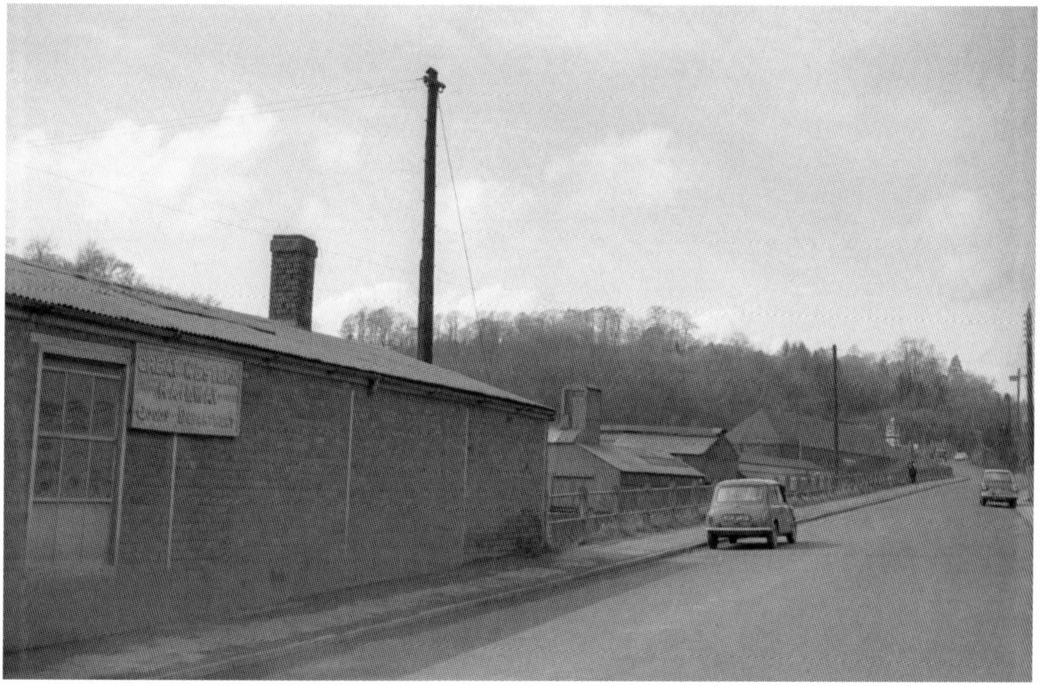

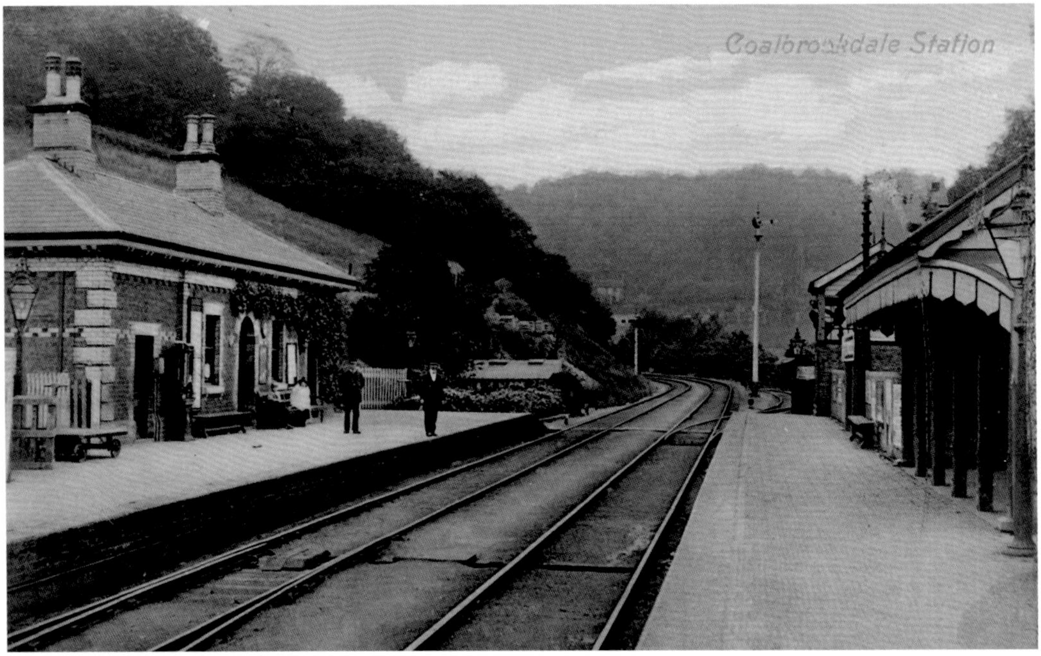

Coalbrookdale Station

The attractive station building, with its yellow brick and tiled roof (above), the work of Joseph Fogerty, Assistant Engineer of the Wenlock & Severn Junction Railway, was opened in 1864. The building survived the closure of passenger services in 1962, and is now the office block of the Green Wood Centre. A train carrying biomass to Ironbridge power station is seen passing (below), but with the likely closure of the power station in 2015, this traffic will cease.

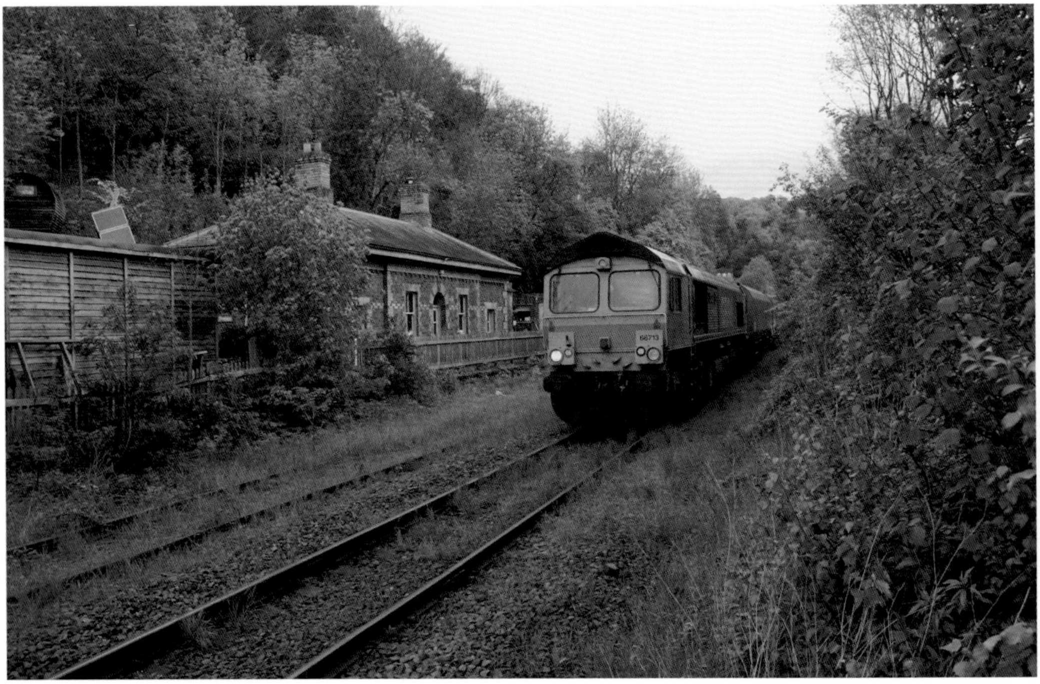

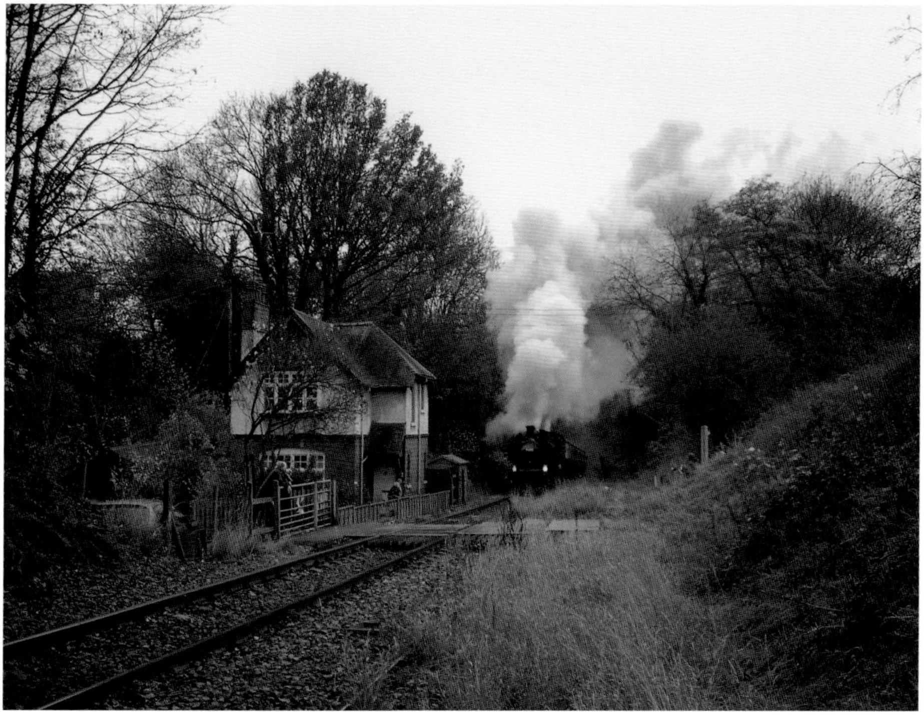

Crossing the Severn

Before the line reaches the river, it crosses Strethill Road at Chunes Crossing. In 2009, a returning enthusiasts' special train approaches the unmanned level crossing (above), hauled by double-headed, restored ex-GWR 0-6-0 pannier tanks. The Severn is crossed by the Albert Edward Bridge (below), which was designed by John Fowler, built by the Coalbrookdale Company and, when opened in 1864, was claimed to be 'the largest cast-iron arch carrying a double line of railway that has yet been erected anywhere in the world'.

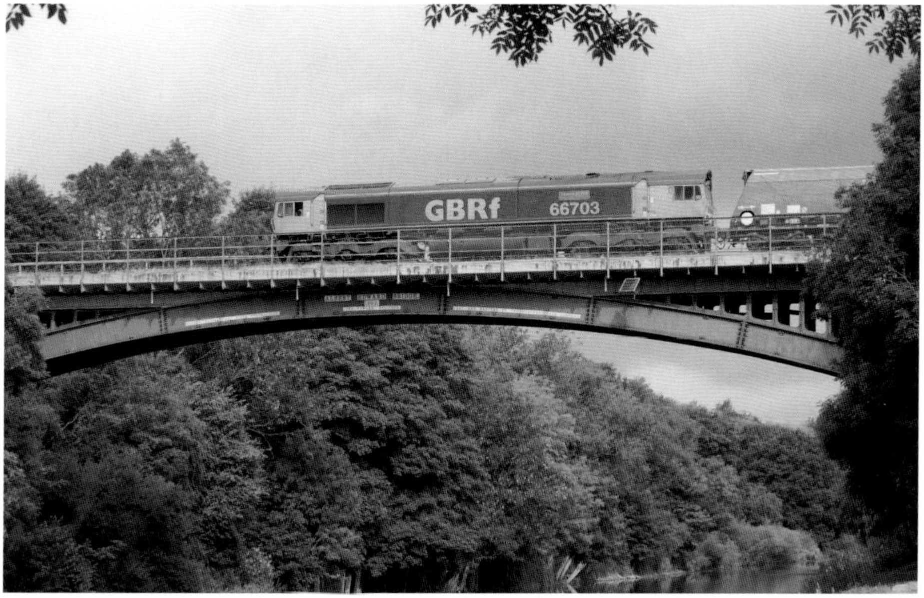

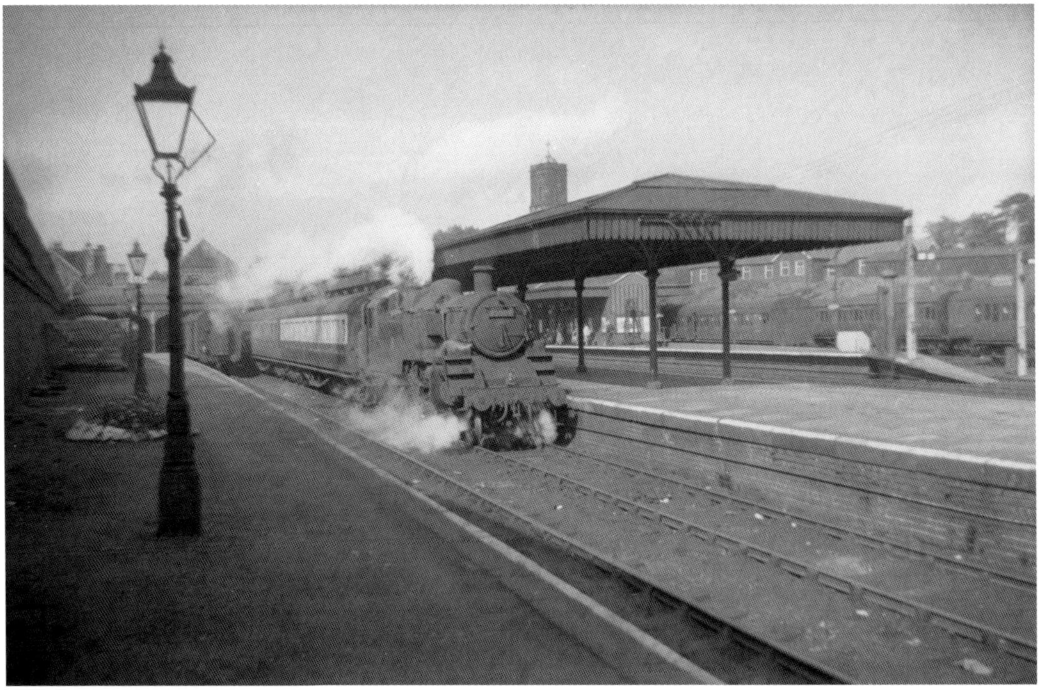

The Line to Wenlock

The Wenlock & Severn Junction line from Buildwas to Much Wenlock, which opened in 1862, climbed up Farley Dingle (where a halt was opened in 1934) at a gradient of 1 in 40. In September 1956, the train that had earlier left Wellington (above) returns from Much Wenlock and is seen approaching Buildwas Junction station (below).

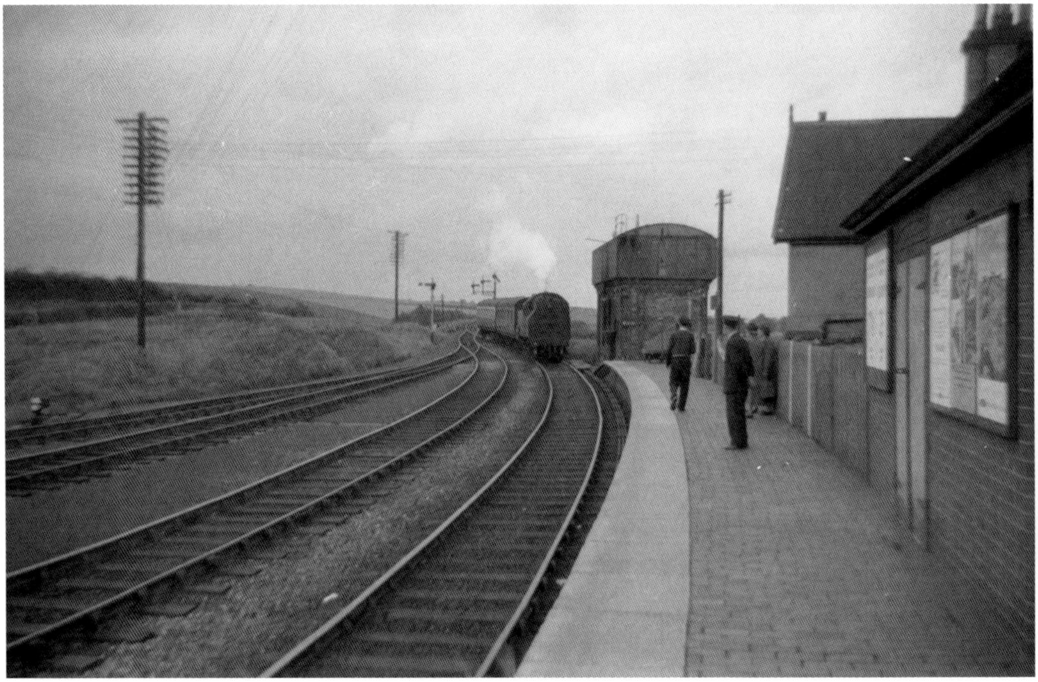

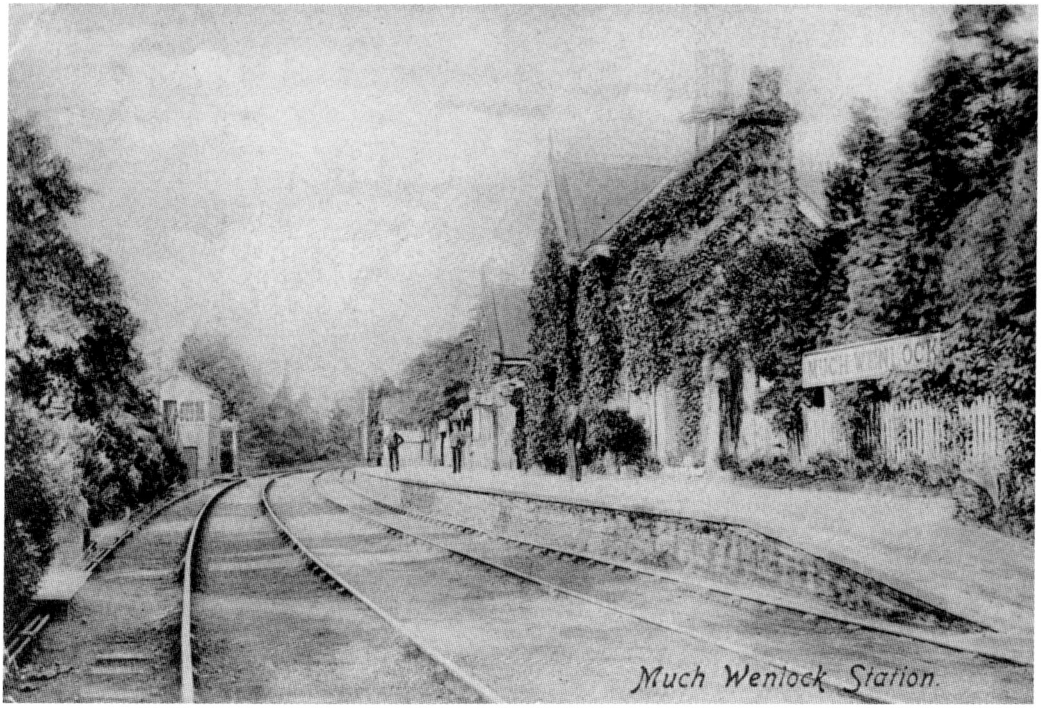

Much Wenlock

Much Wenlock was the terminus for trains from Wellington following the withdrawal of services to Craven Arms in 1951. The brick and stone station buildings, seen over a century ago (above), included the station master's house. Passenger services between Wellington and Much Wenlock ended in July 1962. Semi-derelict in the years that followed (below), the building was later restored for residential use.

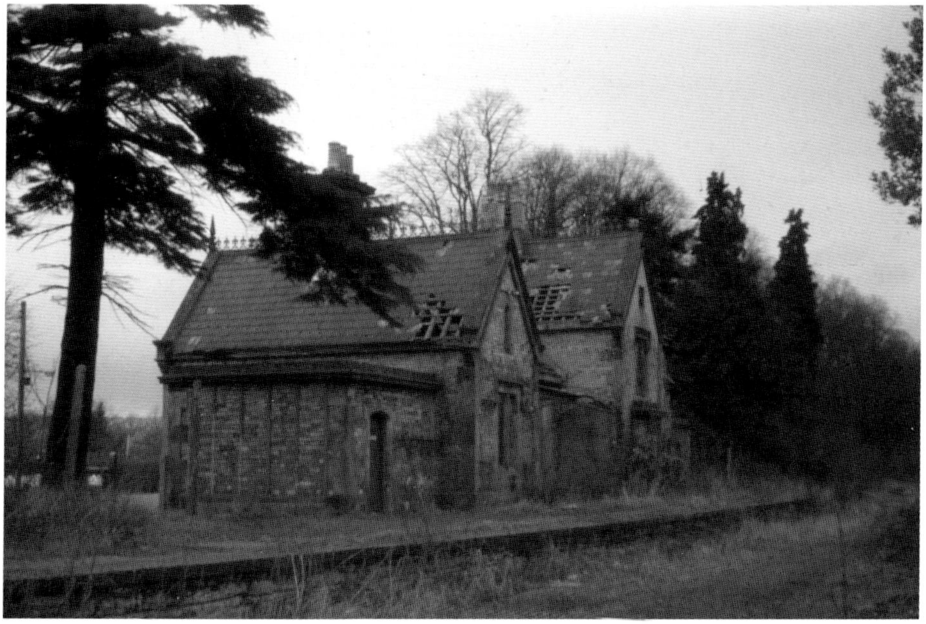

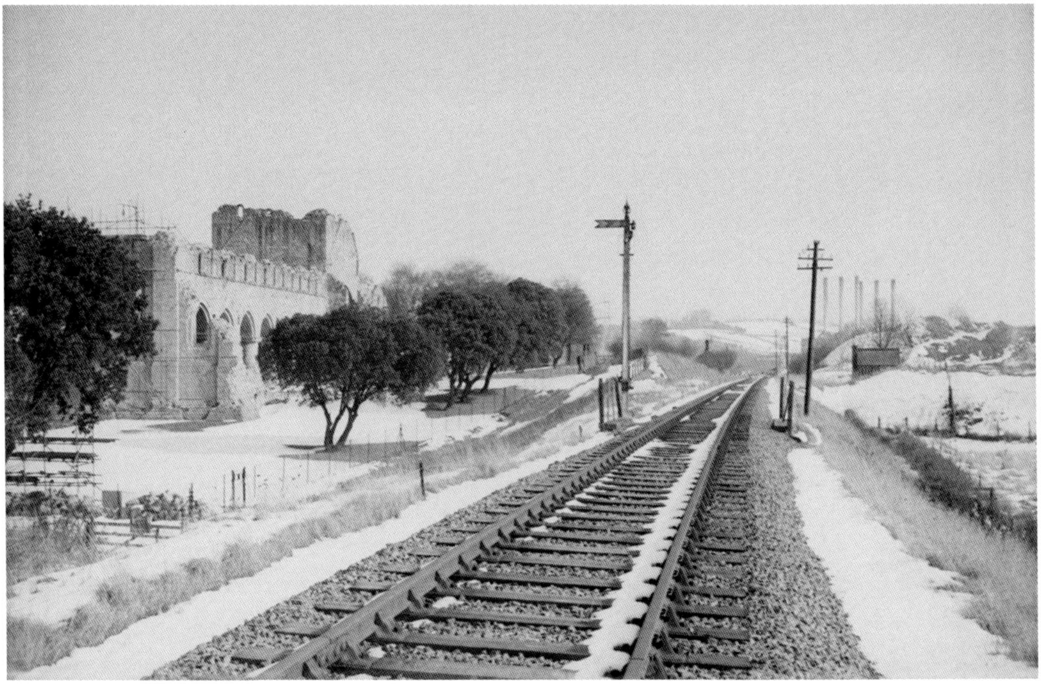

The Severn Valley Line

The railway from Shrewsbury to Hartlebury opened in January 1862. On the approach to Buildwas Junction, and before crossing the Much Wenlock road, the line passed Buildwas Abbey (above). At the junction (below), it linked with lines to Wellington and Much Wenlock/Craven Arms. Passenger services were withdrawn from the Severn Valley line in September 1963.

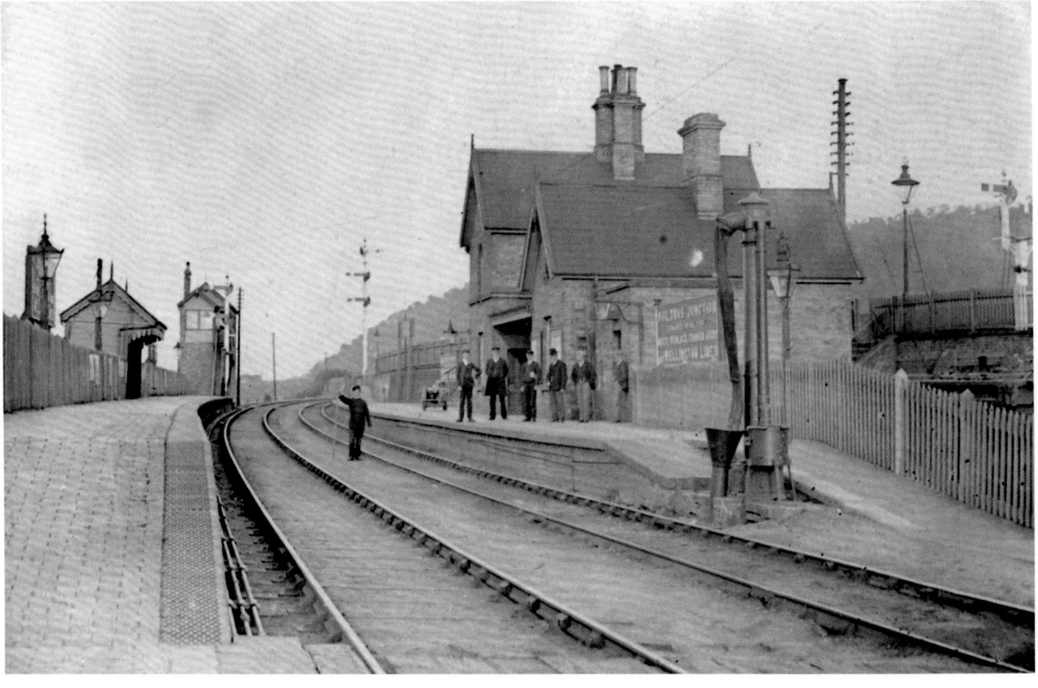

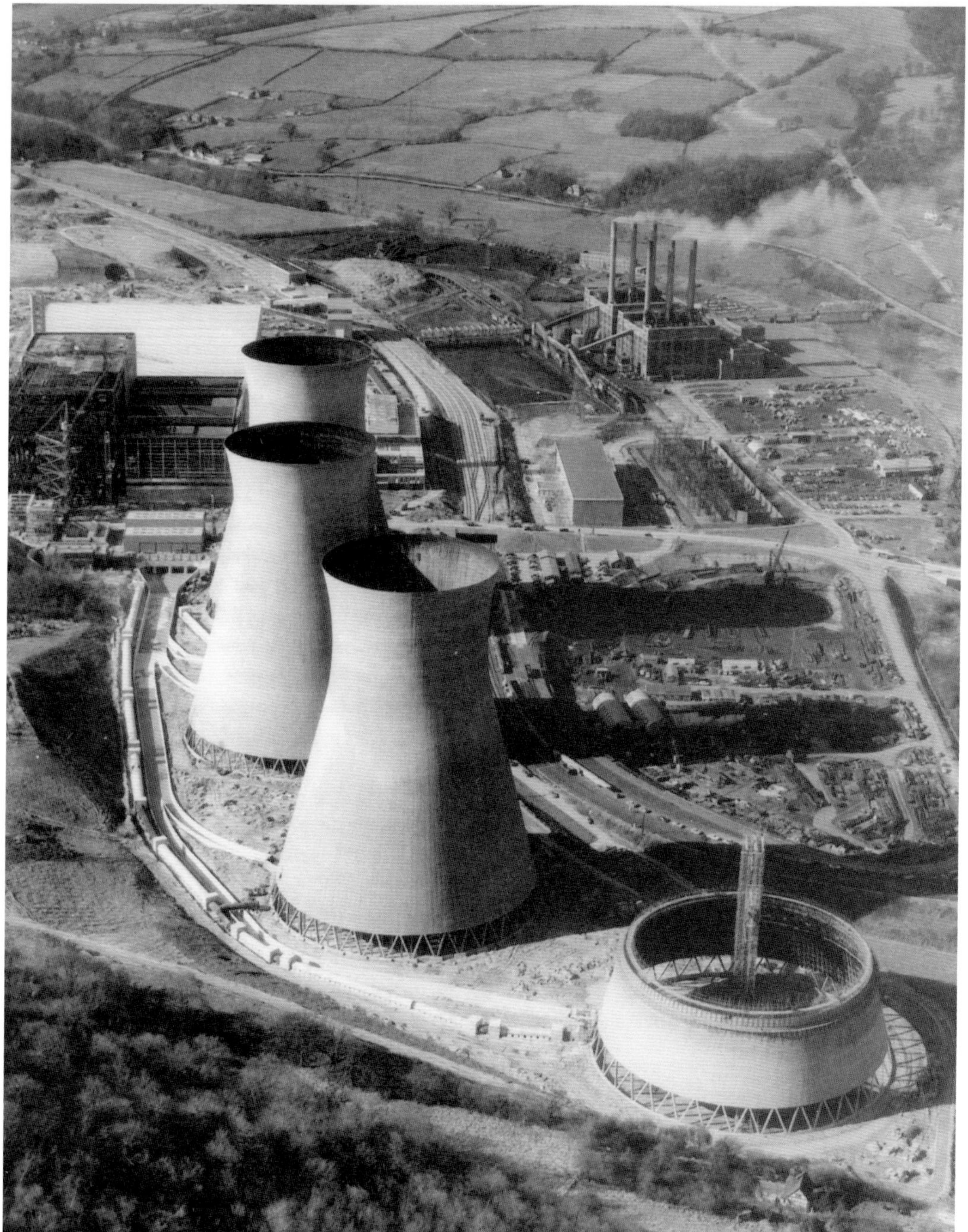

Ironbridge Power Station

The first power station here opened in 1932 and was supplied with coal from local pits by rail. With the closure of the branch to Wenlock and the Severn Valley line, a realignment of the track at Buildwas Junction was made in preparation for the construction of a new power station adjacent to the existing one. The new power station, termed 'Ironbridge B', was commissioned in 1969, and the original one closed in 1978.

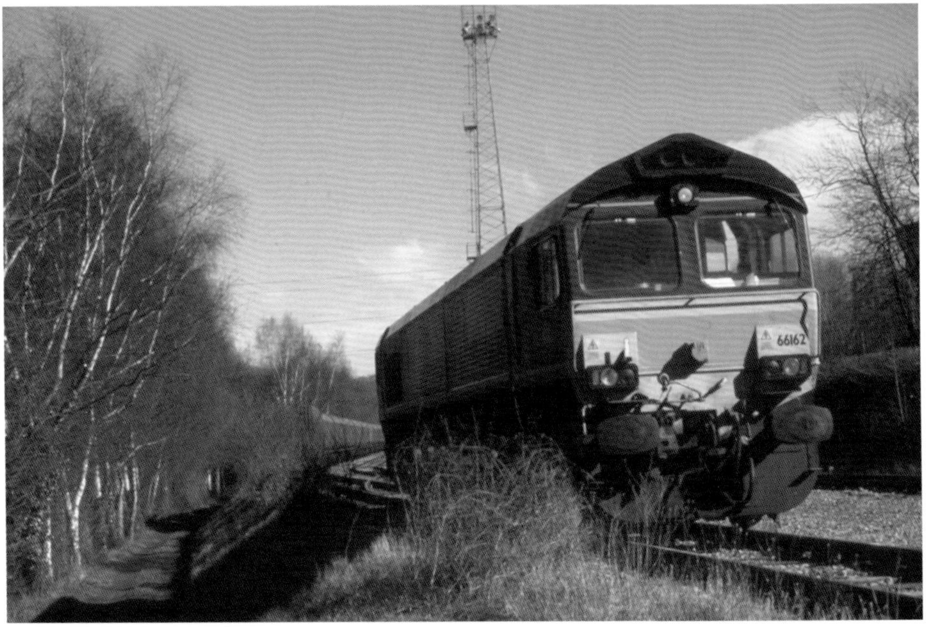

Coal to the Power Station

From 1969, coal continued to be supplied to both power stations along the line from Madeley Junction via Coalbrookdale. When a 'merry-go-round' coal train arrived at the power station's headshunt (above), the locomotive ran around it, prior to hauling the wagons through the unloading plant (below), where they discharged their load while moving slowly over hoppers.

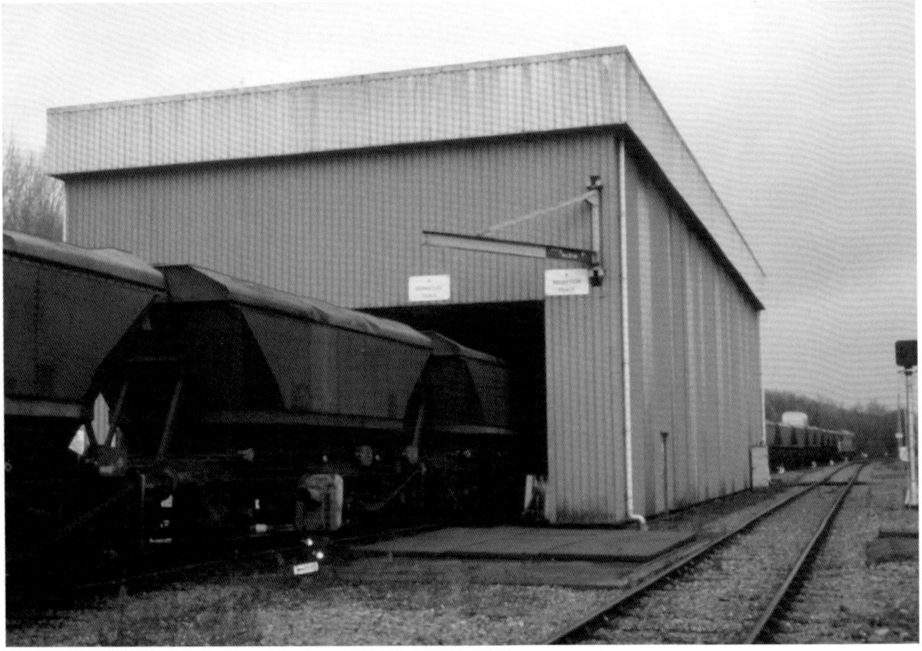

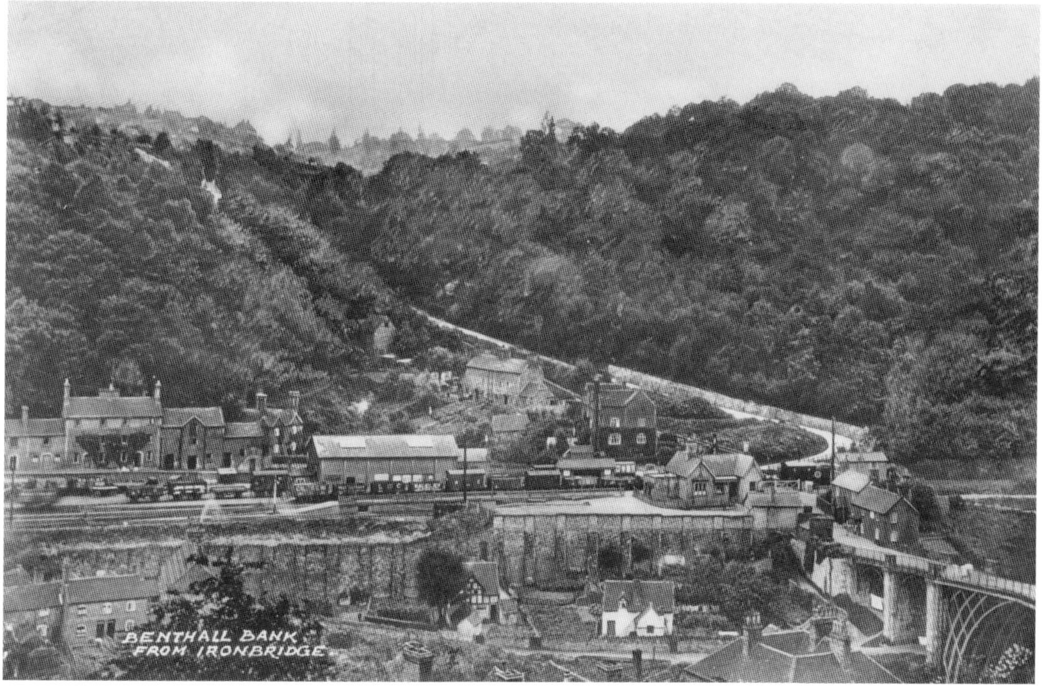

Ironbridge & Broseley Station (1)

The station was on the south side of the Iron Bridge and comprised station building, signal box, goods shed and sidings (above). A century ago, a Shrewsbury-bound train is about to pull out of the station (below). Today, rails are still embedded in the road at the site of the level crossing.

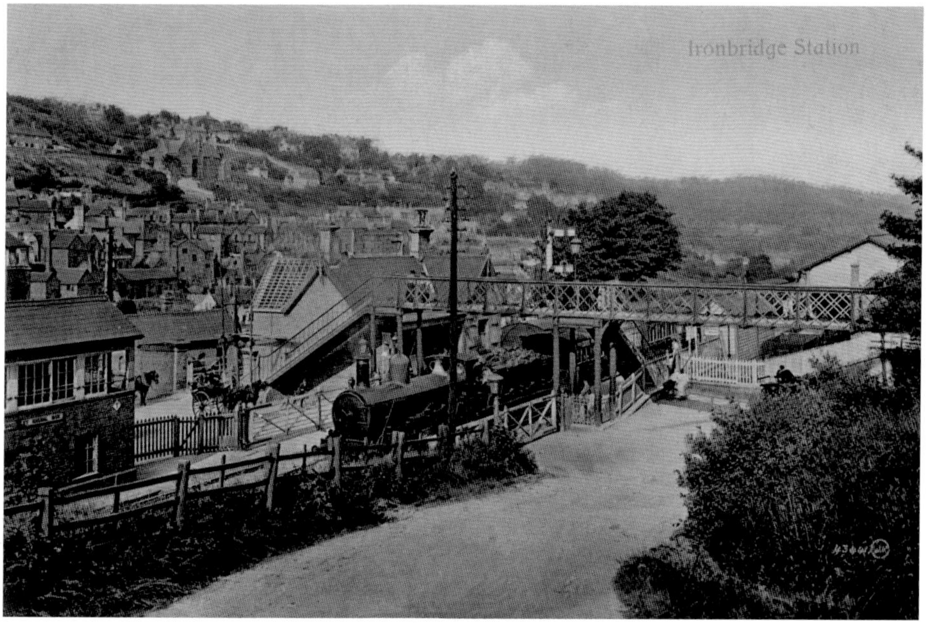

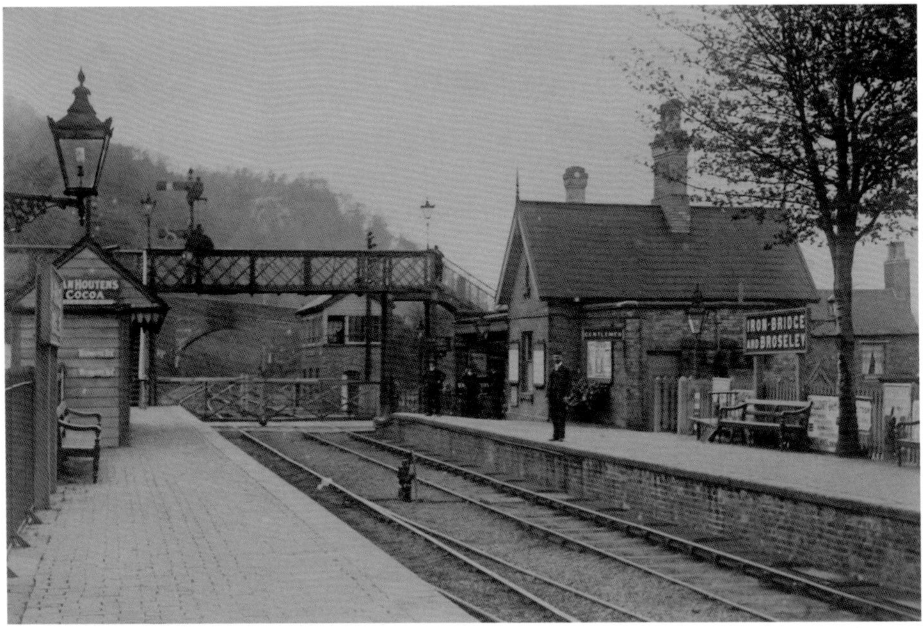

Ironbridge & Broseley Station (2)

Another early view of the station (above, 1908) shows the original spelling 'Iron-Bridge'. The station closed in September 1963 and the track was soon removed, but the station building, signal box and goods shed were still intact the following year (below). The site is now a car park.

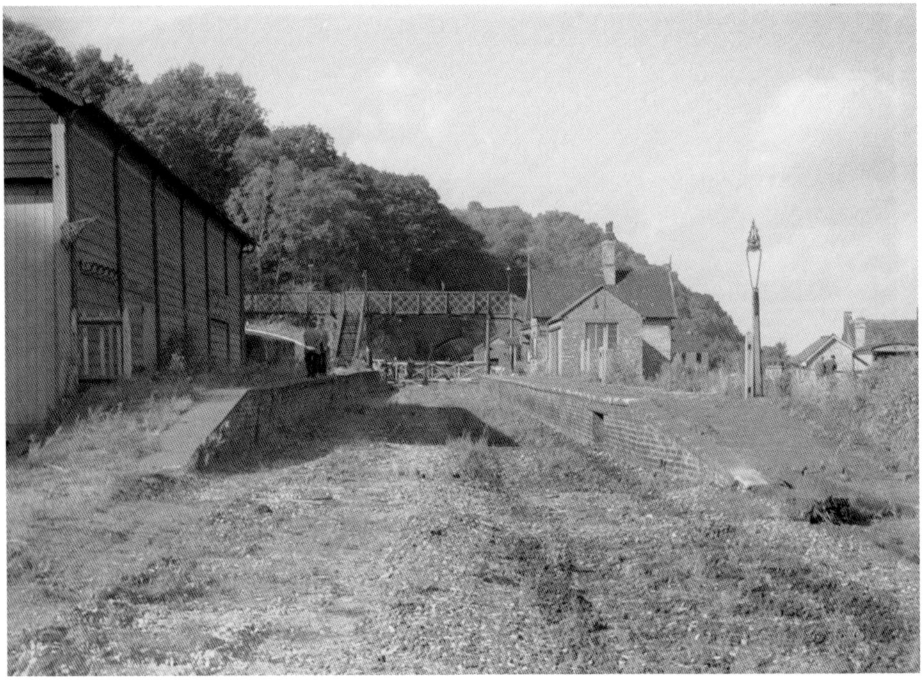

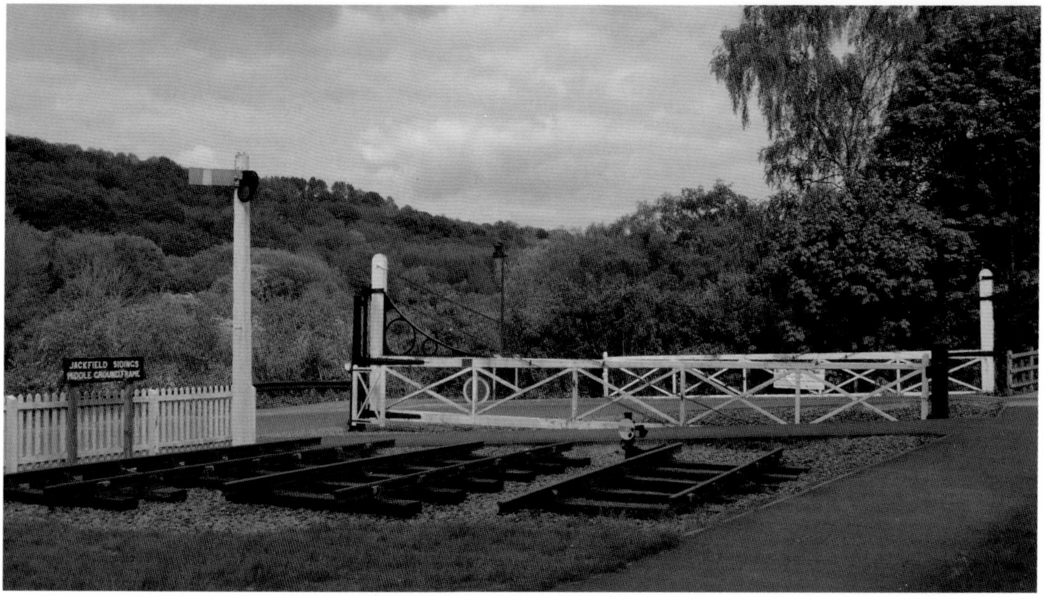

Jackfield

At Jackfield, sidings served local brickworks and the tile works of Craven Dunnill and Maw & Co. The restored Jackfield Crossing (above) shows the large single gates that spanned three tracks, two of which were sidings. The first Jackfield Halt opened in December 1934, but, following a serious landslip in 1952, a new halt was opened 400 yards further east on the reinstated track in March 1954. Below, a train heads south from Jackfield before closure in 1963.

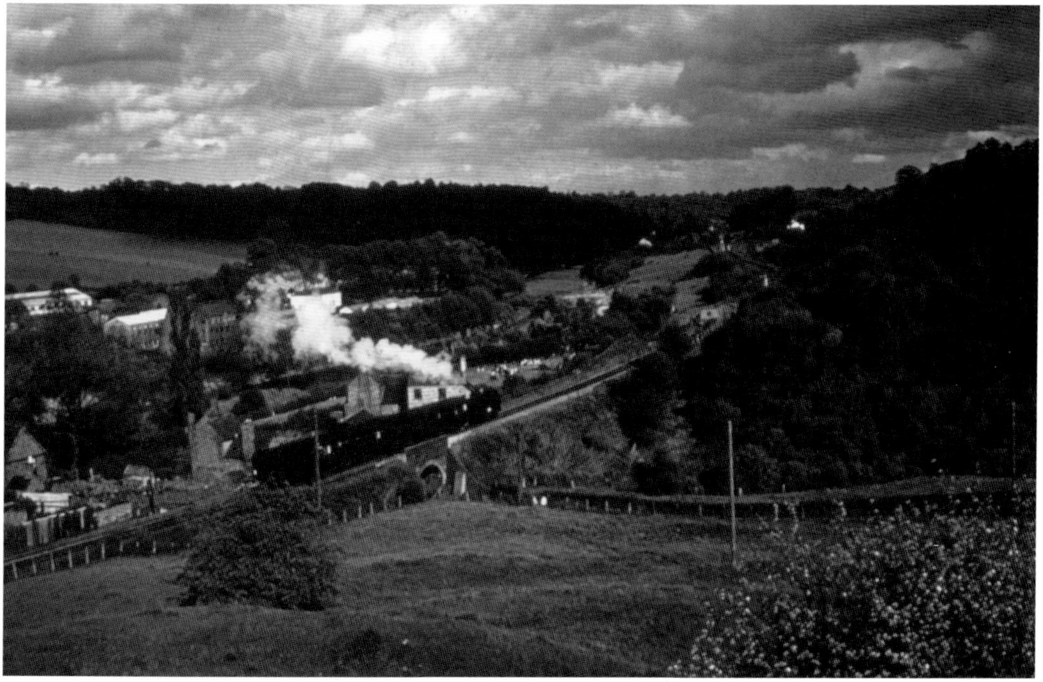

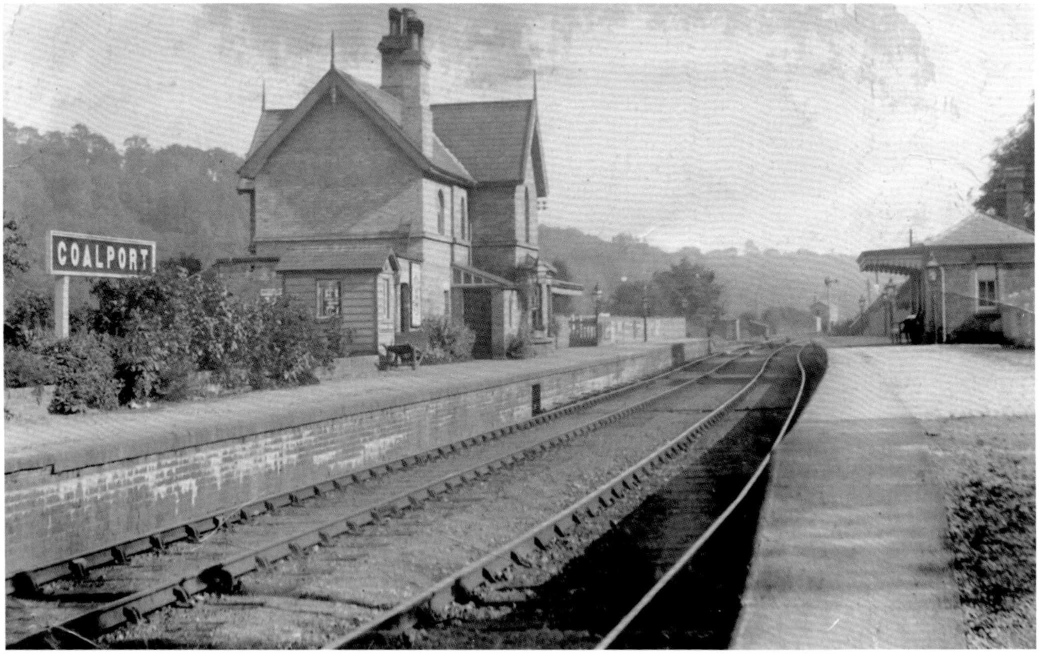

Coalport (GWR)
The village of Coalport had a railway station on each side of the river; the more inconveniently situated one was that on the Severn Valley line (above). On closure the main station building became a residence, but the station site has retained its railway character with a re-laid section of track and the acquisition of coaches which are let out for hire (below).

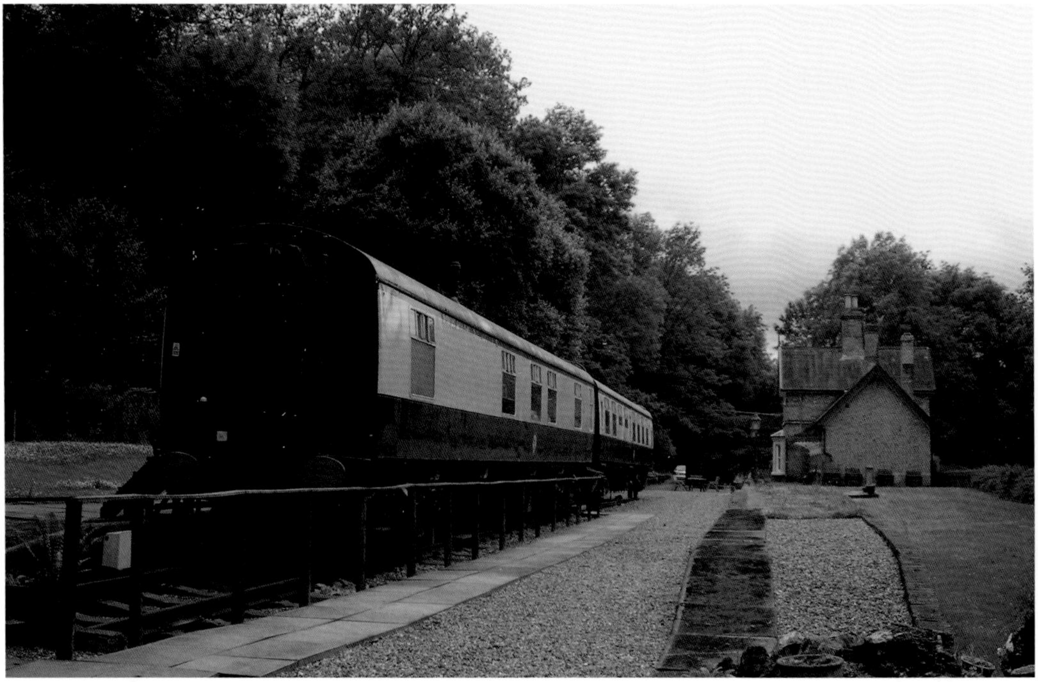

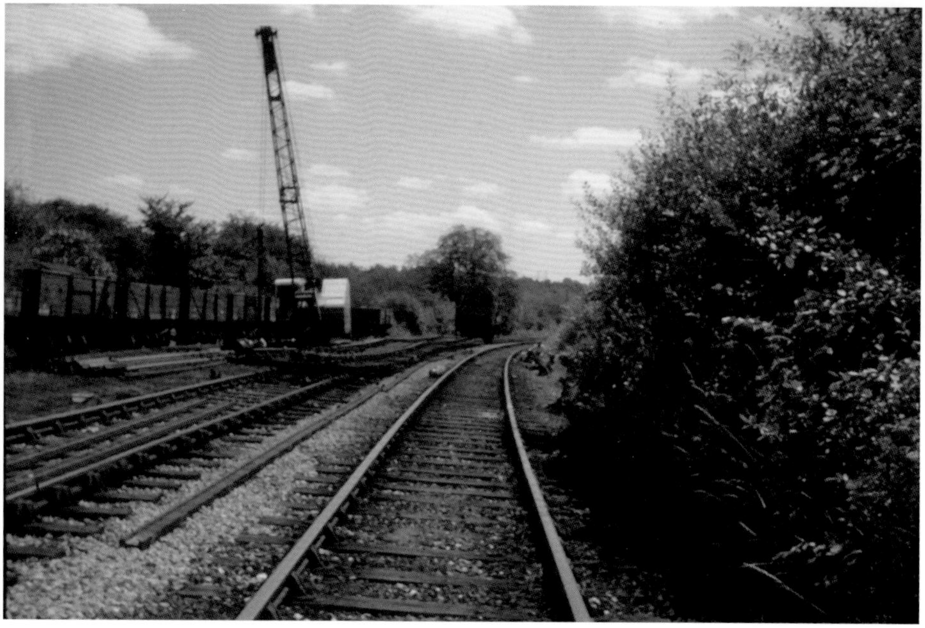

South of Coalport
The railway tracks, including the long siding to Exley's roofing tile works, were lifted soon after closure (above). Between Coalport and Bridgnorth, the station at Linley was opened to appease local landowner Thomas Whitmore of Apley Park, who had opposed the building of the railway. This, too, survived closure to become a private residence (below).

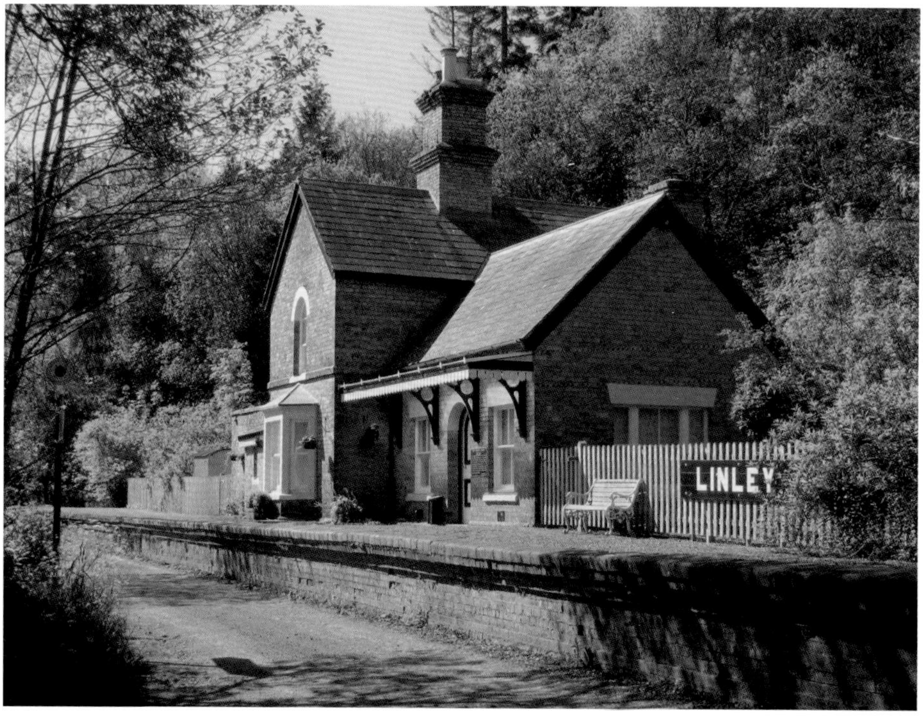

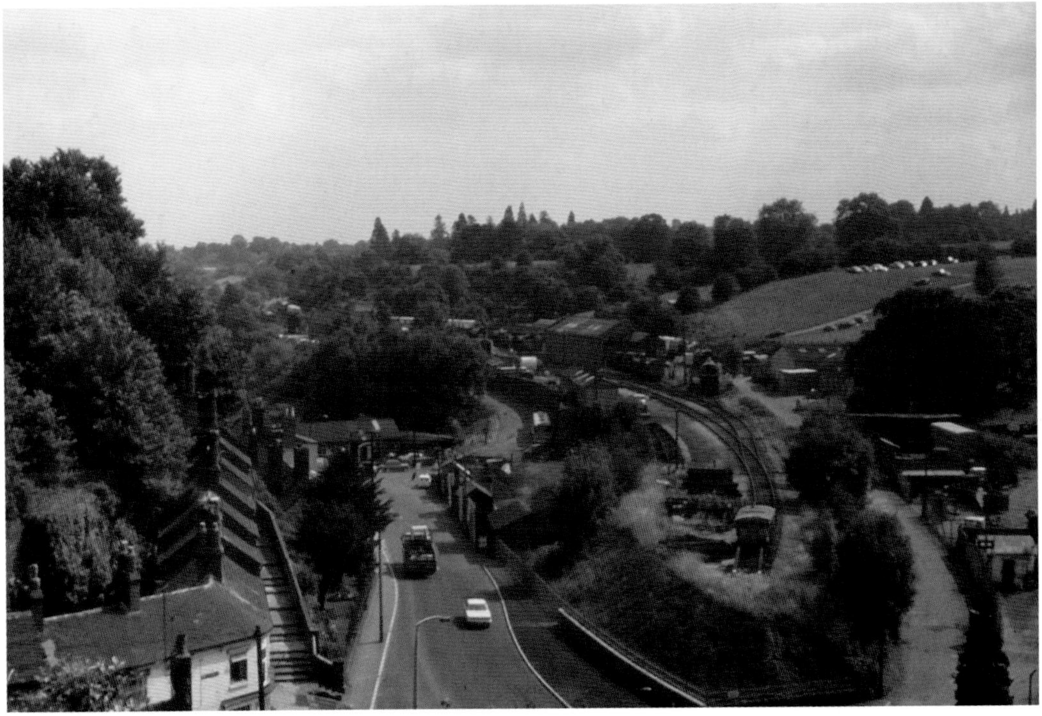

Bridgnorth
The railway ran in a 550-yard tunnel under High Town at Bridgnorth. This was sealed when the line closed and the bridge over the road into the town was demolished. The 1972 view from above the mouth of the southern portal of the tunnel looks towards the station and yard (above). The site had been taken over by the Severn Valley Railway Society two years after the last British Railways passenger train left in September 1963 (below).

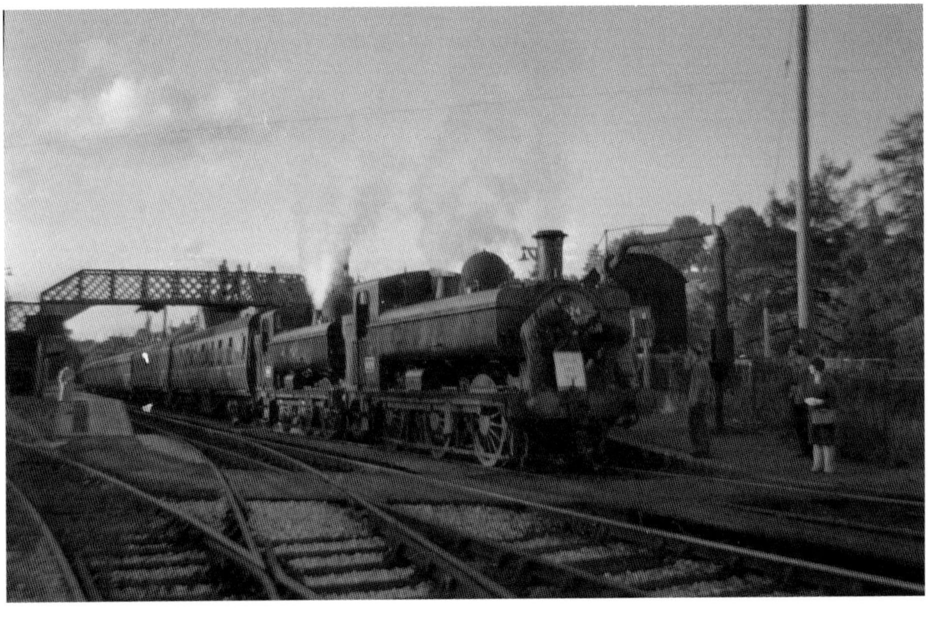

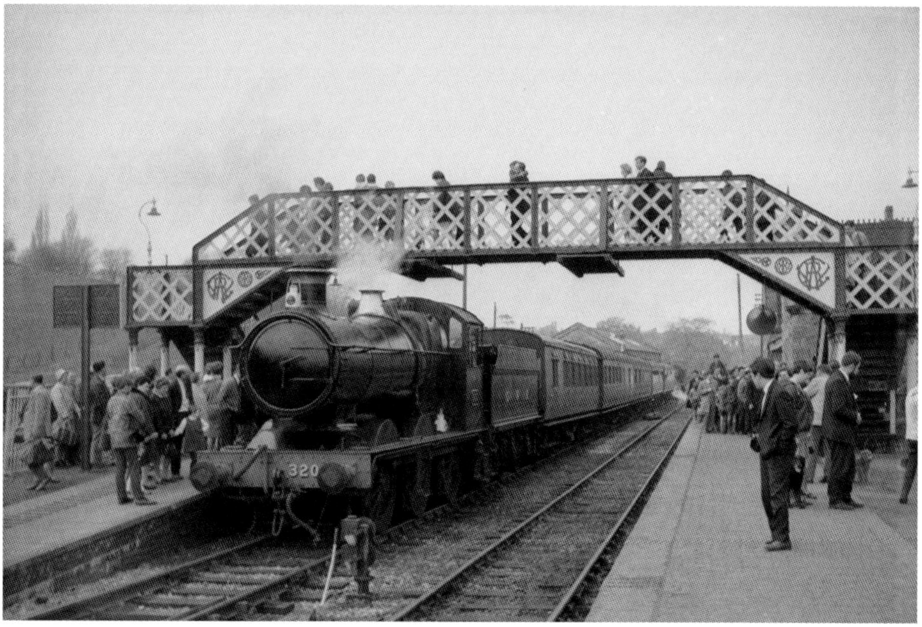

The Severn Valley Railway

A stalwart of the early days of the preserved line was ex-GWR 0-6-0 locomotive, No. 3205 (above). Now operating a limited all-year round timetable between Bridgnorth and Kidderminster, the SVR is today one of the most popular of the country's preserved railways. In 2008, to celebrate the bicentenary of the building of Richard Trevithick's *Catch Me Who Can* in Bridgnorth, the replica of the locomotive was on display in the yard at Bridgnorth station (below).

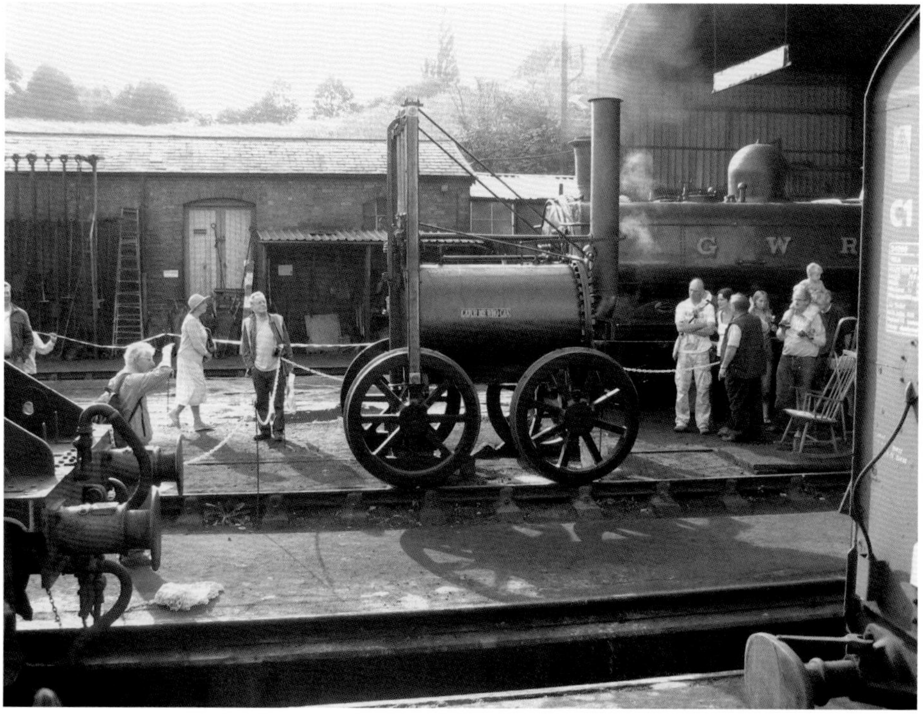

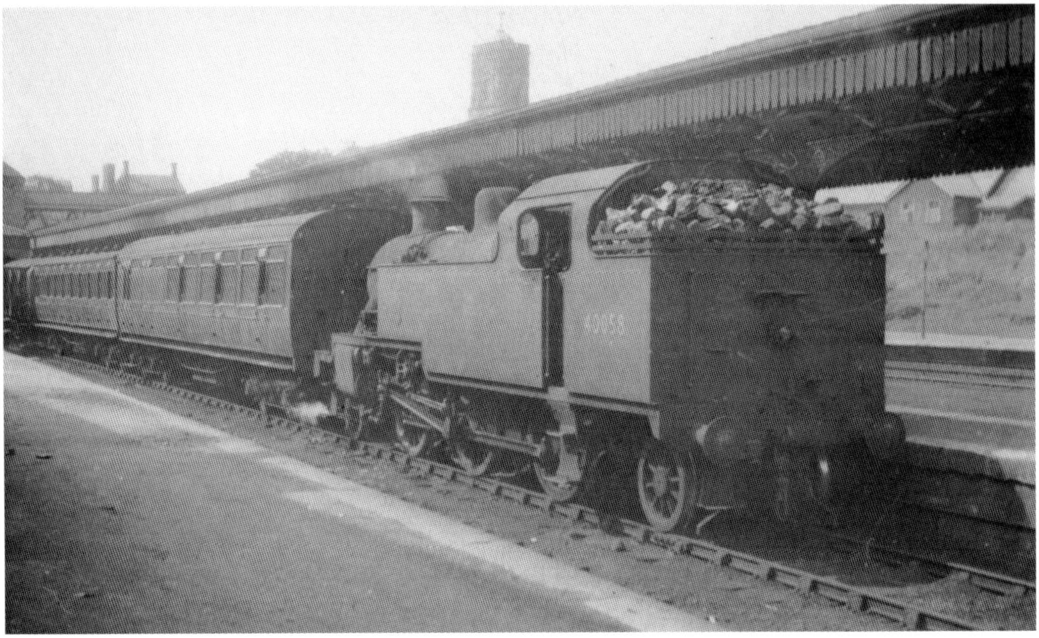

The Coalport Branch

Built by the LNWR to replace the ailing Shropshire Canal, this eight-mile branch line opened throughout in 1861. Known locally as 'The Coalport Dodger', passenger trains from Wellington (above, 1951) called at Hadley station before leaving the Stafford line at Hadley Junction (below) and climbing to Oakengates.

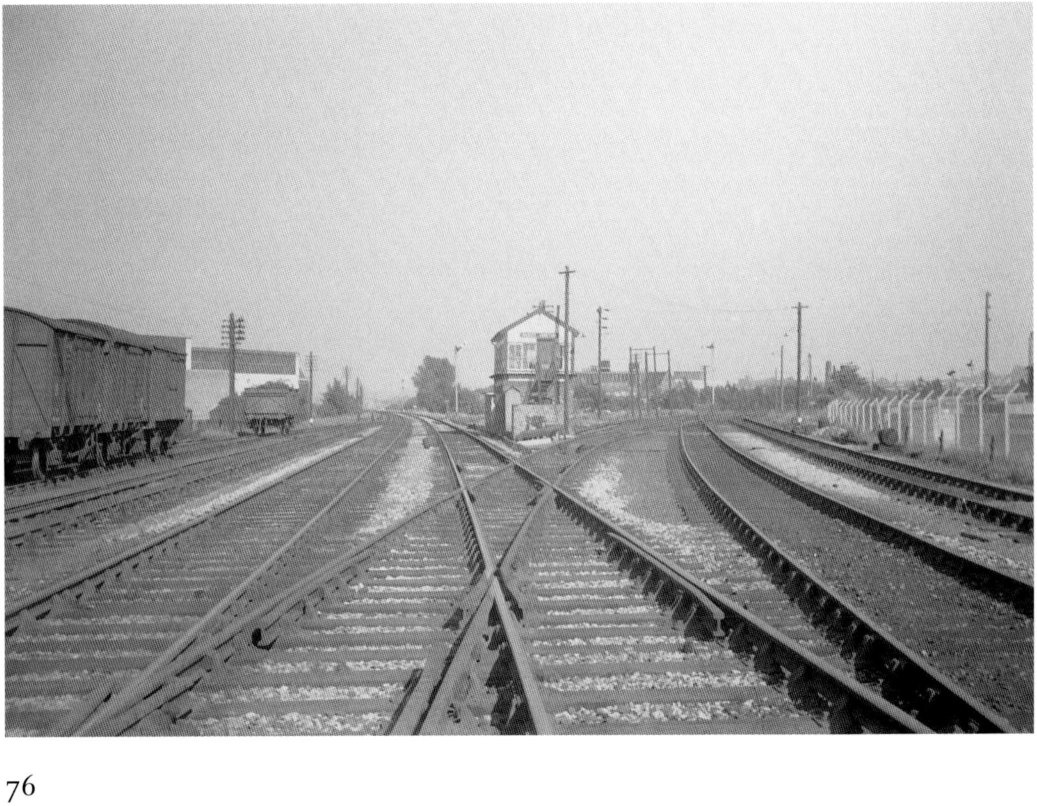

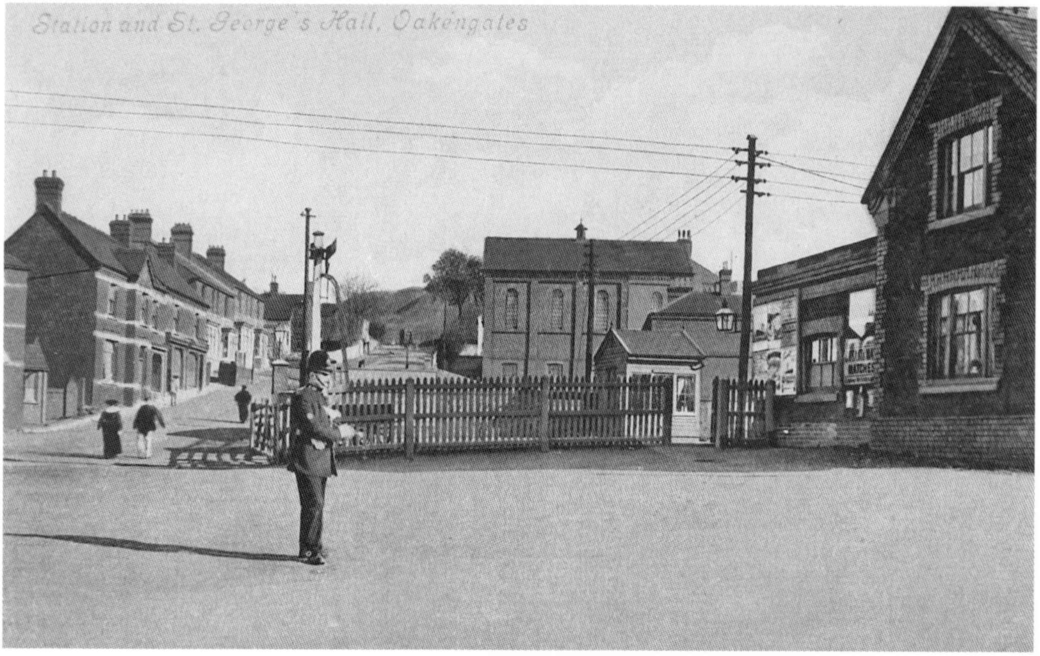

Oakengates (1)
The station in Oakengates was built at the top of Market Street (above). To celebrate the opening of the railway on 10 June 1861, a public dinner was held at the Caledonia Hotel (below), which had been opened when the SBR reached Oakengates in 1849.

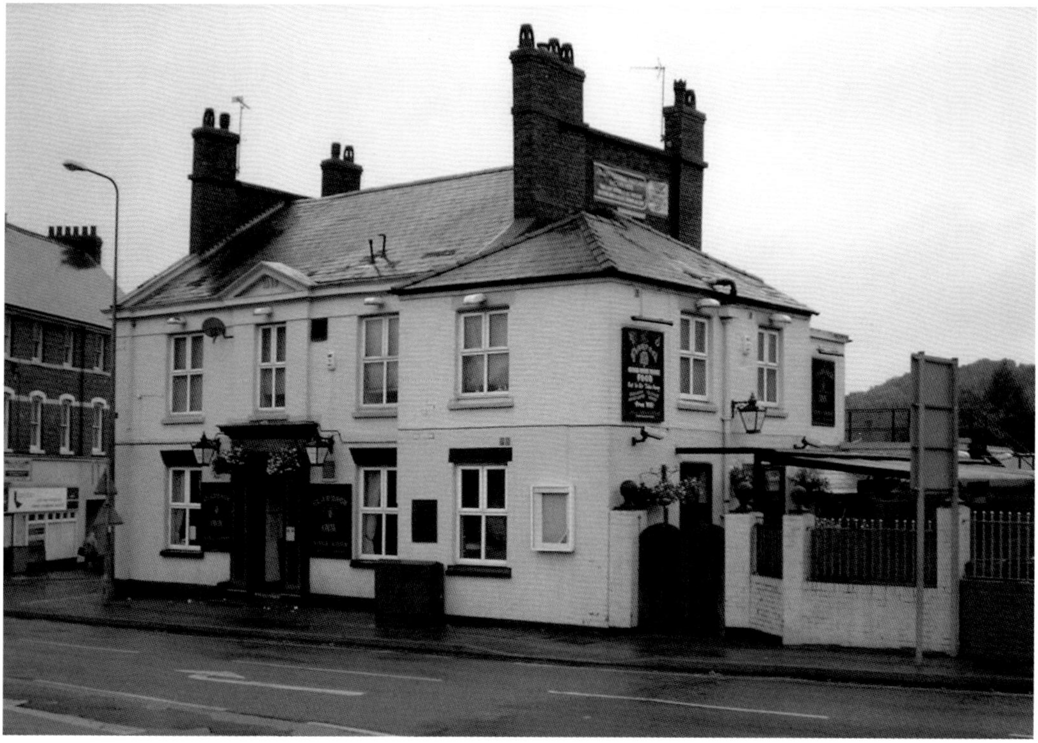

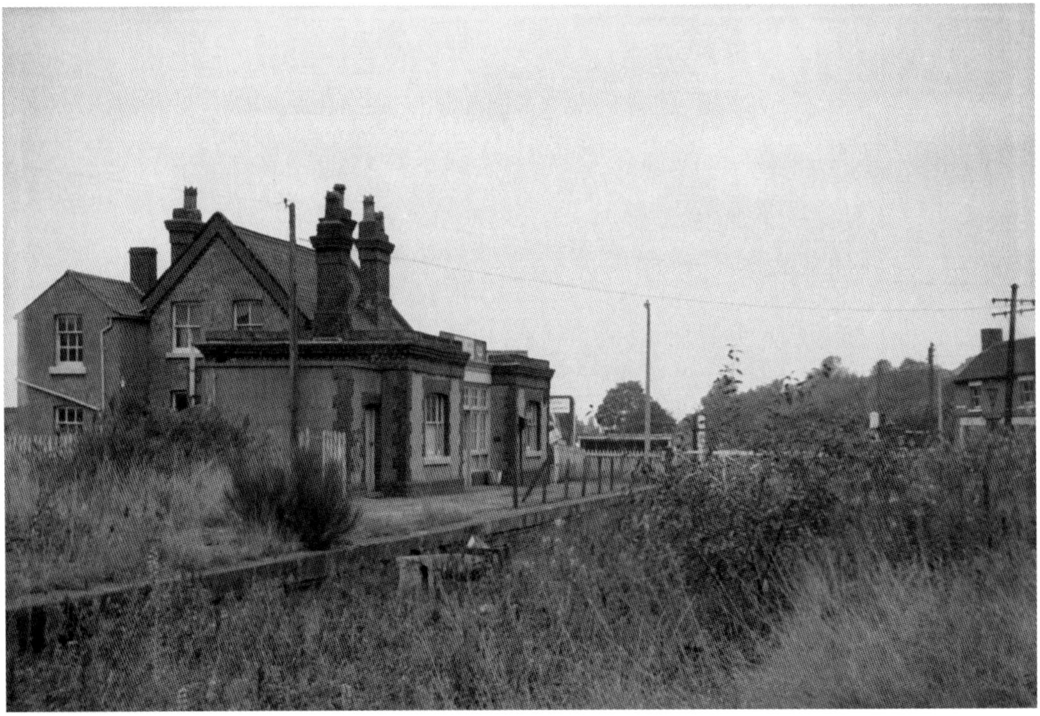

Oakengates (2)
The station was renamed Oakengates Market Street in 1951, a year before closure. It was still intact over a decade later (above), but the site was eventually obliterated by a new road system. The goods shed has survived in commercial use (below).

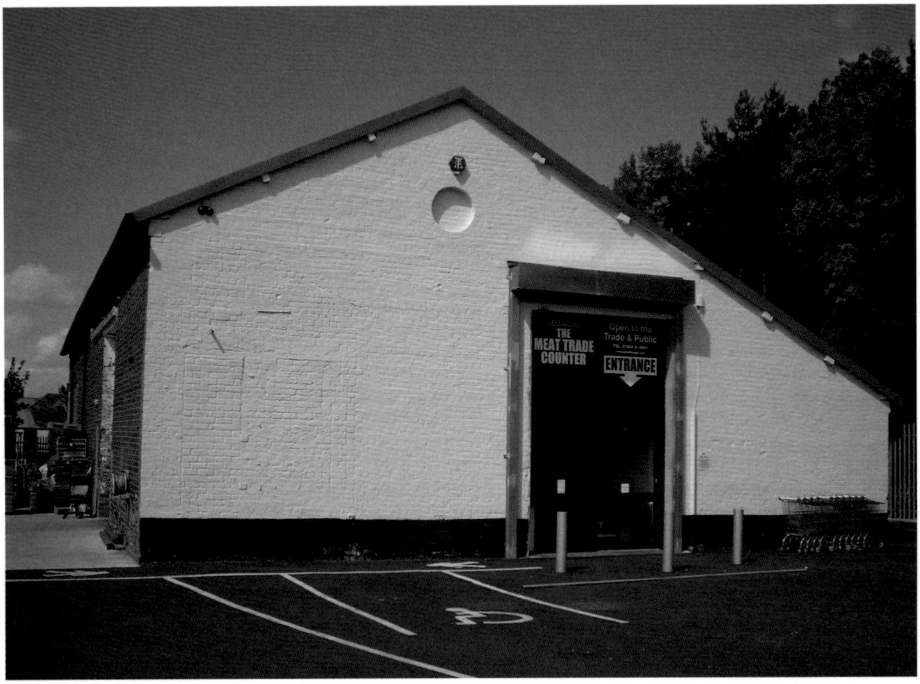

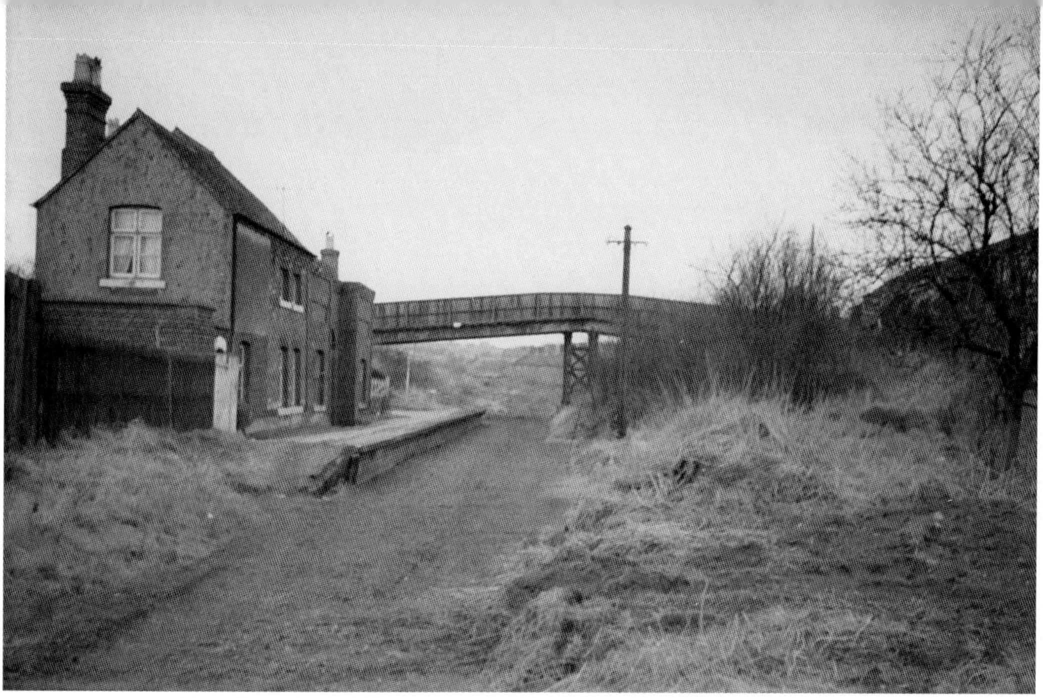

South of Oakengates

Just south of the station, the railway crossed the SBR tunnel and was built on or near the bed of the Shropshire Canal for the next 2½ miles. Malinslee station, opened in 1862 to serve the small industrial settlement of Dark Lane, is shown (above) following removal of the track and before the area was completely redeveloped with the building of Telford New Town Centre. South of Malinslee station was a siding to Randlay brickworks (below, around 1890), and further sidings served the mines and ironworks of the Old Park Iron Company and its successors.

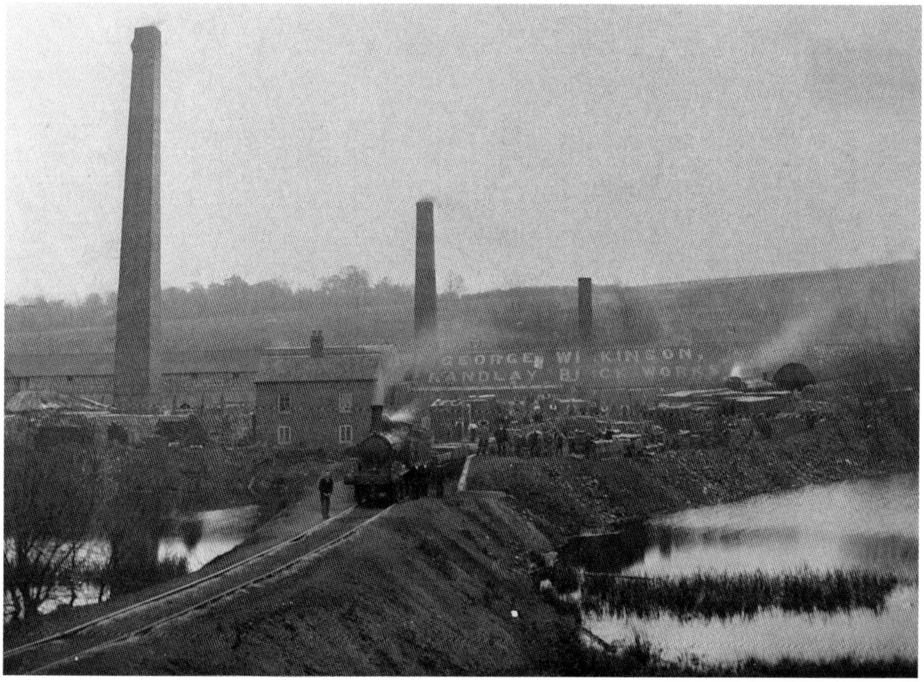

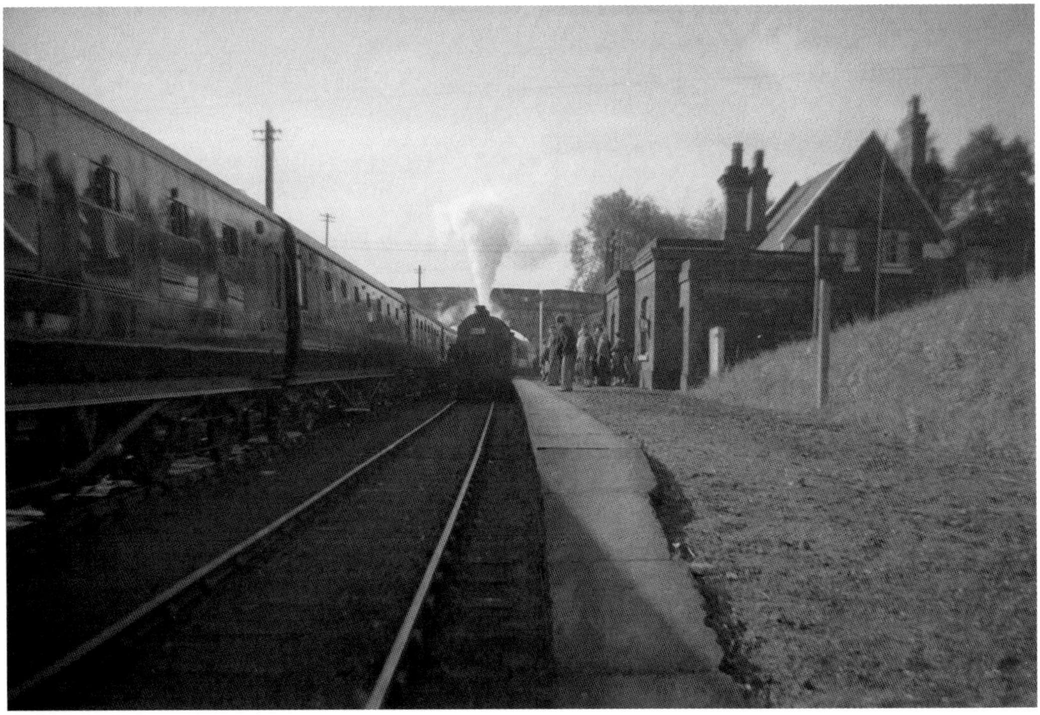

Dawley & Stirchley Station

Until 1923, this station was simply 'Stirchley'. After passenger services were withdrawn at the end of May 1952, there were several excursion trains on the branch in the years that followed. A Madeley Market–Llandudno Sunday School excursion enters Dawley and Stirchley station in September 1956 (above). Today, the restored platform is a feature on the southern section of the Silkin Way footpath (below).

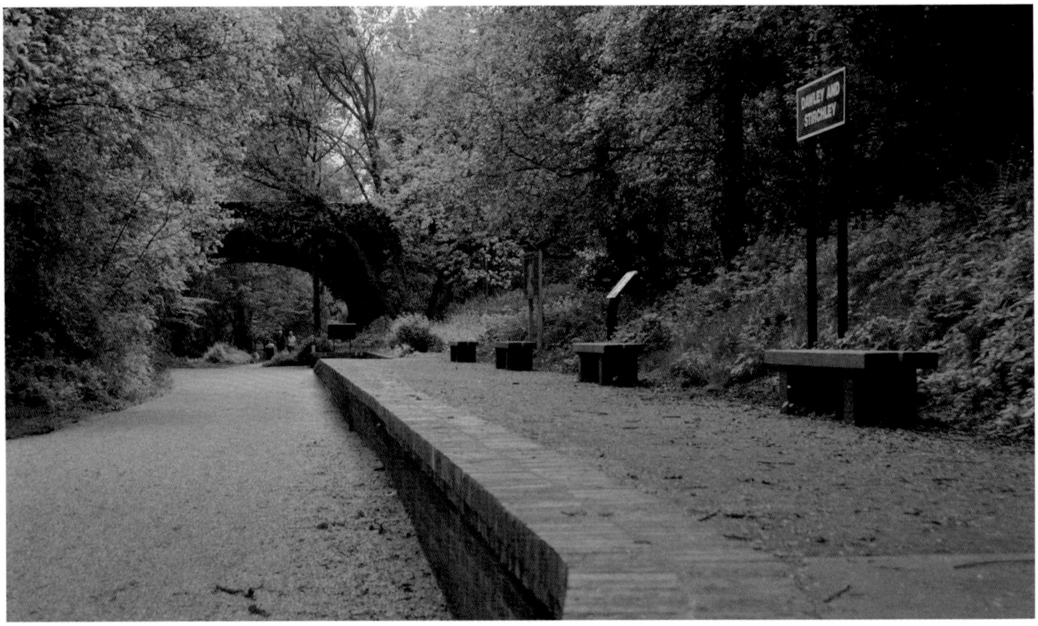

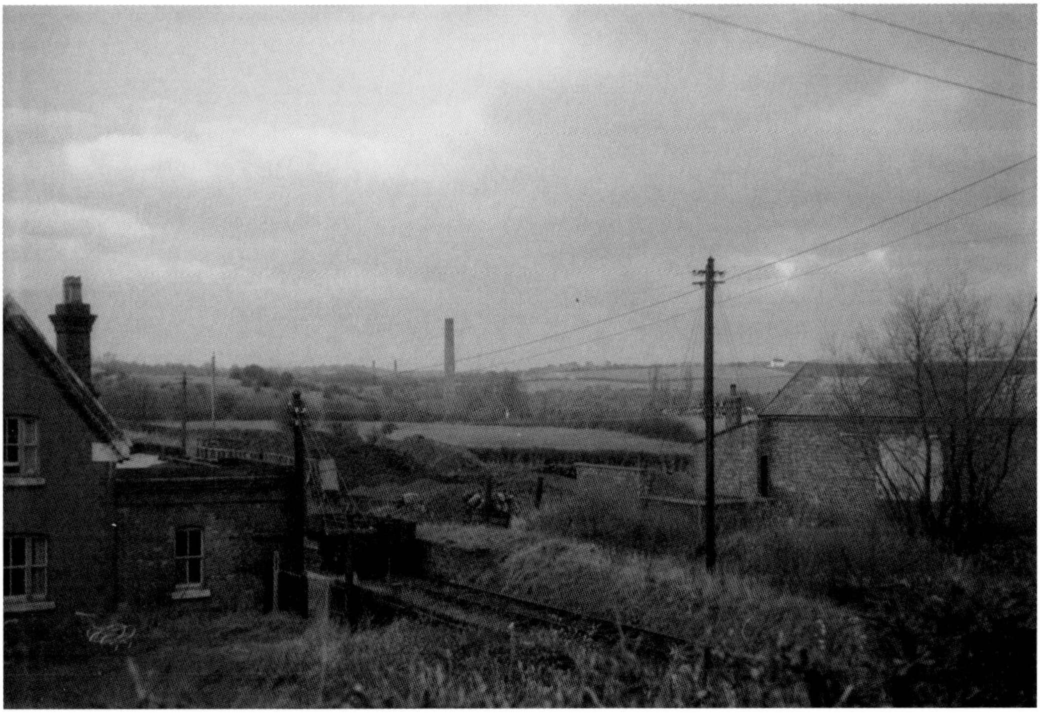

Stirchley

The goods shed and yard at Stirchley (above) were used for many years by a local coal merchant. Freight traffic south of Stirchley ended in 1960, and the rest of the branch was finally closed and the track lifted four years later. The demolition train is shown north of Stirchley in late 1964 (below).

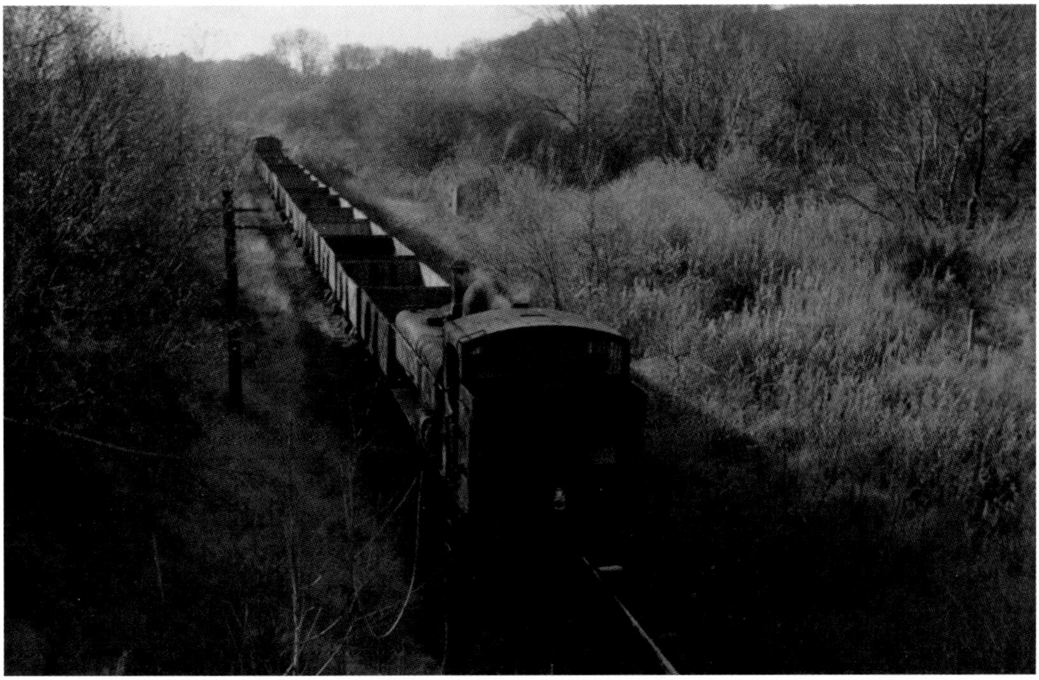

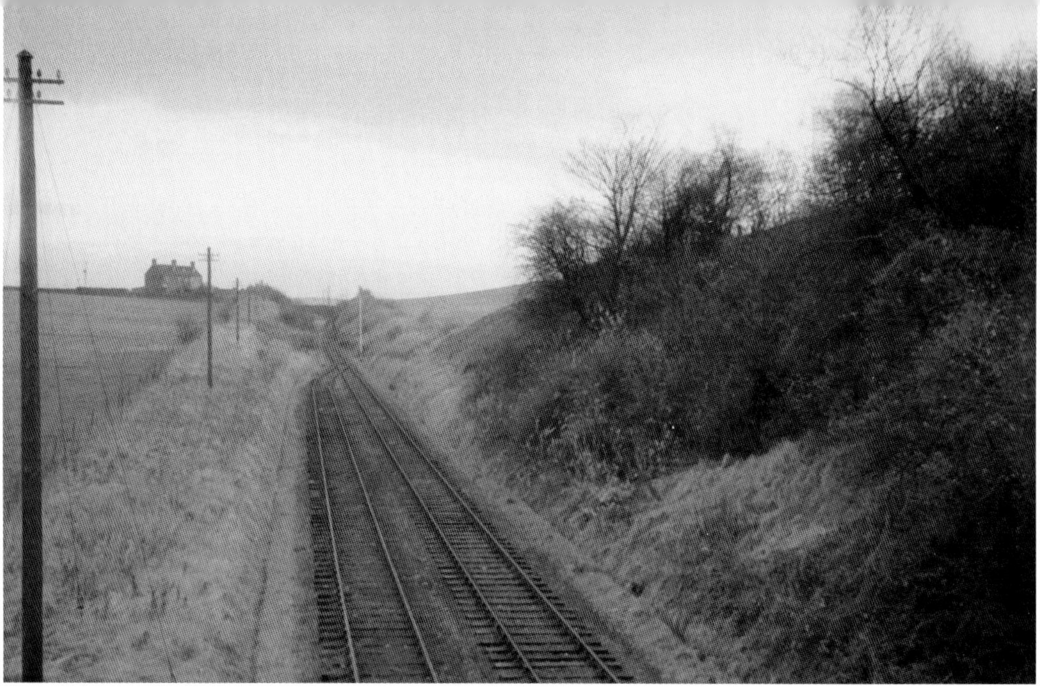

South of Stirchley

The railway opened up the old Shropshire Canal tunnel south of Stirchley, running in a cutting (above) before descending for the next three miles to Coalport. The cottages on the horizon retain the name 'Tunnel Row'. The different levels at this point can be seen in an artist's impression of the redundant aqueduct on the Coalbrookdale branch of the Shropshire Canal (which gave its name to the small industrial settlement here), and a train crossing the low bridge on the Coalport branch railway (below).

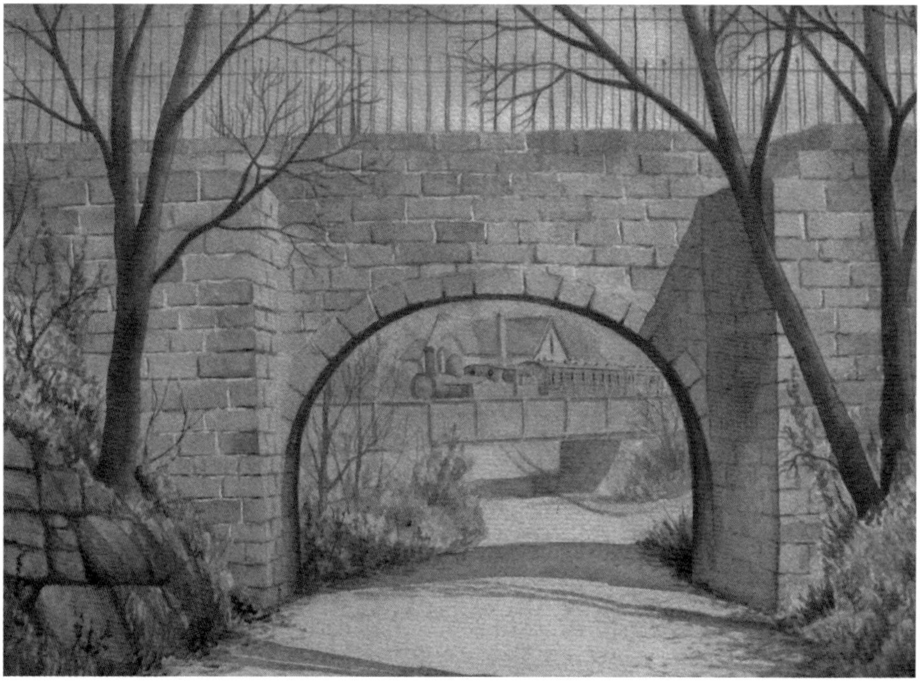

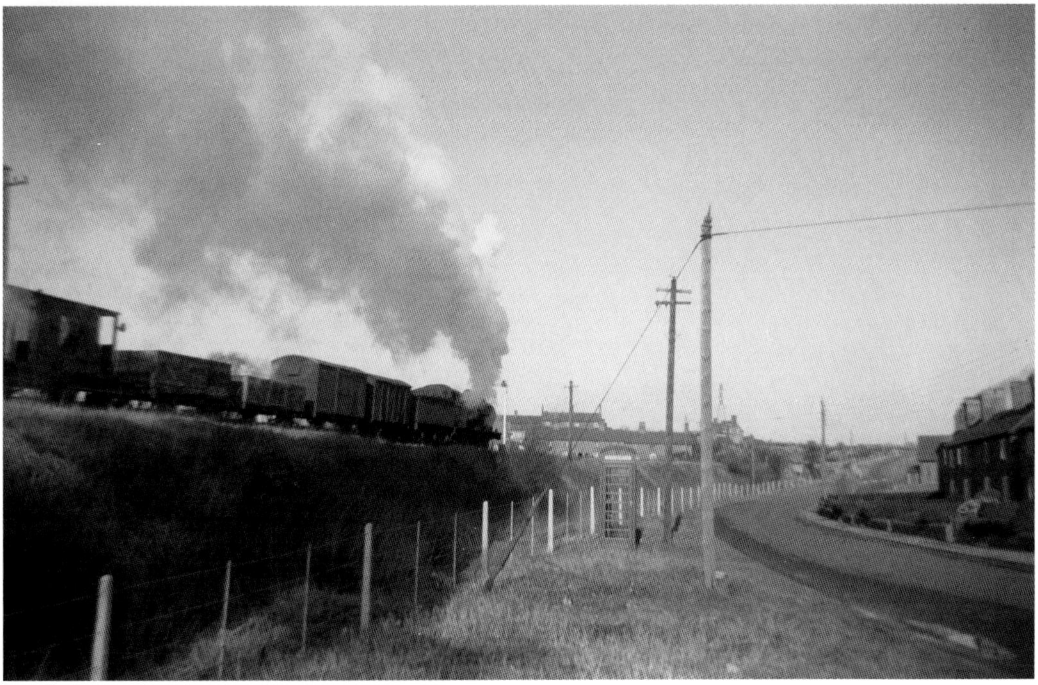

Low Bridge at Aqueduct

In the late 1930s, with the increase in road traffic and the threat of war, the section of the A442 road that passed under the narrow aqueduct and low railway bridge (which had a clearance of just 10 feet!) was replaced by a new stretch of highway. In 1954, the daily goods train is seen approaching the low bridge, with the new section of road in the background (above), and an inspection train crosses the low bridge in September 1956 (below). The low bridge was demolished in the early 1960s.

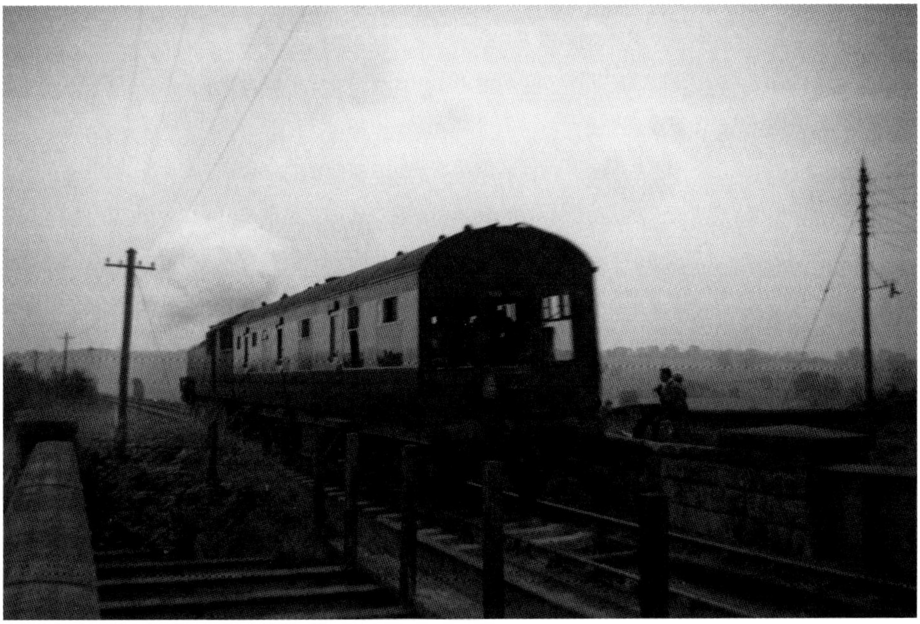

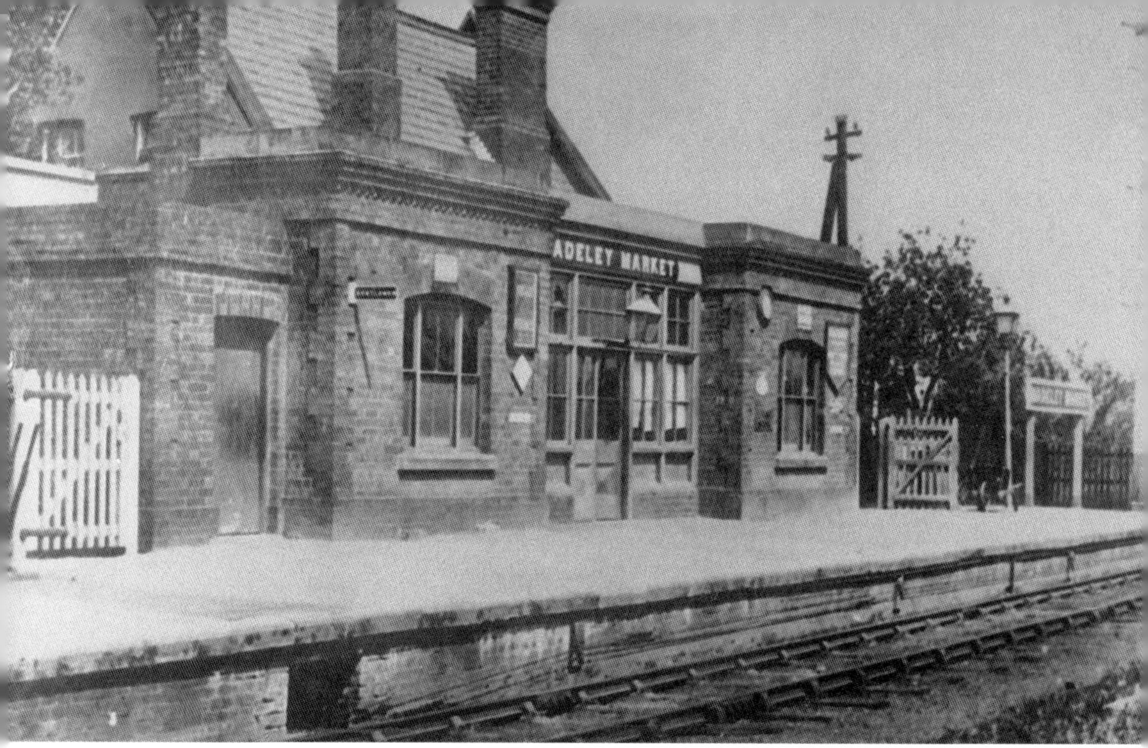

Madeley Market Station

After crossing the GWR Madeley branch, the line reached Madeley Market station (above), situated in the lower part of the town. The design of this building was the same as others on the line, except that at Malinslee. Unlike the others, though, it has survived and had many commercial uses over the years (below).

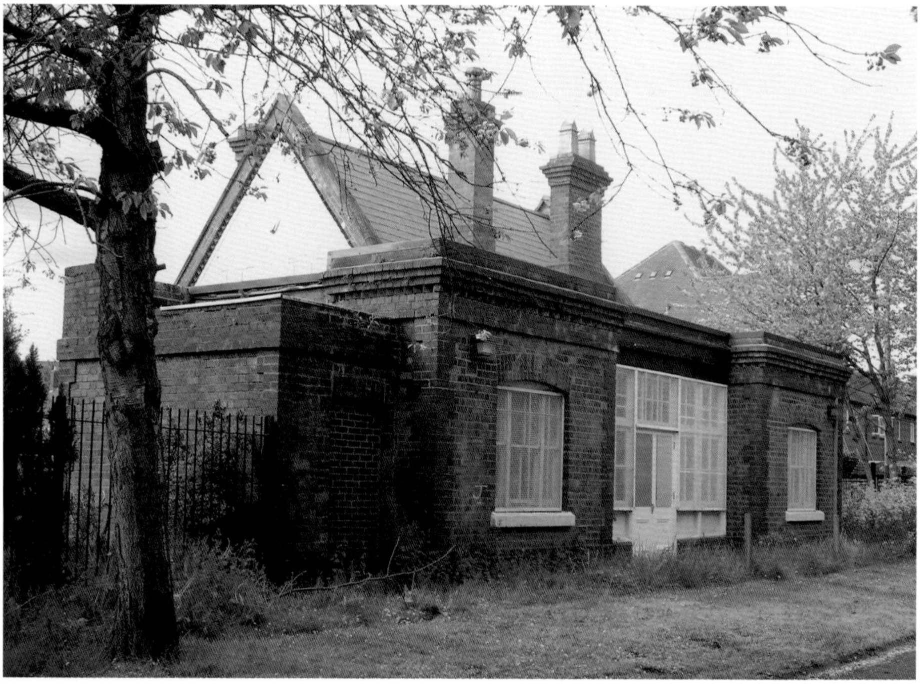

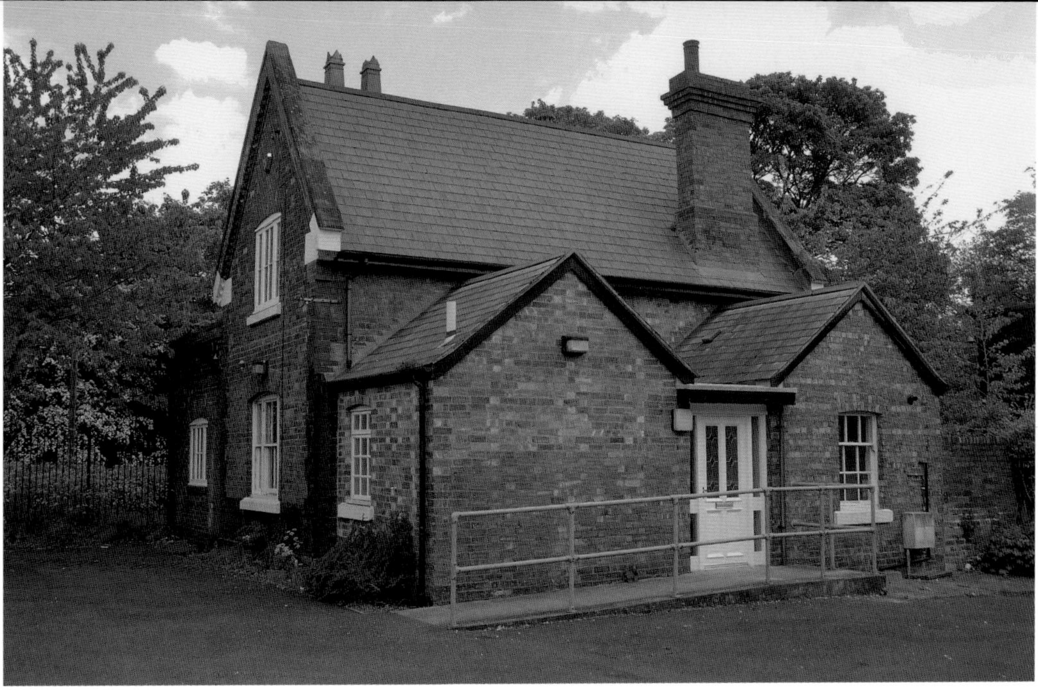

Station Master's House and Goods Yard

Its continued commercial use has kept the former station master's house in good order (above), but the goods shed and sidings at Madeley Market (below), which closed in 1960, have long since gone and been replaced by a small industrial estate. Between Madeley and Coalport, sidings served a brickworks, an ironworks and a chinaworks, and the line passed through a short tunnel at Blists Hill and under the Hay canal inclined plane.

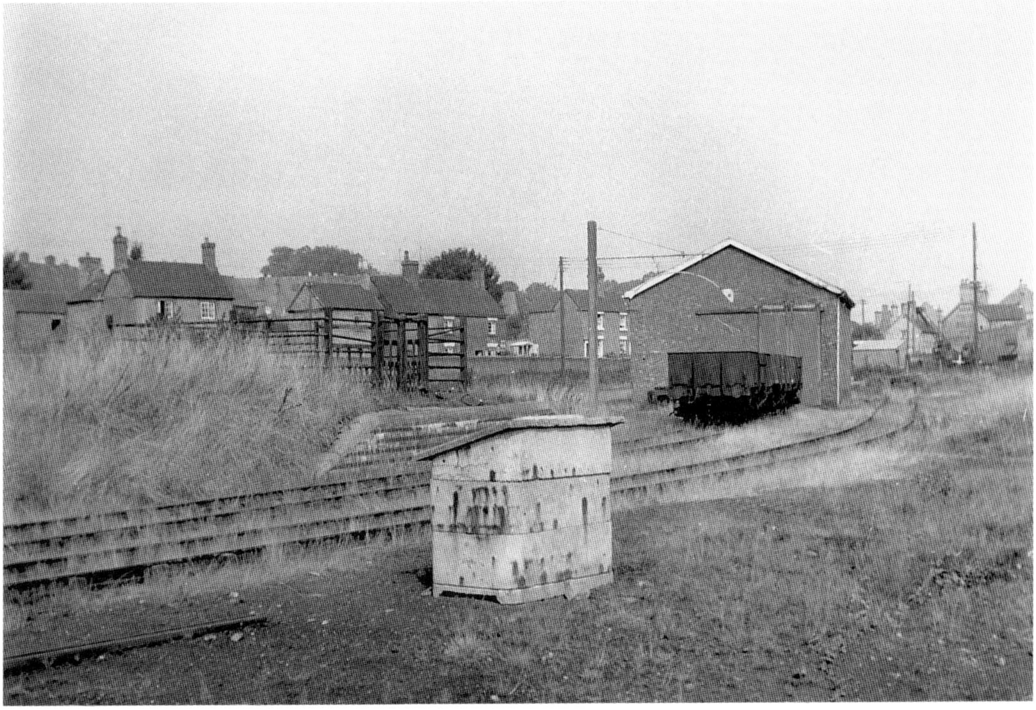

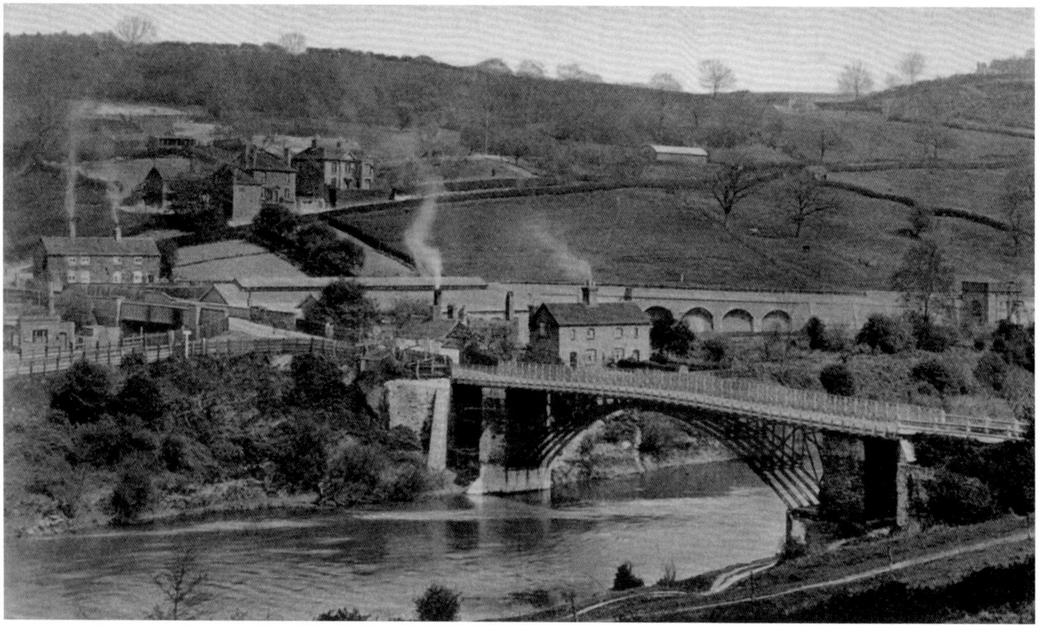

Coalport (1)

The terminus of the line at Coalport consisted of a station building, goods shed and sidings, and an engine and carriage shed (above). The station was also known as Coalport East, to distinguish it from the GWR station across the river. A Webb 0-6-2 'Coal Tank', which was used for passenger traffic on the line, is being prepared for a return journey to Wellington sometime in the 1940s (below).

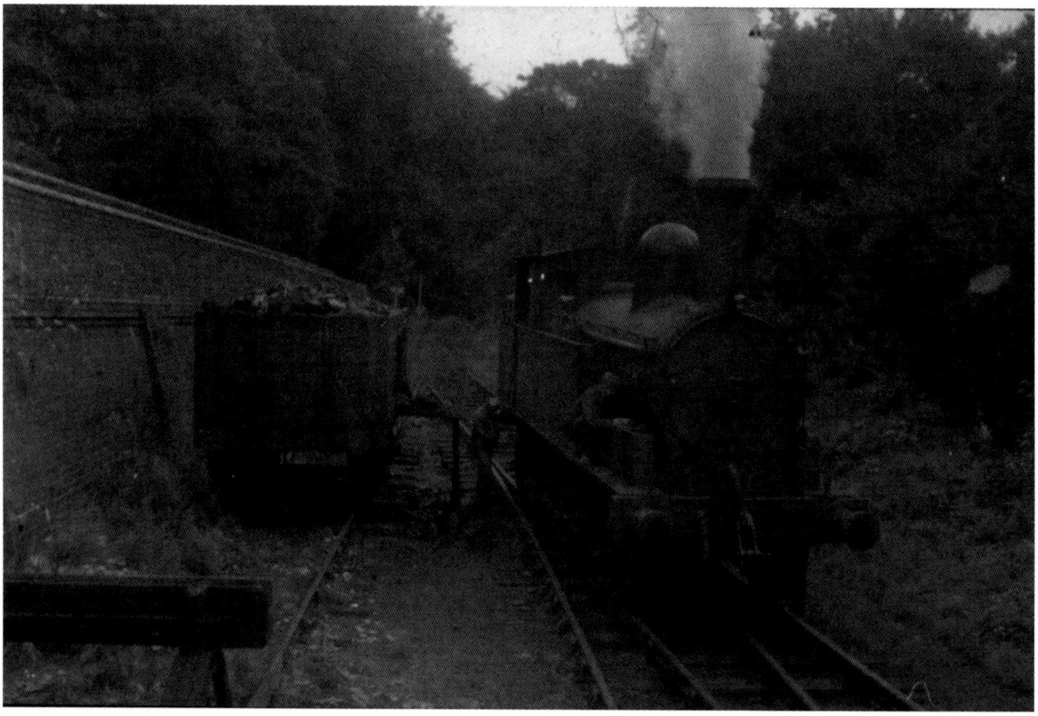

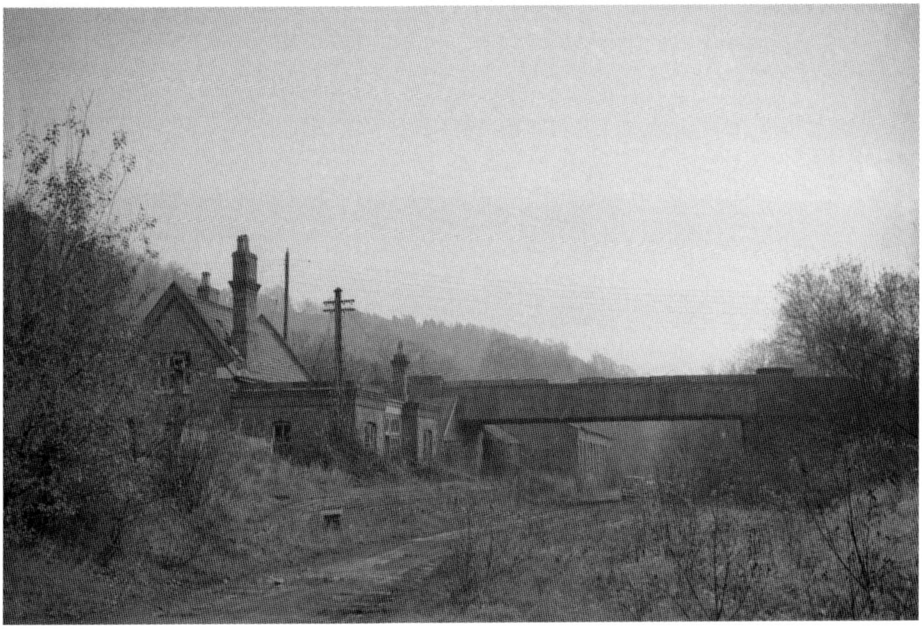

Coalport (2)

The station building remained intact for over a decade after passenger services were withdrawn (above, 1965), but the construction of a large sewage pipeline by Telford Development Corporation in the late 1960s led to the clearance of the site. The only sign of the railway today is the row of former railway workers' cottages (below), together with LNWR cast-iron plate No. 36 on the adjacent road bridge.

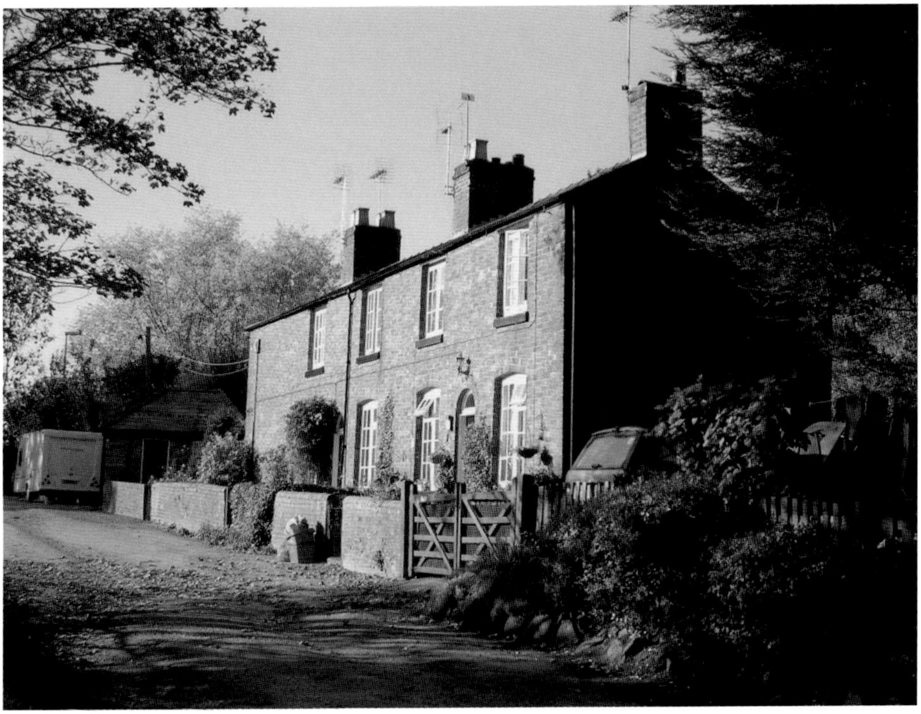

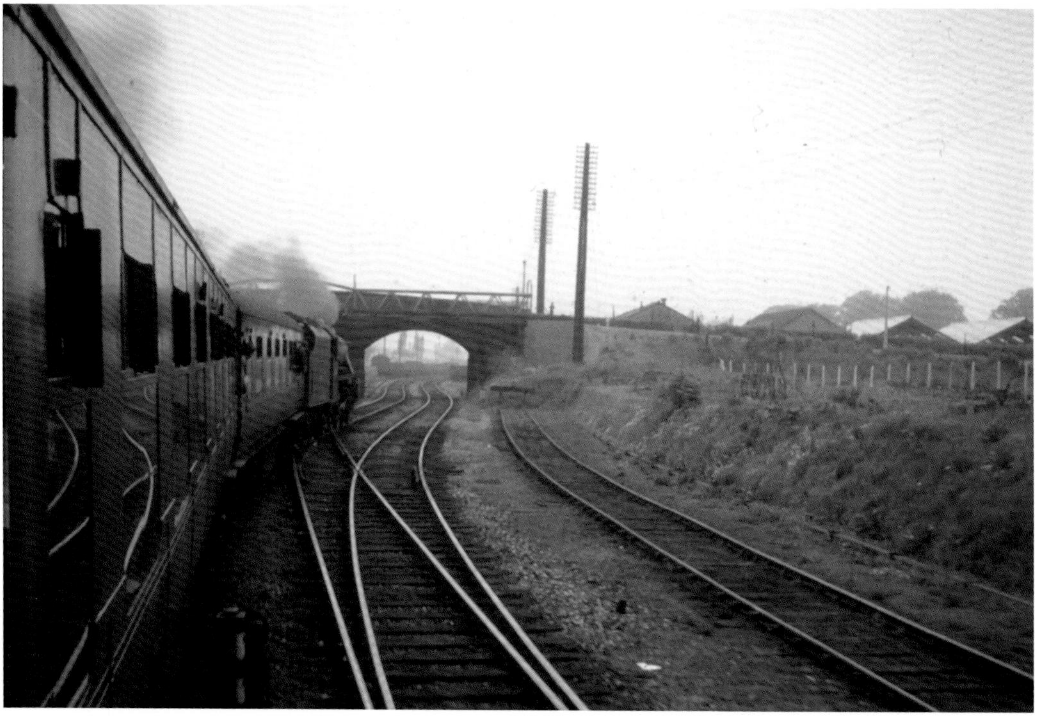

The Market Drayton Branch

The Wellington & Drayton Railway opened in October 1867 and, via connecting lines, provided the GWR with a route to Crewe and Manchester, and, in 1870, to Stoke on Trent. At Market Drayton Junction (Wellington) in June 1964, an excursion train heading for North Staffordshire crosses onto the double-track branch (above). At the same location, a goods train from Crewe comes off the branch the following year (below).

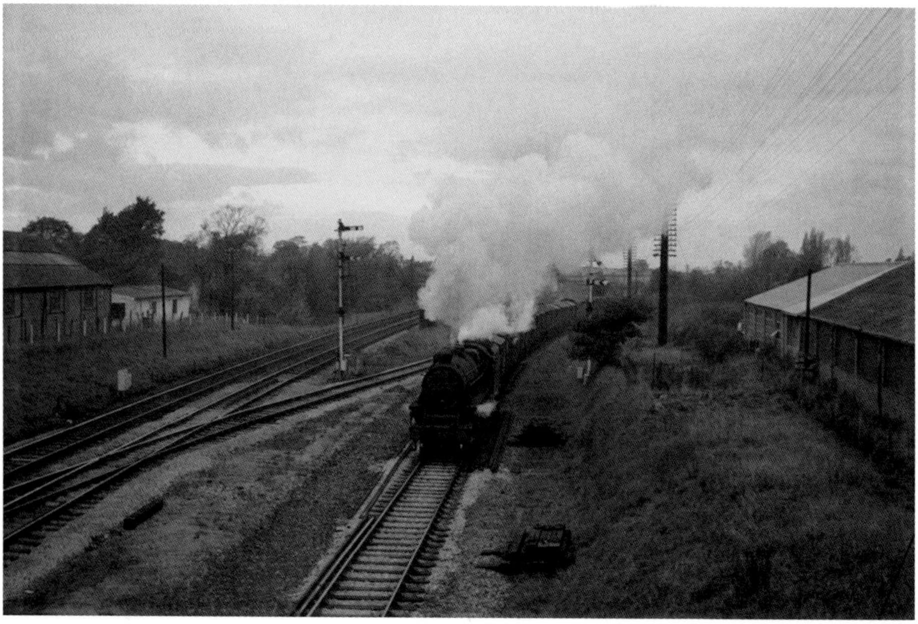

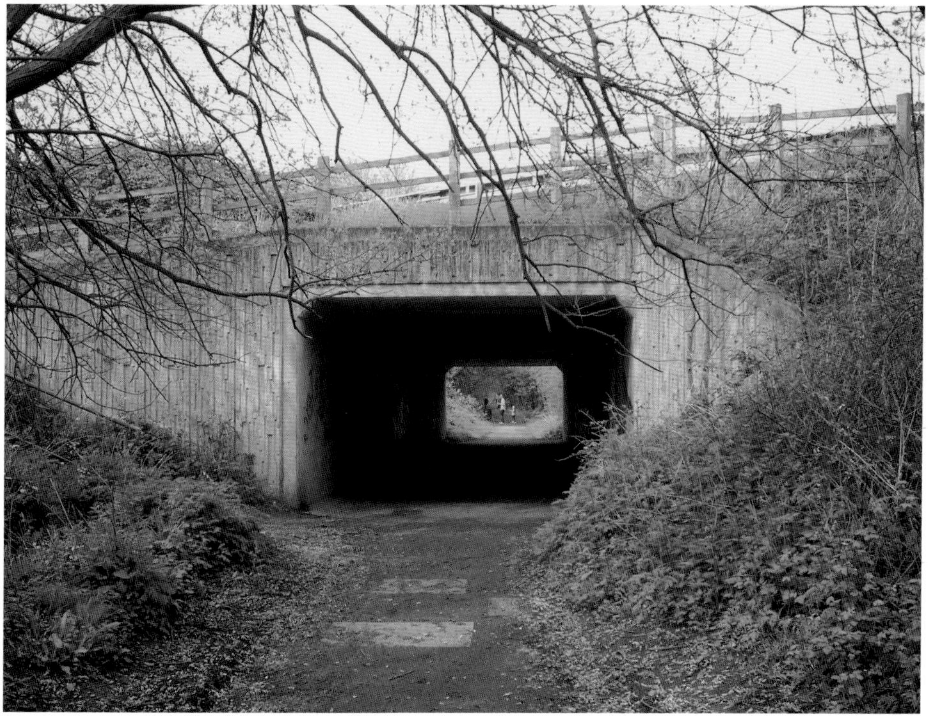

Longdon Halt

Passenger services were withdrawn on 9 September 1963, and the line between Wellington and Nantwich closed completely four years later. Today, the first mile of the former track bed (above) links with the northern end of the Silkin Way footpath. Longdon Halt, the first station on the line, was opened in October 1934 and is shown below after closure. The B5063 overbridge was demolished following the removal of the track.

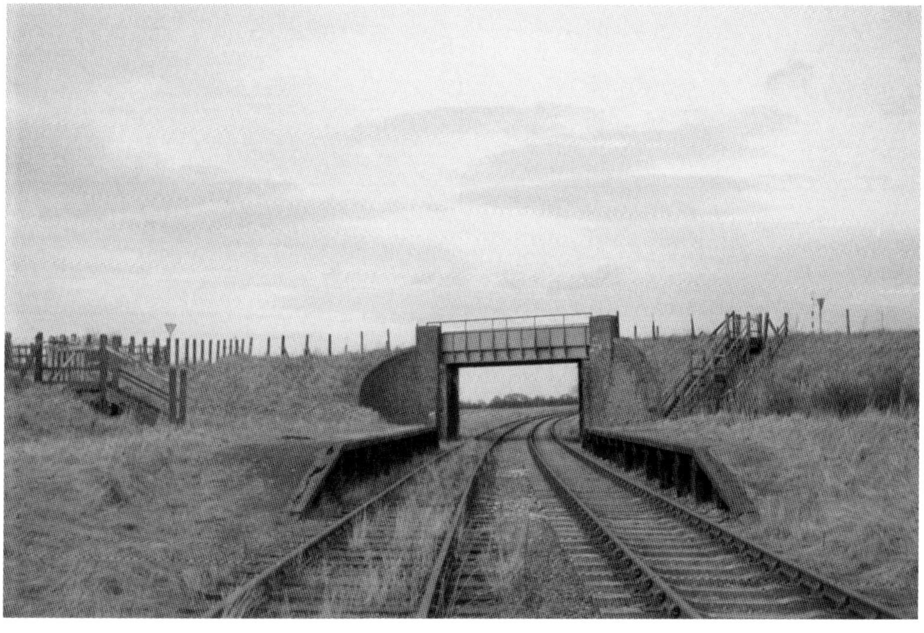

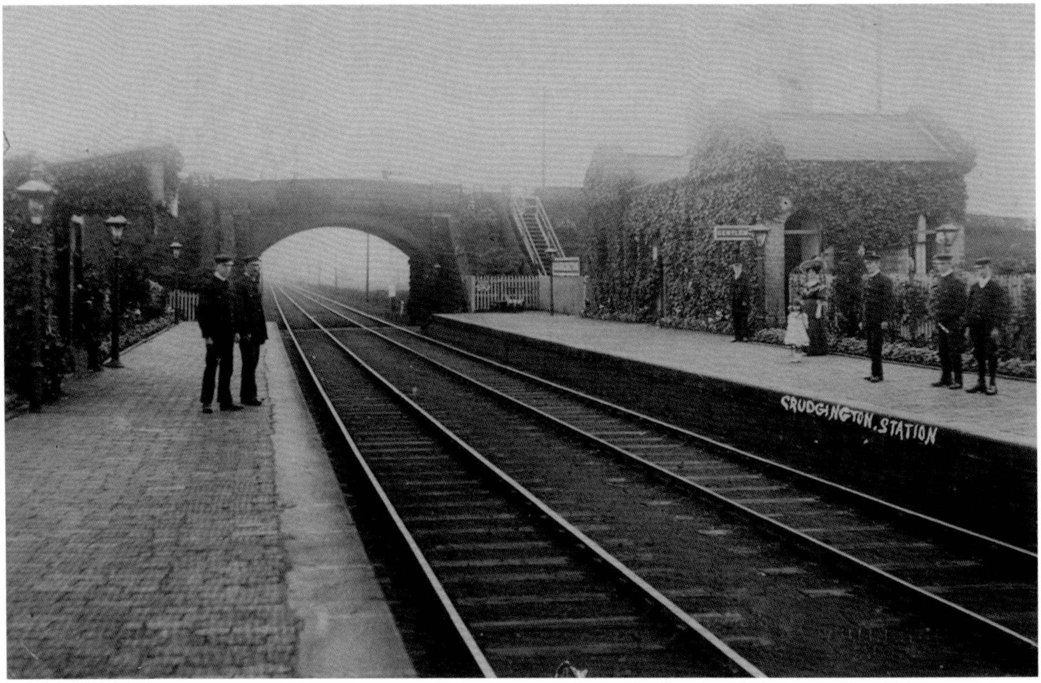

Crudgington

Crudgington's station building was, a century ago, covered in foliage (above). After closure and before demolition (below), its attractive features can be seen; the goods shed is in the middle distance. Among the more unusual items handled here were local damsons dispatched for the London market and incoming rags for nearby Tibberton paper mill.

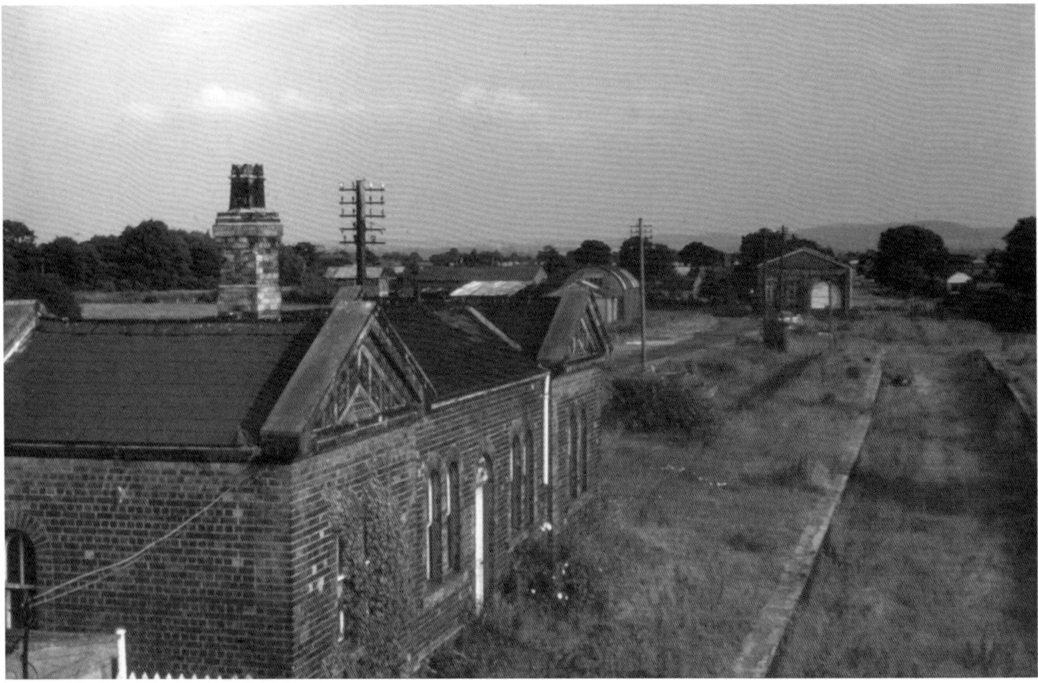

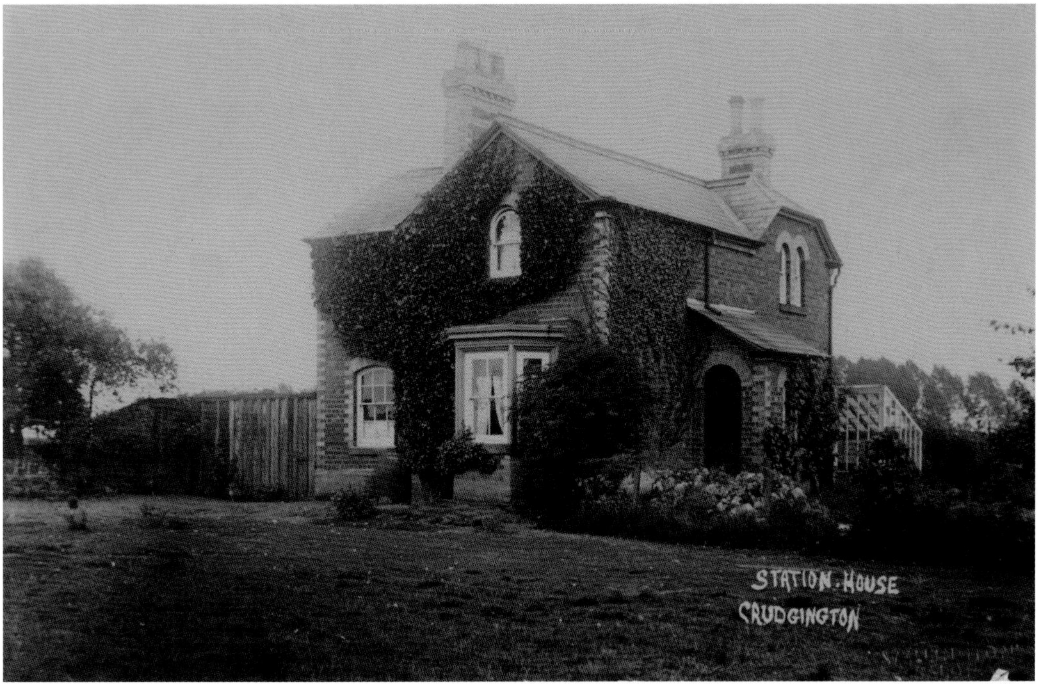

Crudgington Station House

The station master's house, some 50 yards behind the station building, is also partially covered in foliage in this 1905 view (above). Today, the house has been extended and the owner has built a replica signal box in his garden (below).

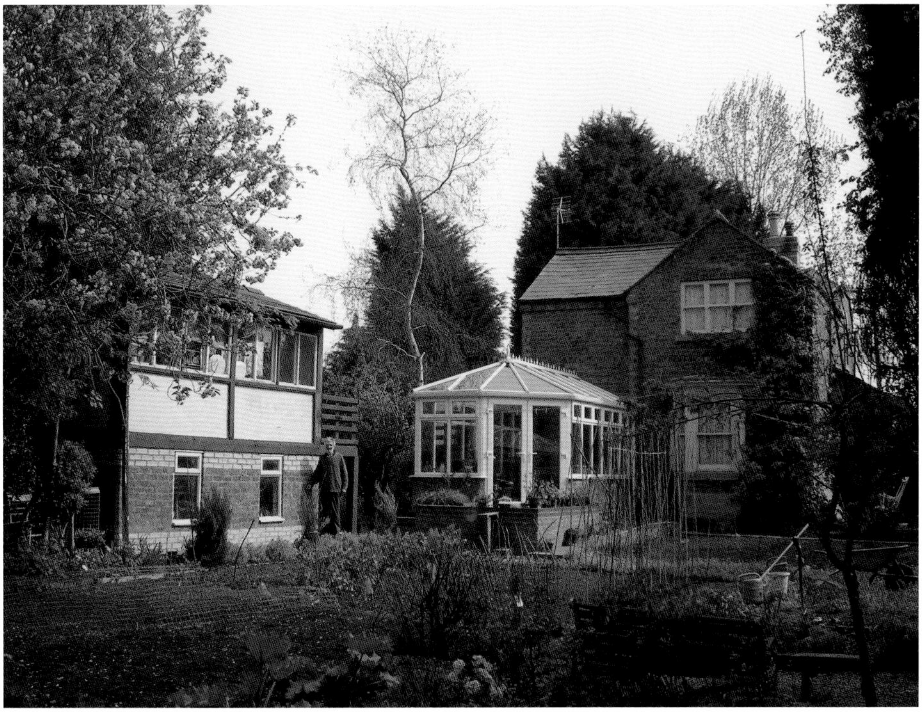

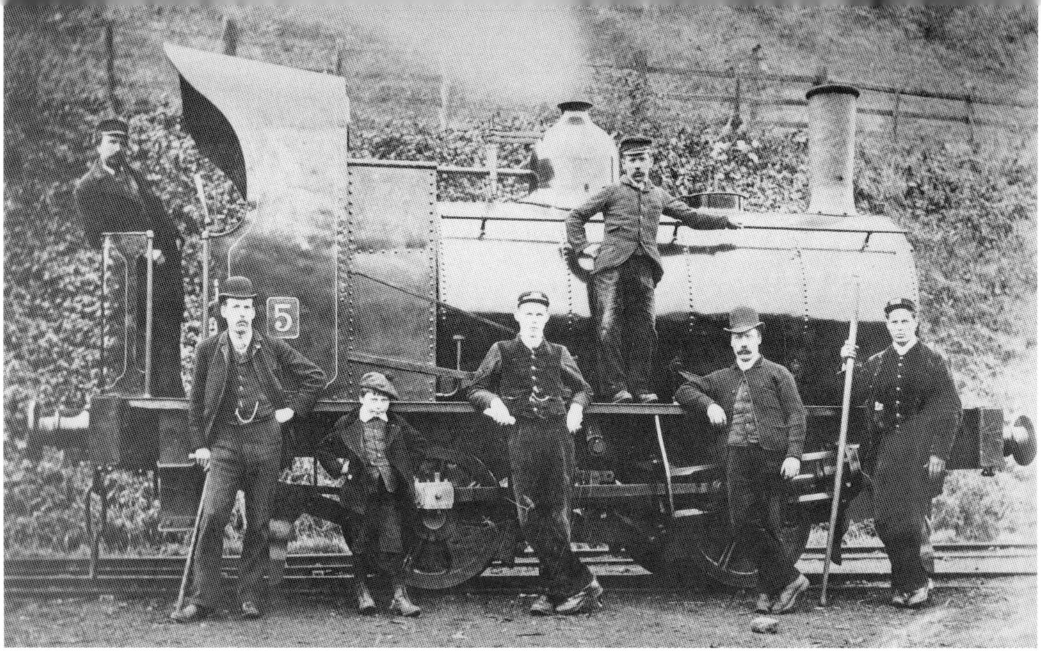

Mineral Railways and Private Sidings

Many local works were linked by sidings or their own mineral lines to the railways that had developed on the Coalfield. Between 1864 and 1866, the Coalbrookdale Company built six standard-gauge 0-4-0 saddle-tank locomotives, two for shunting duties at the works. One of these, No. 5 (above), was sold in 1930 and, after use elsewhere, was brought back to the newly opened works museum in 1959. Today it is on display in Enginuity, part of the IGMT complex (below).

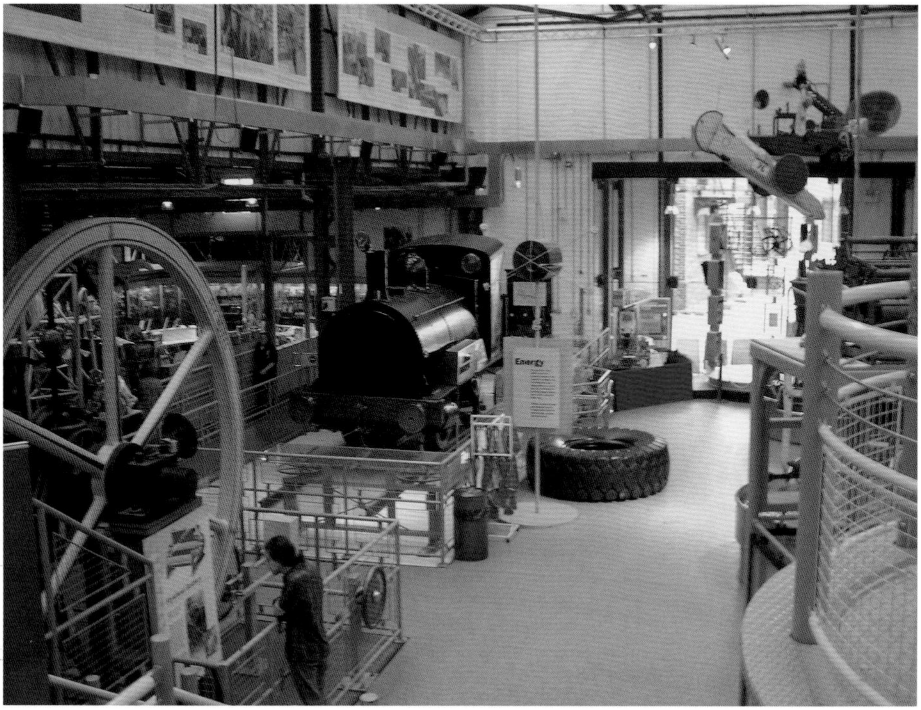

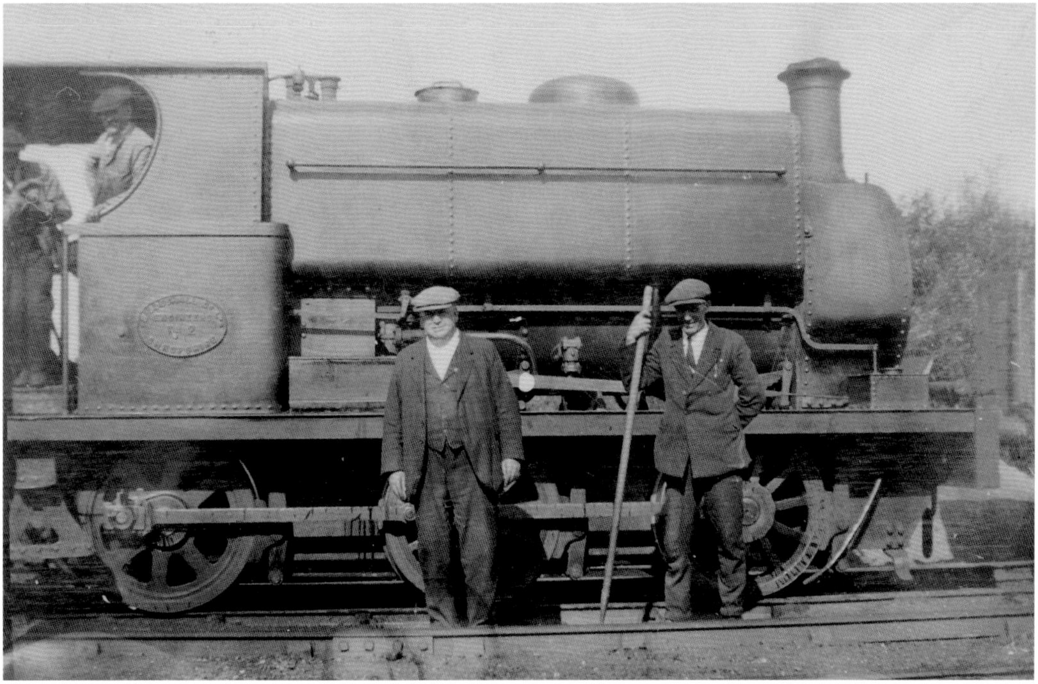

Lilleshall Company

The Lilleshall Company developed an extensive railway system to serve its ironworks, mines, brickworks and engineering works. From 1862, the Company built locomotives for its own use and for others. This is home-built 0-4-0ST No. 2 (above), the worse for wear, at work locally in around 1920. The Company also purchased locomotives to operate on its system, and one of these, 0-6-0T Andrew Barclay No. 11, can be seen at Priorslee furnaces in 1956 (below).

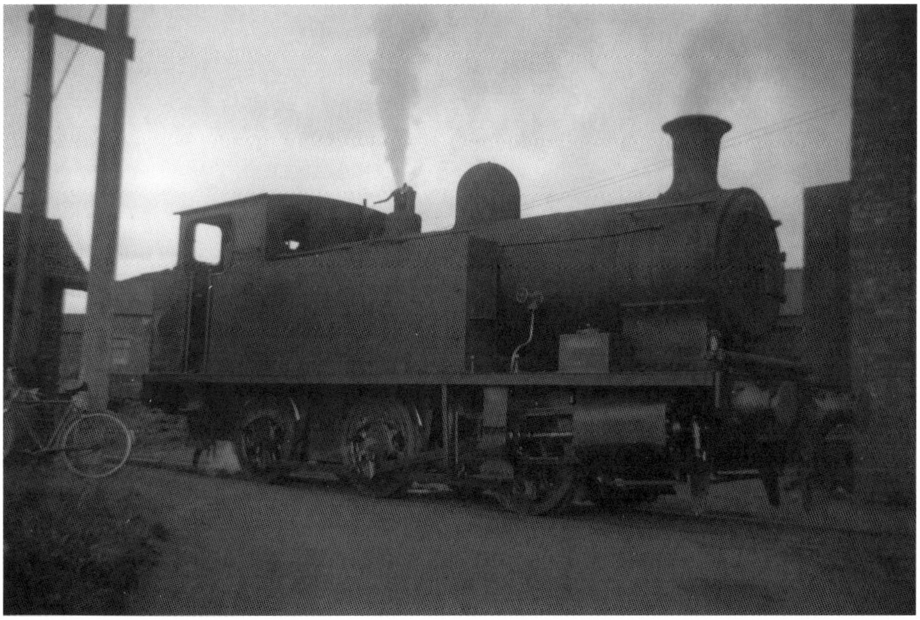

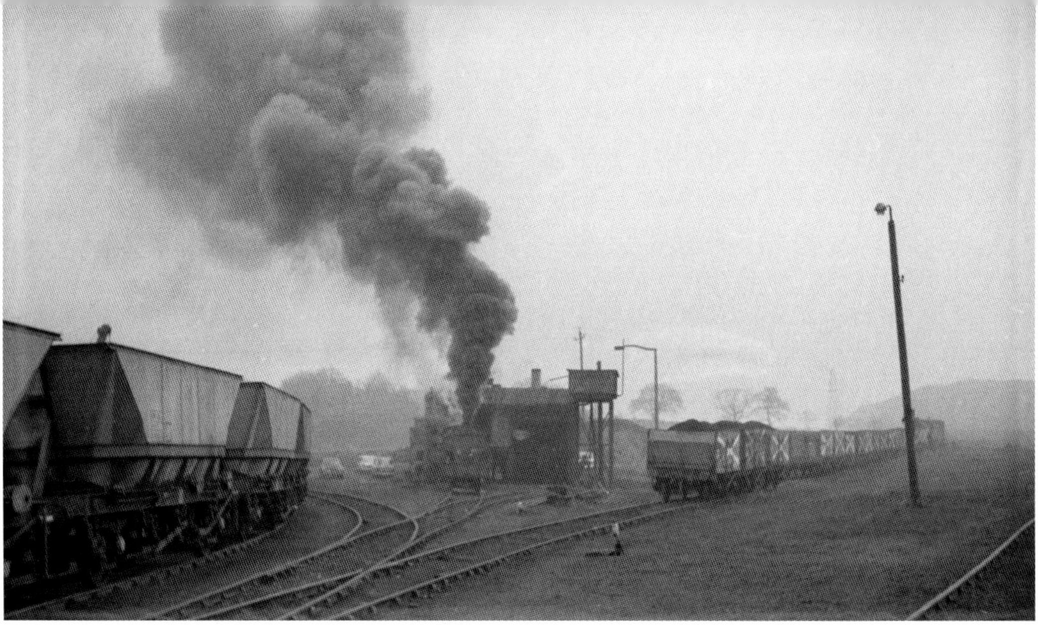

National Coal Board

Although the Lilleshall Co. railway system closed in 1959, the siding from Granville Colliery to Donnington on the Stafford line remained open for coal traffic until the closure of the pit in 1979. The NCB loco shed near the colliery (above, 1967) housed several Hunslet 0-6-0ST locomotives, which were later replaced by diesel mechanical locomotives. One of these is shown during the removal of the Granville Colliery brake van to Telford Steam Railway (below), prior to closure of the NCB line.

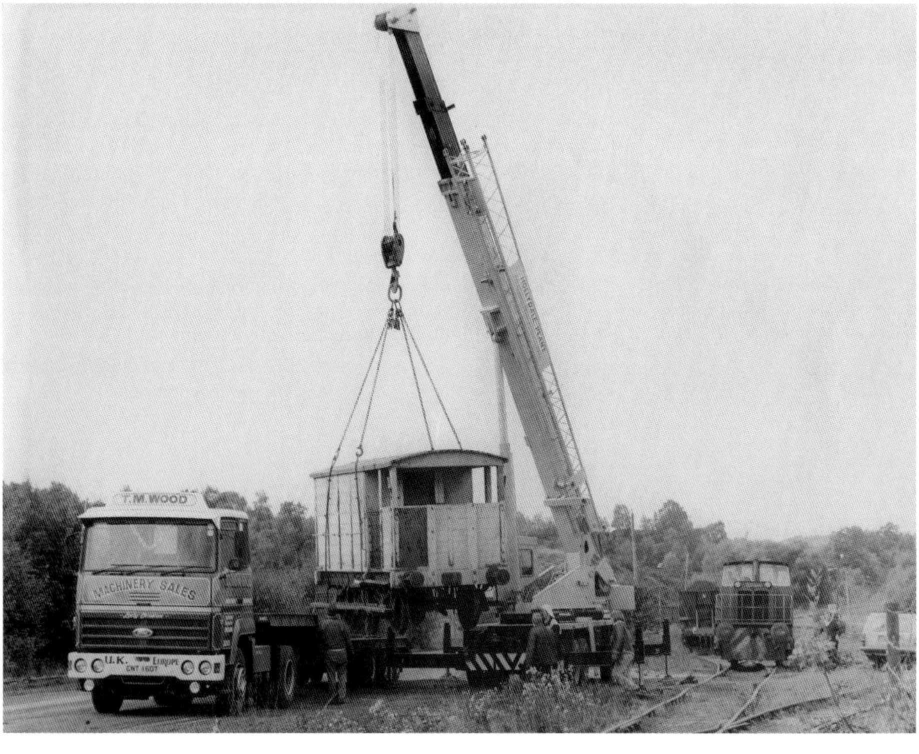

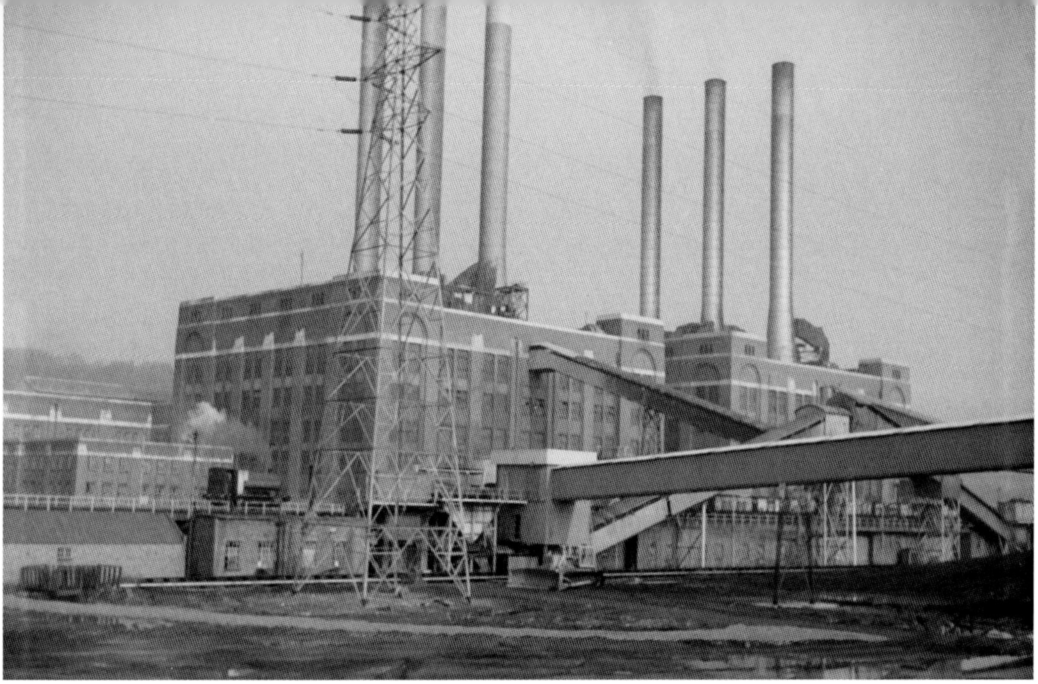

Central Electricity Generating Board

Until 1969, coal for the original power station at Buildwas (which later became 'Ironbridge A') was, on arrival, handled by one of three saddle-tank locomotives (above). Wagons were hauled over a concrete viaduct to the tippler, and the unloaded coal was stored in the open, picked up by an overhead transporter with bucket chains, and fed into hoppers. In February 1968, a Peckett 0-4-0ST busies itself on these duties (below).

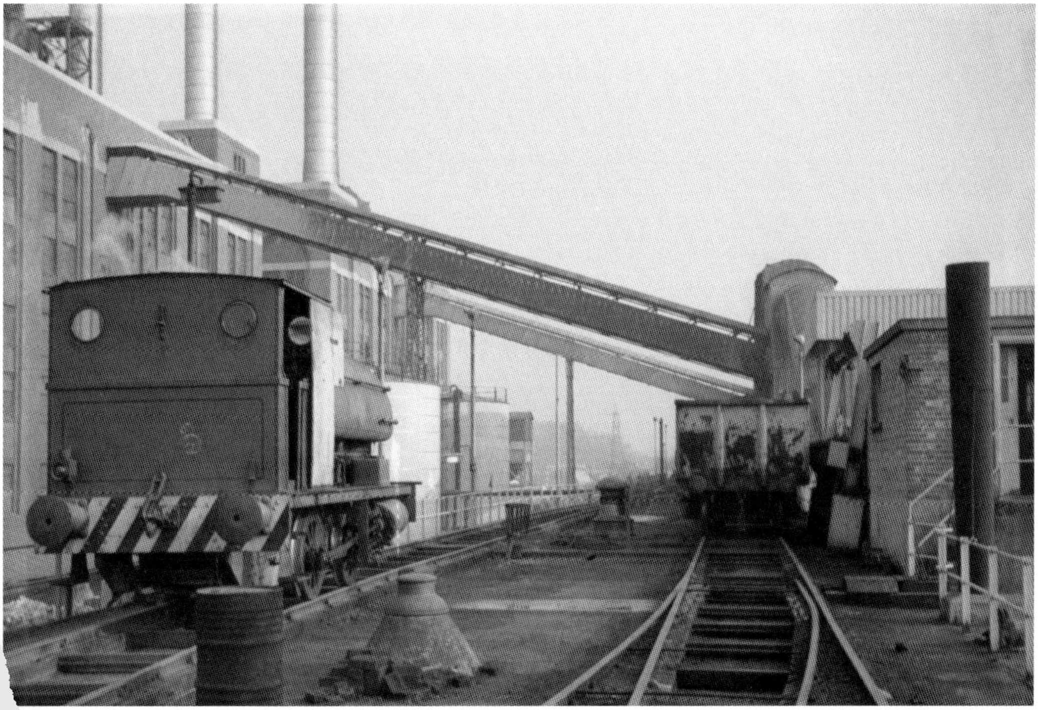

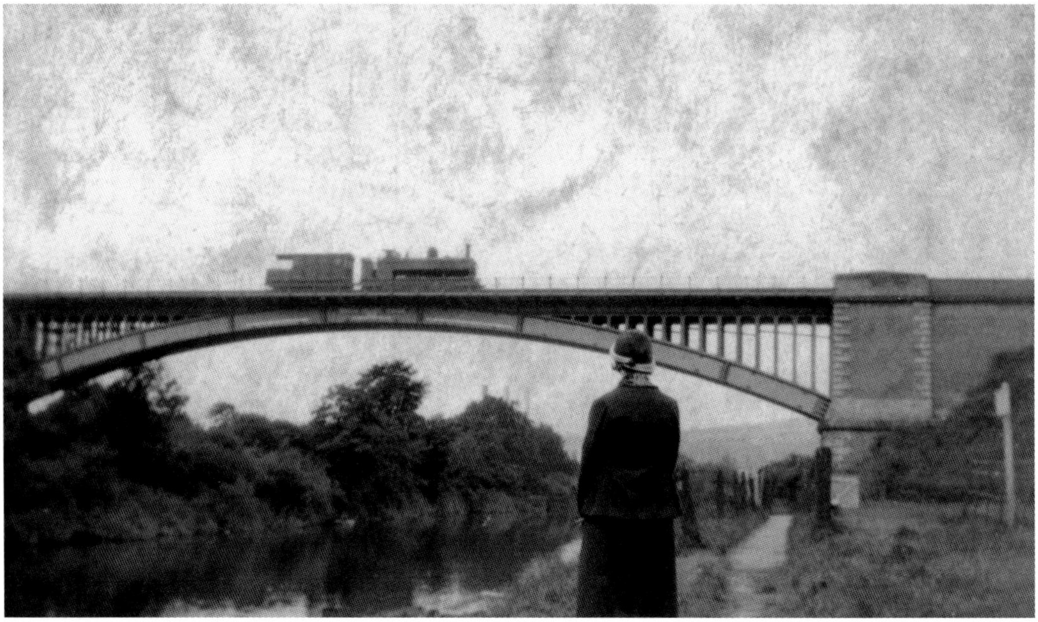

A passer-by watches a GWR pannier tank crossing the Albert Edward Bridge in the 1920s.

Acknowledgements

Many of the photographs in this book are from my own personal collection, taken over the last sixty years and not previously published. I would particularly like to thank Allan Frost and Joanne Smith (Ironbridge Gorge Museum Trust) for providing photographs from their extensive collections, and also Alan Lees and John Powell for photographs of the current scene. For other photographs, information and advice, I am grateful to the following: Ivor Brown, Diana Clarke, Tony Clayton, Jim Cooper, Steve Dewhirst, S. H. Keyse (Owen Prosser Collection), Ron Miles, Stephen Rowson Collection, Shropshire Archives, Barrie Trinder and Ida White.

Every attempt has been made to trace copyright where appropriate, and apologies are extended to anyone who may have inadvertently been omitted from these acknowledgements.